1979

THE BRADFORD BOOK OF COLLECTOR'S PLATES

RAND McNALLY

1979

THE BRADFORD BOOK OF

COLLECTOR'S PLATES

THE OFFICIAL GUIDE TO ALL EDITIONS
TRADED ON THE WORLD'S LARGEST EXCHANGE

EDITED BY

Donna Benson   Curt Johnson
Robert E. Drey   Patricia Kral
Harriet B. Dalaskey   Livingston Platt
Lisa M. Hill   Susanne Southwood

Paul M. Traiber

Photographs by Gerald Hoos
Art Direction by Robert Bowman, Richard Hustad

RAND McNALLY

Chicago   New York   San Francisco

THE BRADFORD EXCHANGE
NILES CHICAGO, ILLINOIS 60648

Library of Congress Catalog Card No. 77-77526

ISBN 528-88188-4

ISSN 0161-2794

CONTENTS

INTRODUCTION

BRADEX LISTED PLATES

APPENDIXES

THE WORLD'S MOST TRADED ART

By J. Roderick MacArthur
Director of the Board of Governors
of the Bradford Exchange

Revised, expanded, and completely updated for 1979, this is the fourth edition of what has been considered the "bible" of plate collecting since it was first published in 1976—the *Bradford Book of Collector's Plates.*

If you regard limited-edition collector's plates as an art form like oils, lithographs, and etchings, then their vastly expanded market in recent years has made them both the single art form most widely collected in America and the most traded art in the world.

And this *Bradford Book,* then, is the official directory of this most traded art.

Best estimates at the end of 1978 placed the number of plate collectors in the United States at more than 3,500,000. Included in this figure are an estimated 500,000 new collectors — a record number. The total number does not include hundreds of thousands more who casually own collector's plates but do not yet think of themselves as "collectors."

A major event of 1978 was the opening of the Bradford Museum of Collector's Plates at the Exchange headquarters in the Chicago suburb of Niles, Illinois. The museum houses the only complete collection of all Bradex-listed plates in the world, and, like the *Bradford Book,* is compelling evidence that plate collecting has truly come of age.

As you leaf through the miniature gallery of plate art

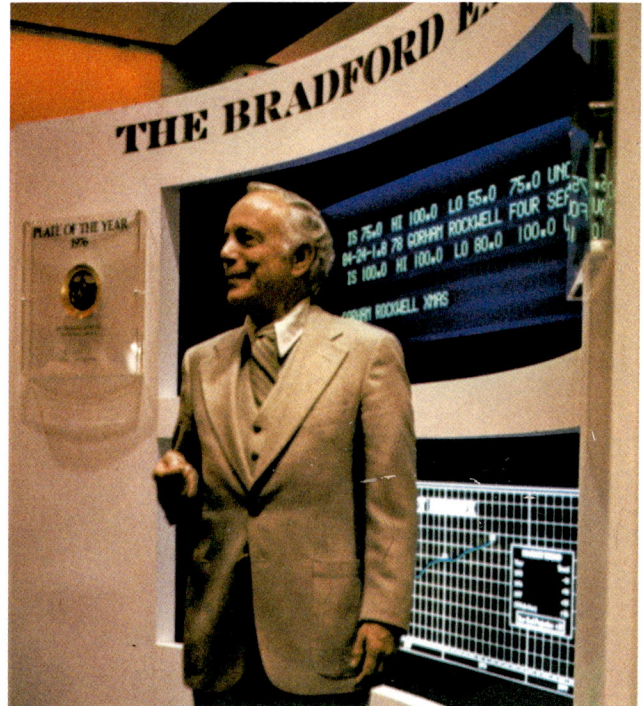

J. Roderick MacArthur

in this book, you'll find every major collector's plate now traded in the market—right up to the 1979 first issue in the D'Arceau-Limoges *Book of Hours* series (pictured on the inside back cover of this book). All illustrations are in full color, and are larger than ever before.

GROWTH OF COLLECTOR'S PLATE MARKET FROM 1960 THROUGH 1978

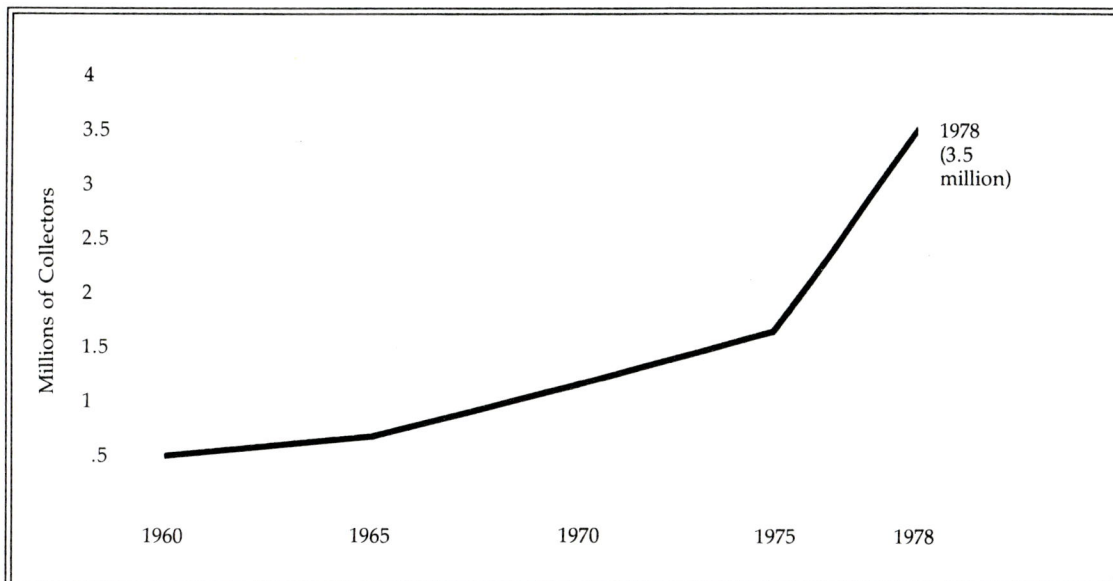

This 1979 *Bradford Book* includes one hundred thirty new issues, seventeen new series and five new makers who are newly listed on the Exchange. In addition, the book now provides a comprehensive index to plate makers and sponsors, and another index of series, titles, and subjects.

In short, the book continues to be what it has been since the first edition was published — the definitive reference work for the current market in limited-edition collector's plates, a resource book needed more acutely than ever as the number of collectors continues to grow.

The largest identifiable concentration of collectors— more than a million in the United States and twenty-one other countries—is served by the world headquarters of the Bradford Exchange in Niles, Illinois, the largest single trading center for collector's plates in the world. Last year, transactions on the Exchange averaged more than 5,000 a day—a 25% increase over the previous year.

The Bradford Museum houses the world's first permanent exhibit of all 1,080 limited-edition plates now listed on the Bradex and valued at more than a quarter million dollars.

THIS BOOK

The Bradford Book is organized to give you the official identification of the maker, artist, edition limit, series, issue price, and year of every plate in the mainstream of the market. The indexing by Bradex number permits quick, precise identification of all 1,080 plates currently traded. The Bradex number is a plate's code on the Exchange and immediately identifies it by country of origin, maker, series, and plate number. (For a fuller explanation of Bradex numbering, see page 39.)

Over the past decade as the "hobby" of plate collecting has expanded to almost every corner of North America and Europe, no other form of art has shown such dramatic market appreciation.

Stories of huge profits are commonplace. People who bought the Lalique *Annual* in 1965, for example, or the Goebel *Hummel Annual* in 1971, or the Rockwell Society *Christmas* in 1974, have seen their plates multiply in value from 469% to as much as 7,000%. And literally scores of other plates have at least doubled in price. Last

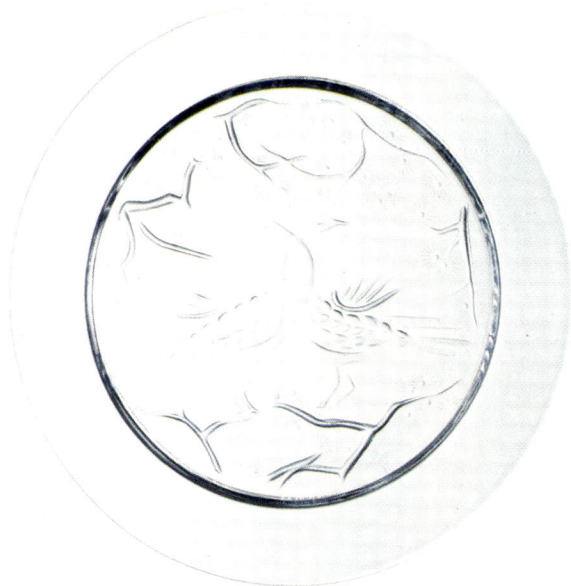

1973 Royal Doulton *Mother and Child*
(26-69-2.1)
Issue Price: $40.00
Price at January 1, 1979: $510.00

1965 Lalique *Annual*
(18-46-1.1)
Issue Price: $25.00
Price at January 1, 1979: $1,750.00

1971 Goebel *Hummel Annual*
(22-27-1.1)
Issue Price: $25.00
Price at January 1, 1979: $1,200.00

1974 Rockwell Society *Christmas*
(84-70-1.1)
Issue Price: $24.50
Price at January 1, 1979: $115.00

year the entire Market Bradex, the "Dow-Jones" index of plate prices, hit 329, establishing a new all-time high. (The Market Bradex is a reflection of overall market performance determined by the current quote-price/issue-price ratio of the twelve most significant plate series.)

Back in 1972, when the market in collector's plates was not advancing—was, in fact, experiencing a brief recession—our analysts here at the Exchange reached two conclusions. First, despite the setback, the market was fundamentally strong and growing stronger. Second, nowhere was there an authoritative book that collectors could rely on for complete, factual information on the hundreds of plates that were already being traded.

I searched everywhere and found a few "guides," but none of them contained straight-forward information backed up by facts. Instead, they were filled with descriptions of "lovely" and "priceless" plates and cluttered with "personal favorites" that were never actually traded. They gave "current market prices" that were hopelessly out of date even before the book came off the press.

That was when we decided to compile an authoritative book ourselves—this book, the *Bradford Book of Collector's Plates*—and to publish it annually.

We laid down some rules. One, there would be no "lovely" plates. The beauty of a plate's design would be left to the judgment of the collector.

Two, there would be no "priceless" plates. If a plate is traded, it has a price.

Three, there would be no personal favorites. If a plate is a favorite with collectors, that too will be reflected in the market trading, the only true reason for listing.

Finally, there would be no attempt to give current market prices. The market moves so quickly that to remain current you must consult a dealer or the Exchange quotations published six times a year.

So the *Bradford Book* contains only issue prices. You won't find a plate called "lovely" or "priceless" anywhere in its pages. You won't find someone's "favorite" plate that was once quickly promoted and just as quickly forgotten. You won't find a plate issued to commemorate the anniversary of your bank, your school, or your state (and there have been many). You won't even find more than six of the scores of plate series that were issued for the American Bicentennial; only these six are regularly traded in the market.

And you won't find listed any of the plates known as "supermarket plates" and "coterie plates."

As the name implies, supermarket plates are sold in supermarkets, discount stores or chain stores, or are given away as premiums at fast-food franchises or by banks, for example. They are poorly made, have practically no artistic value, and are limited only by the manufacturer's idea of how many can be sold. They imitate collector's plates but are not at all the same.

Coterie plates, on the other hand, can be true collector's plates, but they are made in such small or obscure editions that in today's vastly expanded market they remain unknown except to a small coterie of collectors.

A plate is listed on the Exchange and in this book, *by the volume of continued trading*—either past or expected—*not by whether or not it will increase in market price.*

A new plate that continues a series already traded is listed before trading begins. And a new series from a maker whose other series are widely traded may be listed if demand is expected to carry over to the new series.

A SINGLE SHAPE...A REMARKABLE VARIETY

1977 Arabia "Aino's Fate"
(16-5-1.2)

One of the squared plates listed on the Exchange

In case you're new to the subject, collector's plates bear pictures or sculpture and are made in a dozen countries in various sizes but mainly in only one shape—round. A few plates have been introduced in squared shapes, but so far only three—the Rorstrand *Christmas* series **(76-69-1)**, the Royal Doulton *Christmas* series **(26-69-1)** and Arabia's *Kalevala* series **(16-5-1)** — have "made the Bradex," that is, have been listed on the Exchange.

Nearly all listed plates can be considered handmade (although some are more so than others) and many are completely hand painted.

They can be made in wafer-thin china like the Belleek **(26-8-0)** or in heavy sculptured stone like those by di Volteradici of Italy **(38-90-0)** and Incolay of California **(84-31-0)**. They can be metal (silver, silverplate, copper, and pewter), crystal like Lalique **(18-46-0)**, even wood like the Anri **(38-4-0)**. But most are made of ceramic, from simple terra cotta to true hard-fire porcelain.

1979 Studio Dante di Volteradici
Living Madonnas
(38-90-2.2)
(Ivory Alabaster)

1979 River Shore
Famous Americans
(84-69-1.4)
(Copper)

1976 Franklin Mint
Mother's Day
(84-19-2.5)
(Sterling Silver)

1978 Anri
Christmas
(38-4-1.8)
(Wood)

Many can be used as dinner plates, but few ever are. Instead, you'll find them hanging on the walls of museums or homes or displayed with great pride on plate rails or in shadow boxes, in small stands or display cases on side tables. They are sold in department stores, gift shops, specialty shops, and antique stores. Some few can only be imported from abroad one at a time by individual private collectors.

1976 D'Arceau-Limoges
Women of the Century
"Scarlet en Crinoline"
(18-15-3.1)

Series originally available only by subscription directly from France

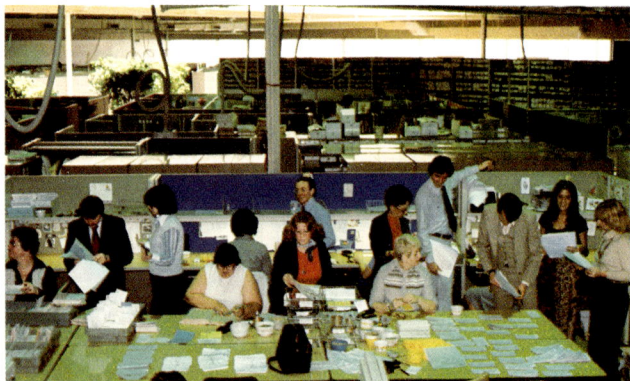

The Bradford Exchange (trading floor)

And always you find them moving with their changing prices on and off the floor of the Exchange. Here, however, they are represented merely by thousands of pieces of paper called "buy-orders" and "sell-orders" which change hands without an actual plate in sight.

The action is fast, and the rewards can be great. (But don't be too tempted to speculate—wait until I tell you what happened to some pretty smart speculators seven years ago.)

EDITION LIMITS AND MARKET VALUE

One thing all collector's plates have in common, of course, is that they are "limited editions."

There has been much debate as to what this means. Some manufacturers give the precise number of their editions; others, particularly those with the widest following, like Bing & Grøndahl **(14-8-0)**, insist that edition size be kept a deep, dark secret.

But there is one thing you can be sure of: with only a single exception,* *no plate in the Bradford Book (or listed on the Exchange) has ever been reissued once the edition closed.*

The range among edition sizes is vast. The smallest *announced* edition limit listed in the *Bradford Book* is five hundred for three issues from two Veneto Flair series **(38-84-1)** and **(38-84-9)**; the largest is 30,000 for the Haviland *Christmas* **(18-30-1)**. But the *undisclosed* editions are by far the largest, ranging from less than one thousand for the earliest into the hundreds of thousands for the later ones.

There was a time, when the market was small, that a new plate series in an edition of two thousand or less could become established and sometimes trade up in price to dizzying heights. Today, with the market so vastly expanded, this is unlikely. With the rare exception of a series like the Rosenthal *Oriental Gold* **(22-69-8)**, an unknown new series launched with an edition of less than ten thousand would probably remain unknown except as a coterie plate.

Don't let me discourage you from adding an obscure plate you really like to your collection—*but don't expect it to go up in market value just because the edition is small—the*

1979 Bing & Grøndahl *Christmas*
(14-8-1.85)
Eighty-fifth plate in an open-end series

*The one exception is the Rosenthal *Traditional Christmas* series **(22-69-1)**. Editions from 1910 to 1971 in this series were reopened briefly between 1969 and 1971. These plates are now Bradex-listed on the firm assurance by the maker that the practice ceased forever in 1971. Thus, they are limited editions at last, and current trading prices now reflect all plates in the editions regardless of when they were made.

market value of a plate is *never* determined by the size of the edition alone. Rather, it is determined by the *ratio* of supply to demand, and a very small edition can't create much demand.

Most plates are produced in series—either "closed-end" in a predetermined number of editions, or "open-end" to continue indefinitely. The Limoges-Turgot *Durand's Children* series **(18-52-1)** is a closed-end series scheduled for four editions, while the Bing & Grøndahl *Christmas* series **(14-8-1)** is open-end. Most collectors specialize in one or more of these series. (In fact, they *must* specialize in something; there are 1,080 listed plates in this book and the only complete collection anywhere is in the Bradford Museum.)

The first plate in a series is usually—but not always—the most wanted. Some collectors used to refer to these plates as "first editions," but this was a misnomer. Practically all plates listed are first editions since an edition is normally never reopened; the first in a series is now properly called a "first issue."

THE UNEXPLAINED PHENOMENON

Because these plates have gradually become the most widely collected form of art and prices for the prized editions have outstripped the most glamorous stocks and bonds, I suppose it was inevitable that amateur sociologists would try to explain this phenomenon. At any rate, we have not lacked for "explanations" that compare plate collecting to other fields—but always with a certain strained logic.

At Bing & Grøndahl—the very oldest manufacturer of collector's plates and therefore presumably an authority on the subject—it has been said that collector's plates are "closely connected with the traditions of interior decorating." While plates certainly do decorate an interior, to suggest that this is their primary function is to lose sight of the joy of acquisition, the searching, bidding, and trading that collectors delight in—to lose, in fact, the very idea of collecting.

Others call collector's plates "giftware" and bring us no closer to an answer. Of course, collector's plates make fine gifts—that's what they were originally, before they became collector's plates. But again, we are not collecting merely by giving or receiving a gift.

What is more confusing—and most widespread—is the comparison of collector's plates with antiques. A surprising number of dealers, manufacturers, and collectors — all of whom should know better — persist in suggesting that plates can somehow become "instant antiques." It is easy to see how some people might prefer them to real antiques because they are so easily identified. Usually the plate itself carries its own identification. Even the danger of copies and counterfeits is close to nonexistent. (I've seen only one counterfeit, a copy made in Portugal of the famous 1962 Royal Copenhagen "Little Mermaid" **[14-69-1.55]**.) But not even the oldest

1978 Limoges-Turgot
Durand's Children
"Marie - Ange"
(18-52-1.1)

1979 Limoges-Turgot
Durand's Children
"Emilie et Philippe"
(18-52-1.2)

collector's plates are yet old enough to be considered antiques by the generally accepted definition, and the fast-moving market in plates can hardly compare with the slow, involved trading of antiques.

Still others compare plate collecting with stamp collecting and coin collecting — and there are comfortable similarities: a defined national market, for instance, with fast-changing prices and occasional wild speculation. But there, I think, the similarities end. No plate collector would compare the art of his plate with the art that appears on a stamp or coin. And, in fact, art has virtually no bearing on the value of a stamp or coin. Both stamps and coins are usually hidden away in albums, while collector's plates are intended for display. And there is another, most vital difference — no stamp or coin is normally issued as a limited edition. It becomes so only after it is discontinued.

The comparisons with other forms of art are little better. There is not the same uniform, codified market in other art as there is in collector's plates, and no concerted trading other than the occasional spectacular auction.

So that leads us to compare the continuous trading in plates with that of stocks and bonds. Of course, many plates are collected as investments, but unlike stocks and bonds they are not collected *only* as investments. To do so would be to ignore their aesthetic appeal entirely.

In most respects, plates cannot be compared with stocks and bonds. The activity of stocks is rarely reflected in the plate market. When stocks fall, plates tend to go up. In fact, after some disagreement with the U.S. Securities and Exchange Commission back in 1973, the official view of the Bradford Exchange has been that, if collector's plates are to be considered investments, they should be defined as commodities, not securities, preferably art commodities, and modern art at that.

THE STANDARD YARDSTICK

There is no denying that many plate editions have proved to be spectacular investments. But how can you know which plates will succeed and which will fall by the wayside?

No one knows with absolute certainty. However, in 1972 analysts at the Bradford Exchange compiled what ultimately became known as the Eight-point Checklist for evaluation of any plate. Since then, with minor evolutionary modification, this checklist has become something of a standard yardstick.

1. *Maker:* Is the maker known for its standards of fine workmanship and continuity of other plate series?

2. *Artistry:* Is it original art created especially for this plate by an artist of note? Is the subject one of broad, but not trite, appeal?

Plate III, Limoges-Turgot
Durand's Children
(Not yet issued)

Plate IV, Limoges-Turgot
Durand's Children
(Not yet issued)

The four-plate *Durand's Children* collection is an example of a closed-end series. (Only the 1978 and 1979 plates have been issued as yet.)

3. *Rarity:* Is the edition tightly limited yet not too limited to create a market? If the edition is closed, are dealers bidding in the secondary market?

4. *Collectibility:* Is it one, preferably the first, of a collectible periodic series or merely a single issue?

5. *Time of Acquisition:* Can you get it at the right time —at issue—or while the price is still rising?

6. *Sponsorship:* Is it issued in association with a government or an official nonprofit institution?

7. *Commemorative Importance:* Does it commemorate a seasonal event or a historic event? If so, does it bring new insight to the event? Or is it an event in the history of the artist or of the maker?

8. *Material:* If made of ceramic, is it true hard-paste (or "hard-fire") porcelain, bone china or fine china? If made of metal, is it solid gold or silver? If made of glass, is it genuine 24% lead crystal?

These points are intended to be listed in order of importance, but for purposes of investment, point five—*Time of Acquisition*—is crucial. If you pay too much for a plate, it may take years to break even. Yet even at a high aftermarket price, a plate can be a bargain if it is still going up.

FROM QUAINT DANISH CHRISTMAS CUSTOM TO WORLD'S MOST TRADED ART FORM

Every history ever written about collector's plates agrees that they originated in Denmark eighty-four years ago with a small blue and white plate issued by Bing & Grøndahl. Two semi-official histories say the idea was inspired by an old Danish custom of presenting gifts of food on beautifully decorated wooden plates to the common folk at Christmastime. After the food was eaten, the plate remained to remind the people of the spirit of Christmas giving throughout the year. This is a pretty story, but to the best of my knowledge no one has ever seen one of these wooden plates that supposedly represented such a widespread custom.

Officials at Bing & Grøndahl have said, instead, that the custom had its beginning in the Renaissance when an honored guest was given the plates from which he had eaten his meal. This suggests the rather unlikely scene of a nobleman coming home from dinner with a large, clanking "doggy bag" full of tableware.

Although there were earlier commemorative plates, such as the 1892 Royal Copenhagen plate for the fiftieth wedding anniversary of the king and queen of Denmark, they are one-of-a-kind issues, not part of a series, and Harald Bing, the son of one of the founders of Bing & Grøndahl, did in fact issue what most historians now accept as the first collector's plate—the 1895 "Behind the Frozen Window" **(14-8-1.1),** and was the first to identify

the plate as a Christmas plate with the year of manufacture on the front.

But it is doubtful that Mr. Bing thought of the now-famous plate as a "limited edition." More probably he limited his edition merely because he believed it would be hard to sell a plate dated 1895 in 1896.

Harald Bing

"Behind the Frozen Window" was hand painted in cobalt blue underglaze on bas-relief porcelain, a technique which came to be known as "Copenhagen blue on white" and set the fashion for all collector's plates for the next seventy years, no matter where they were made.

Bing & Grøndahl claims to have kept secret the number of plates produced each year, but knowledgeable estimates are that about four hundred of the historic 1895 plates were made. I believe the majority of these still exist, many as part of complete collections of the Bing & Grøndahl *Christmas* series, and most now in the United States. The plate, which originally sold for about 50¢, traded in 1978 at more than $3,000.00 on the Exchange.

In her book, *Modern Porcelain* (Harper & Row, 1962), Alberta Tremble tells us this first collector's plate was issued to commemorate the reorganization of the Bing & Grøndahl company and the opening of its new, greatly enlarged plant. I must, however, correct Ms. Tremble's claim that "the plates caught on like wildfire. Potters everywhere copied the idea."

In fact, no one successfully copied the idea until Royal Copenhagen **(14-69-0)** did it in 1908, thirteen years later. Rorstrand in Sweden began a series in 1904 and hung on until 1926 before giving up; the recently discovered 1907 Rosenthal plate from Germany (see page 37) seems to have had no successor; Porsgrund in Norway tried it in 1909, but abandoned the effort after one issue for lack of success. (Both Rörstrand **[76-69-0]** and Porsgrund **[54-61-0]** resumed production in 1968, but only after the new American market had developed.) It was not until 1910 that Rosenthal issued "Winter Peace," the first in its German *Traditional Christmas* series, and that series, like Bing & Grøndahl's and Royal Copenhagen's, has continued to the present day despite wars and economic crises.

THE MODERN MARKET

Although the early Christmas plates are true collector's plates as we understand them, they were not collected at their time of issue as they are today. Danish families collected them but never thought that one edition might be more valuable than another, and the idea of acquiring a complete collection was yet to come.

As Danes emigrated to the United States, they brought collector's plates with them. But until the late 1940s the plates were little known in America except in a few antique shops in Scandinavian neighborhoods. Only two importers, the U.S. representatives of the Georg Jensen company (which later became a plate maker) and the Stanley Cocoran company, were bringing in plates for Danish immigrants.

The first American dealers entered the market with no idea of what they were starting.

"If you had told me in 1947 that someday there would be millions of plate collectors, I just wouldn't have believed you," says Chicago antique dealer William Freudenberg, Jr. Yet in 1947, he became the very first to recognize the possibilities in Danish plates when he began reselling them to other antique dealers.

William Freudenberg, Jr.

"I simply found them at an auction house," he says, "and took a few to see what I could do." Freudenberg's asking price for the oldest Bing & Grøndahl at that time was only $4.50 (the same plate that was quoted at $3,170.00 in the market in 1978).

In 1949 Pat Owen in Fort Lauderdale, Florida, became a collector's plate dealer through a fluke. An American company wanted to sell cash registers in Denmark, but exporting Danish currency was prohibited. To get around this, the purchasing company used

Pat Owen

Danish kroner to buy collector's plates from young Danes who had no interest in their families' collections. These were then resold for U.S. dollars to Mrs. Owen, and she became the first American dealer to sell plates to gift shops and department stores.

That same year Rev. Elias Rasmussen, a Norwegian-born pastor from Minneapolis, was traveling in Denmark when he met an elderly lady who was trying to sell her plates. As he told it, no one in Denmark wanted them at any price. So Rev. Rasmussen brought them back to America to see if he could sell them for her. Within a few years he was reselling plates by the thousands. After Rev. Rasmussen's death, his son continued the business.

In 1950 Jon Nielsen settled in Dearborn, Michigan and began importing Danish plates along with antiques from the old country. He sold them all for about $3.50 apiece regardless of the year of issue.

"Not until 1953 did dealers want any current plates," he remembers. "The next year I raised my prices to $3.75, and you should have heard them complain that I was charging too much."

Elias Rasmussen

Svend Jensen

Antique dealers and gift shops around the country were soon quoting Svend Jensen's prices, and other price lists began to appear. Collectors with recently issued plates tried to complete their collections with earlier plates. Prices were bid up well beyond those of Svend Jensen's early lists; yet as late as 1955 the historic Bing & Grøndahl plate from 1895 could still be bought for only $75.00.

Jon Nielsen

But the event that really moved collector's plates out of the realm of antiques and giftware took place in 1951. Svend Jensen in Rye, New York, had begun importing Danish plates the year before. He was the first to charge different prices for various back issues. In 1951 he printed and circulated the first back-issue price list based on his estimates of the rarity of each edition. With this simple act, the modern American market in collector's plates was born.

1945 Royal Copenhagen
Christmas
(14-69-1.38)

1951 Royal Copenhagen
Christmas
(14-69-1.44)

Earl Falack

Two "winners" on the early plate market were the 1945 Royal Copenhagen Christmas issue, "A Peaceful Motif," and the 1951 Royal Copenhagen Christmas issue, "Christmas Angel." Both plates were designed by artist Richard Bocher, and many collectors found his sentimental portrayals of youthful angels a refreshing departure from the customary landmarks, cathedrals and Danish countryside scenes featured in the series. The plates, which were issued in Denmark at prices equivalent to $4.00 and $5.00, respectively, traded widely throughout the early 1950s, and by 1958 both were trading as high as $300.00 in the U.S.

By 1960, with the supply of antiques dwindling and more and more plate collectors asking for current editions of the Danish Christmas plates, antique dealers began to add the new editions to their lines even though they were hardly antiques. As the new editions also began to appear in specialty gift shops, new customers began looking for still earlier issues, and a circular trading pattern developed from one kind of dealer to another.

Some enterprising dealers found they could still bypass American distributors and go directly to Denmark for plates. As late as 1960, Earl Falack of Edward's 5th Avenue, Ltd., New York, found some Danish dealers still blithely unaware of the boom occurring across the Atlantic. Royal Copenhagen back issues of random years could still be purchased in lots of 1,000 or even 2,000 at a time at from only $2.00 to $5.00 per plate.

In 1962, a combination of demand—from Americans who had visited Copenhagen, transplanted Danes, the growing numbers of plate collectors, and other people who were simply attracted to the Hans Christian Ander-

sen story — centered on the 1962 Royal Copenhagen Christmas plate, "The Little Mermaid at Wintertime" **(14-69-1.55)**. Issued at about $11.00, it immediately began to rise in market price (the plate traded in 1978 as high as $235.00), and this in turn increased prices for all earlier editions (an appreciation also due in part to the fact that the mold broke before the edition could be completed).

CRYSTAL SHATTERS MARKET

In 1965 Lalique of France, whose crystalware was selling in shops where Danish plates were unheard of, brought out an etched crystal plate of two entwined birds. The plate, "Deux Oiseaux" **(18-46-1.1)** — now legendary among collectors for its rise from $25.00 to more than $1,700.00 in little over a decade—shattered the previously accepted boundaries of plate collecting: it was not porcelain, not Danish, not blue and white, not even a Christmas plate. It was simply called an "annual" (the series closed in 1976), and its issue finally set the stage for limited-edition plates as true "collector's items."

1962 Royal Copenhagen
Christmas
(14-69-1.55)

1969 Wedgwood
Christmas
(26-90-1.1)

In 1967 Bareuther of Germany introduced a Christmas series **(22-6-1)**, and in 1968 it began a Danish Church series **(22-13-1)**. In that same year Rorstrand of Sweden **(76-69-1)** and Porsgrund of Norway **(54-61-1)**, re-entered the growing market with Christmas series.

When Bing & Grøndahl issued the first Mother's Day plate, "Dog and Puppies" **(14-8-3.1)**, in 1969, U.S. collectors scrambled to buy it at the issue price of $9.75. They were now aware that earlier Bing & Grøndahl Christmas plates were selling at many times issue price and thus bought the newest plate as an outright investment and saw their hunches pay off when the plate began to appreciate (it traded at $490.00 in December 1978).

In Denmark, however, Danish dealers had little interest in the first Mother's Day plate, and in 1969 Jon Nielsen, returning from a Danish buying trip, was still able to buy eighteen plates at the gift shop in the Copenhagen airport for $3.50 each. The manager said he had 125 more if Nielsen wanted them. Nielsen did.

His foresight paid off: the issue sold out quickly both here and in Denmark, and went up in price immediately. But unfortunately for Nielsen, the Danish dealers soon caught on, and when he returned to Denmark, he was unable to buy a single 1970 Bing & Grøndahl Mother's Day issue.

Late in 1969 Wedgwood of England issued its first Christmas plate, "Windsor Castle" **(26-90-1.1)**, at the issue price of $25.00. It, too, sold out quickly and began to climb in value. Within a year, "Windsor Castle" was trading at twice its issue price, and suddenly it seemed that everyone was buying, selling, and collecting plates.

The following year, in 1970, plate makers rushed into the field to meet the sudden demand. Svend Jensen decided to make his own plates; so did the firms of Haviland, Belleek, Spode, Kaiser, Berlin, Lenox, Santa Clara, Pickard, Reed & Barton, and Orrefors, among others. All were successful and still survive. Franklin Mint made history by issuing the first silver collector's plate, "Bringing Home the Tree" by Norman Rockwell **(84-19-1.1)**, and it, too, was a runaway success doubling in value in a year. Prices increased as soon as editions closed, with demand coming from ever more, and more avid, collectors.

In 1971 still more makers like Fürstenberg, Gorham, and Lladró entered the market. Haviland Parlon began a unique and successful series based on medieval tapestries **(18-32-1)**, Goebel introduced plates inspired by their famous Hummel figurines **(22-27-1)**, and Veneto Flair began a series of handmade plates from Italy **(38-84-2)**. Older makers such as Royal Copenhagen and Wedgwood introduced Mother's Day series.

Even this new surge in supply could not keep up with demand. As the number of collectors and dealers increased, prices continued to rise. News of the boom began to appear in the press. In December 1971, the *Wall Street Journal* ran an article under the headline "While You Were Going Under, Granny Got In At $100, Got Out At $450." The article was based on the spectacular price rise of the first Franklin Mint Christmas plate. Reporter Scott R. Schmedel also singled out the 1969 Wedgwood Christmas plate which was then selling for about $200.00 —800% of issue price. To show this could be momentary inflation, Mr. Schmedel quoted a serious Wedgwood collector as predicting its value would fall back and stabilize at around $80.00. Instead, it has held its price ever since and traded at $270.00 at the end of 1978. The *Wall Street Journal* article and others like it were widely reprinted and set the stage for 1972 as the year of the speculator.

THE CRASH OF 1972

In 1972 still more makers entered the market. Perhaps it was inevitable that some of them should be less than reputable. Plates of poor design and quality were rushed into production. Thousands of new dealers and collectors began speculating with little or no knowledge of plates or of the market. New "mints" sprang up to mass-produce silver plates on the heels of Franklin Mint's success.

One such new mint advertised its silver "Collie and Pups" with pictures of an acid-etched plate and sold thousands before the plate was produced. Prices rose dramatically, but the actual plate was stamped, not etched, and many collectors were sadly disillusioned as the price of the issue plummeted. Another new mint introduced six new silver plates at once.

Suddenly dealers all over the country found themselves overstocked and prices for silver plates fell below

1972 "Collie and Pups"
The plate that set off the
"crash of '72"

the year of the "shakeout." Several "mints" closed their doors. Thousands of plates were melted back into silver. Established makers cut back production dramatically, and the bedroom dealers vanished.

In 1973, thousands of new collectors entered the market to buy two spectacular series begun that year. A French series for the American Bicentennial, the *Lafayette Legacy* Collection from D'Arceau-Limoges **(18-15-1)** was unavailable to dealers but was imported by enough individual collectors directly from France to be widely traded on the secondary market. "Colette and Child" **(26-69-2.1)** from Royal Doulton was the first plate by artist Edna Hibel and quickly led the entire field toward recovery. Although marginal plates disappeared from trading, established plates remained steady and regained their market strength.

issue. All other plates began to fall on the heels of the silver crash. Dealers panicked, and the speculator-collectors, many of whom had gone into part-time business as "bedroom dealers," saw their visions of quick riches vanish.

After the "crash of 1972," the following year became

It was at about this time — in the mid-'70s — that a significant factor contributing to the growth of the American market was finally recognized: demand from European collectors and dealers. As news of the American plate collecting boom slowly spread abroad, plates that originated in Europe but had languished in the market there — issues such as the Rörstrand *Christmas* series **(76-69-1),** for example — were bid up even higher in the American market as European dealers and their agents bought them up for resale back in Europe.

In 1977 the Bradford Exchange established European headquarters in Zug, Switzerland; local national Exchanges reporting to that office were established in 1978 in Cologne, Germany, and London, England.

1976 Studio Dante di Volteradici
Grand Opera
(38-90-1.1)

MARKET MATURES

Since 1974 the overall Market Bradex, the "Dow-Jones" index of collector's plate prices on the American market, has shown a steady increase that reflects growing collector confidence and market stability. The 39-point rise last year, from 289 to 328, was greater than in any year since 1974, and this bodes well for the future.

Though not as spectacular as the boom of 1971, gains since 1974 have long since wiped out the losses of 1972 and are spread over a much broader range of plates. In fact, 145 series were Bradex-listed at the end of 1978, compared with only eighty-two in 1972.

The entry of hundreds of thousands of new collectors into the market has been more than enough to offset this increase in new series, and exceptional new editions can still double and triple in price in relatively short periods of time. "Rigoletto" **(38-90-1.1)**, the 1976 *Grand Opera* plate from Studio Dante di Volteradici (and the first ivory alabaster plate), was already quoted at $100.00 — 286% of its $35.00 issue price — by the end of 1977, and by the end of 1978 had risen to $148.00, 423% of its issue price. The spectacular Pickard "Alba Madonna" **(84-50-2.1)**, issued late in 1976, was at $320.00 by the end of 1978 — 533% of its $60.00 issue price. And the 1977 "Plate of the Year," Incolay Studios' "She Walks in Beauty" **(84-31-1.1)** the first cameo collector's plate, went to 483% of its $60.00 issue price by the end of 1978.

1976 Pickard
Christmas
(84-50-2.1)

1977 Incolay Studios
Romantic Poets
(84-31-1.1)

So I think it's fair to say that prospects for market growth continue to be excellent. In fact, given the ever-increasing volume of trading in recent years — both in North America and Europe—the greatest growth of the collector's plate market may still lie ahead.   □

THE YEAR IN REVIEW

For the third consecutive year the Market Bradex — the index of overall activity in the limited-edition collector's plate market — advanced steadily, breaking the 300 mark in June of 1978 and continuing upward to close at an all-time year-end high of 328. This closing 1978 figure reflected a 39-point increase over the twelve-month reporting period and culminated eighteen consecutive months of advance. During the November-December period alone, the Bradex rose 15 points, spurred by the event that had the single greatest impact on the 1978 market: the death of Norman Rockwell on November 8.

CHART OF BRADEX

289	297	301	306	309	313	328

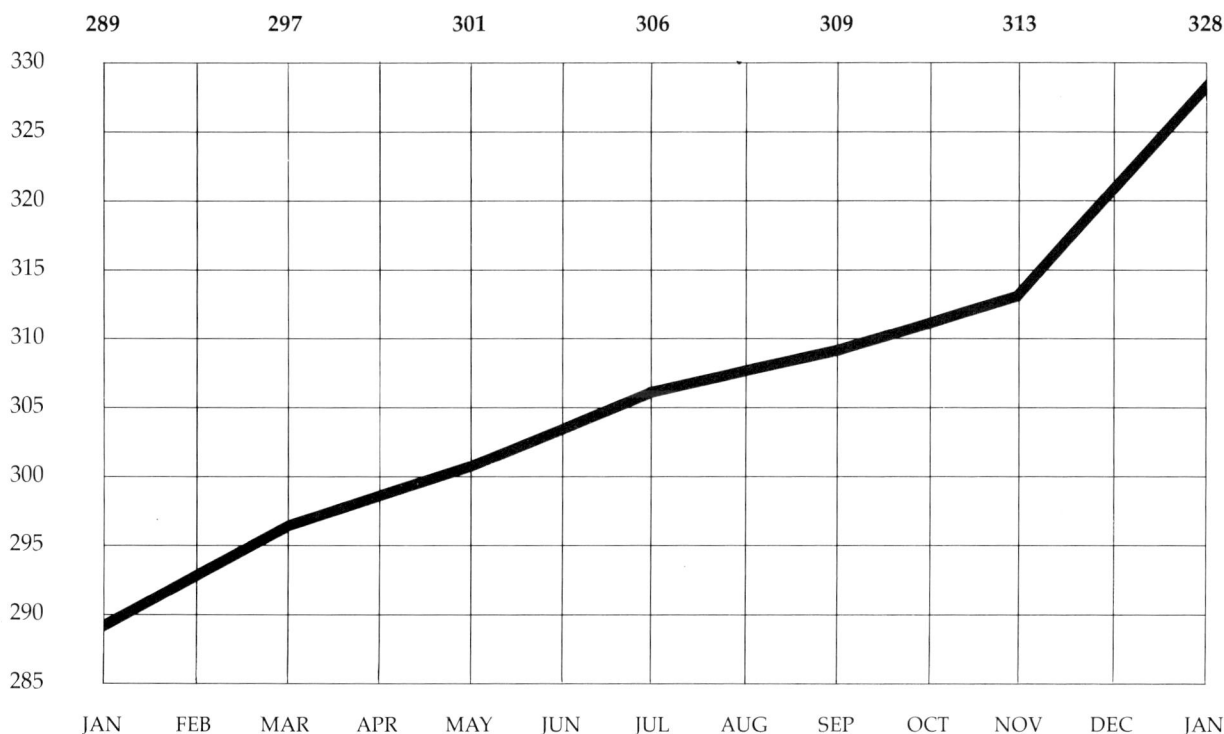

| JAN | FEB | MAR | APR | MAY | JUN | JUL | AUG | SEP | OCT | NOV | DEC | JAN |

Far and away the most collected artist in the plate market, Rockwell is represented by twenty-five series, with eight listed on the Exchange and seventeen traded over the counter. Most of the series traded on the Exchange had shown steady, if not always spectacular, appreciation. But following the artist's death unprecedented trading caused prices to soar. By December, twenty-nine of the thirty-seven individual issues within the Bradex-listed Rockwell series had advanced, with the top five plates appreciating to an average 183% of the price quoted in the reporting period just prior to his death; Christmas trading then pushed many Rockwell series to more than double their previous record highs.

A new market record was set by Rockwell's "The Toy Maker" (Bradex Number **84-70-3.1**), the 1977 first issue in the Rockwell Society of America's *Rockwell Heritage* collection. "The Toy Maker" closed the year at 517% of issue price, rising from $14.50 to $75.00 and becoming the all-time market leader in trading volume on the Exchange.

Significantly, nearly 200% of this increase — $28.00 — came in the last six weeks of the year, following the artist's death. The second issue in this collection, "The Cobbler" **(84-70-3.2)** more than doubled in price during November and December and closed the year at $45.00, 231% of its $19.50 issue price and $24.00 higher than its October quote. Two other Rockwell issues also rose sharply in that period: the 1977 Gorham *Rockwell Four Seasons* **(84-24-1.7)**, a four-plate set which shot up from $80.00 to $150.00, and the 1977 Royal Devon *Mother's Day* **(84-76-2.3)**, which closed the year at $45.00, nearly twice the $24.50 issue price it had sustained since its release.

1978 ROCKWELL SOCIETY
HERITAGE
"The Cobbler"
84-70-3.2

1977 ROYAL DEVON
MOTHER'S DAY
"The Family"
84-76-2.3

Paced by these and other Rockwell issues and spurred by heavy trading in the Goebel *Hummel Annual* series **(22-27-1)** which appreciated 44% in 1978, the overall trading volume for 1978 was up 20% over the previous year (1978's total of 1,300,000 transactions by the Exchange exceeded 1977's by 300,000 and represented a composite increase of 30% — the largest one-year advance ever recorded). Reflecting the continuing expansion of the market, winners outstripped losing issues by 251 to 149. An estimated 500,000 new collectors entered the American market for the first time in 1978. Revised estimates now indicate that there are 3.5 million active plate collectors in the United States alone, and under the headline "Blue-Plate 'Specials' Turn Into Highfliers For Some Collectors," the *Wall Street Journal* commented that Americans collecting limited-edition plates are "spurred on by the expectation of rapid appreciation in a time of rising inflation and a sinking securities market." In 1978, U.S. sales of limited-edition collector's plates reached $250 million, a record high.

1971 GOEBEL
HUMMEL ANNUAL
"Heavenly Angel"
22-27-1.1

The Goebel *Hummel Annual* series **(22-27-1)** closed the year trading at an average of 731% of issue price, making it second only to the famous Lalique crystal series as the most successful modern plate series of all time.* (By comparison, the total average value of Lalique *Annuals* **[18-46-1]**, the top series, stood at 733% of issue price at year's end.) Back issues continued in heavy demand.

During 1978 alone, the '71 issue in the Goebel *Hummel Annual* series rose $204.00, from $996.00 to $1,200.00; the '72 went from $109.00 to $120.00; the '73 from $245.00 to $310.00; the '74 from $90.00 to $172.00; the '75 up $30.00 to $114.00; the '76 from $72.00 to $118.00; the '77 from $80.00 to $255.00.

1978 GOEBEL
HUMMEL ANNUAL
"Happy Pastime"
22-27-1.8

*Long-term changes in world currency values form part of the exceptional appreciation of the late nineteenth-century and early twentieth-century issues by Bing & Grøndahl, Royal Copenhagen, and Rosenthal; these are not included in this comparison.

26

But as a result of this unprecedented trading, problems developed — particularly for the 1978 issue, "Happy Pastime," which was already quoted at $215.00, 331% of its issue price, at year-end. Although Goebel shipped more plates to the United States in 1978 than in 1977, taking them from other markets to favor the U.S. where demand was so great, some dealers received their full allotments on time, many others did not. And in this atmosphere of uncertainty, rumors began to circulate that Goebel of North America might in fact bypass dealers and promote Hummel plates directly to collectors.

In late October, representatives of the National Association of Limited Edition Dealers (NALED) met with Goebel officials to clarify the situation and attempt to forestall speculative buying which was threatening to deprive individual Hummel collectors. Following the meeting, it was announced that in future Goebel would guarantee specified annual allotments to individual dealers and that NALED members in turn would sell only one plate to each customer.

By the end of the year all Goebel *Hummel Annual* prices were finally stabilizing, though at a very high level, and Goebel announced that the issue price of "Singing Lesson," the 1979 issue, would be $90.00, a 38% increase over the previous year's $65.00 (a price at which it was sold by few dealers). This steep hike was in part due to the depreciation of the U.S. dollar which put pressure on all foreign plate prices.

Not all Goebel issues performed well, however. Prices for the *Wildlife* series **(22-27-2)** were static with sparse trading.

At the July International Plate Collectors Convention in South Bend, Indiana, a mood of optimism — spurred largely by the strength of the Goebel Hummel issues — prompted dealers to place increased orders for many other new issues. Although these new 1978 plates were advertised heavily, some of them, including Schmid's "Tranquility" (sold over-the-counter), were delivered months late; others, such as Royal Doulton's "Kathleen and Child" **(26-69-2.6)**, Knowles' "Scarlett" **(84-41-3.1)**, and Wedgwood's "Cherish" **(26-90-4.2)**, were not delivered in 1978 at all. The traditionally heavy fall trading period thus found collectors still waiting for delivery, and when plates failed to materialize, many cancelled their orders entirely. As a result, the September-October reporting period was marked by what some experts called a "mini-recession" in the market. (This downswing was completely reversed, however, in the surge of trading following Rockwell's death.)

1978 KNOWLES
GONE WITH THE WIND
"Scarlett"
84-41-3.1

1978 WEDGWOOD
BLOSSOMING OF SUZANNE
"Cherish"
26-90-4.2

Some observers suggested that the mini-recession might foreshadow a 1979 market "shakeout" similar to that which followed the "crash of '72" (see p. 19). Their theory was based on supposed parallels in the two years, both of which saw many new makers and dealers entering the market, many collectors becoming dealers, many dealers becoming makers, and a significant increase in the number of new plates introduced.

This opinion was discounted by Bradford analysts, however. Almost all 1978 plate issues attracted strong interest and — when they finally reached the market — were actually bought by collectors, a very different situation from that of 1972 when dealers were glutted with plates that never sold.

One hundred thirty-nine issues were newly listed on the Bradex in 1978, additions that were offset by the fourteen issues delisted for lack of active trading, making a total of 1,080 Bradex-listed plates, a gain of 125.

The 1978 first issue in Pickard's *Children of Renoir* series, "Girl with a Watering Can" **(84-50-4.1)**, posted the all-time highest first-year percentage gain in market history and clearly became "plate of the year." Issued at $50.00 in an edition limited to 5,000, the plate was an immediate sellout, jumping to a quoted price of $150.00 within days of its issue. By the end of the year it was trading at $300.00 — 600% of issue price.

The market strength of "Girl with a Watering Can" was so great that by year's end brisk options trading (the buying and selling by dealers of rights to purchase future plates before they are delivered) had already driven the price of its successor in the Renoir series, "Child in White" **(84-50-4.2)**, to $140.00 — 280% of issue price — before the first plate was fired.

"Plate of the Year" for 1978

was Pickard's "Girl with a Watering Can." First issue in the Children of
Renoir series, this gold-rimmed reproduction of a painting by the French
Impressionist was trading at $300.00 by year's end, up 500% from its
$50.00 issue price and a new market record for appreciation in one year.

1978 PICKARD
CHILDREN OF RENOIR
"Girl with a Watering Can"
84-50-4.1

The extraordinary success of plates in Pickard's earlier Christmas series using Renaissance art had paved the way for the Renoir series. The 1976 Christmas issue, the ''Alba Madonna'' **(84-50-2.1)**, was one of the most sought-after plates ever to go on the market and closed 1978 at $320.00, 533% of its issue price; the second issue in the same series, ''The Nativity'' **(84-50-2.2)**, was one of the top new issues of 1977 and closed 1978 at $170.00, 261% of issue price.

Because all of these Pickard issues bear artwork created in another medium by artists now long dead, their popularity still surprised some market observers. It was apparent that collectors were attracted to the excellent quality of the Pickard reproductions and the reputation of the maker and were willing to ignore the fact that these plates are not original art.

Another top-gaining series in 1978 confirmed that collectors are not always finicky about the origin of their art. Plates in River Shore's *Famous Americans* series **(84-69-1)** — sculpted in copper by Roger Brown — carry the signature of Norman Rockwell although they are only interpretations (as indeed are the

history-making Goebel *Hummel Annuals*) rather than reproductions of the artist's original work. Perhaps for this reason, the series as a whole was surprisingly unaffected by the year-end boom in Rockwell issues that followed the artist's death. However, it proved extremely strong when evaluated over the entire twelve-month reporting period. ''Brown's Lincoln,'' the 1976 first issue, advanced 158% over the year, from $165.00 to $425.00; the 1977 ''Brown's Rockwell'' rose 106% from $90.00 to $185.00; and the 1978 ''Brown's Peace Corps'' climbed from its issue price of $45.00 to $140.00, more than tripling in value.

Another new good performer in 1978 was ''Erik and Dandelion'' **(84-91-1.1)**, first in the *Zolan's Children* series from Viletta, which was issued at $19.00, tripled in value, and was trading at $57.00 before the year was out. Also strong was the previous ''Plate of the Year,'' Incolay Studios' 1977 ''She Walks in Beauty'' **(84-31-1.1)**, in its *Romantic Poets* collection. This first cameo collector's plate increased an additional 164% in 1978, closing the year at $290.00 — a total 483% of its issue price of $60.00 — making it one of the highest gainers of all time. The second plate in this series, the 1978 ''A Thing of Beauty Is a Joy Forever'' **(84-31-1.2)**, advanced 33% to $80.00 by year's end.

1978 RIVER SHORE
FAMOUS AMERICANS
''Brown's Peace Corps''
84-69-1.3

1978 VILETTA
ZOLAN'S CHILDREN
''Erik and Dandelion''
84-91-1.1

1978 INCOLAY
ROMANTIC POETS
''A Thing of Beauty Is a Joy Forever''
84-31-1.2

Over the same twelve-month period the 1976 Gorham *DeGrazia Children* plate, ''Los Niños'' **(84-24-5.1)**, appreciated $120.00 to $450.00 for a total of 1,186% appreciation over its $35.00 issue price, and Fairmont's 1978 *Irene Spencer's Special Requests* plate, ''Hug Me'' **(84-14-7.1)**, advanced 155% to $140.00.

Equally impressive was the performance of the 1976 first plate in Studio Dante di Volteradici's *Grand Opera* series, ''Rigoletto'' **(38-90-1.1)** which advanced 48 points to $148.00, or 423% of its issue price. (The 1977 issue, ''Madama Butterfly'' **[38-90-1.2]**, gained 10 points and was quoted at $50.00 at year's end.)

''Innocence'' **(26-90-4.1)**, the first bone china Wedgwood collector's plate and the first plate in artist Mary Vickers' *Blossoming of Suzanne* series, had traded in options at 25 points above its $60.00 issue price even before it appeared in 1977 and advanced an additional 95 points to $180.00 in 1978. The second plate in the series, ''Cherish,'' was originally promised for spring 1978; by year's end, however, plates had still not yet appeared on the market, and options trading had faded.

In September, Limoges-Turgot announced it would complete its *Durand's Children* series **(18-52-1)** despite the death of artist Paul Durand who had evidently completed four canvases only weeks before he died. The first plate, ''Marie-Ange'' **(18-52-1.1)**, had shown little market activity by year's end.

1977 STUDIO DANTE DI VOLTERADICI
GRAND OPERA
''Madama Butterfly''
38-90-1.2

1978 FAIRMONT
*IRENE SPENCER'S
SPECIAL REQUESTS*
''Hug Me''
84-14-7.1

1976 GORHAM
DEGRAZIA CHILDREN
''Los Ninos''
84-24-5.1

1973 D'ARCEAU-LIMOGES
LAFAYETTE LEGACY
"The Secret Contract"
18-15-1.1

In the last week of the year collectors and dealers were saddened anew by the death of yet another — and perhaps the most famous — French plate artist, André Restieau. In the United States he was best known for his six-plate *Lafayette Legacy* series **(18-15-1)** for D'Arceau-Limoges which became the most sought-after collectible of the American Bicentennial. This series closed 1978 at $326.00 for a complete set, nearly three times original issue price, even before news of Restieau's death could have an effect.

The first issue in another Restieau series, the 1975 "Flight into Egypt" **(18-15-2.1)** from the *Nöel Vitrail* collection, was quoted at $110.00, 452% of issue price, at year's end. However, succeeding plates in this "stained-glass" series failed to stir collector interest during 1978. Interest in another plate by a noted French artist — the first issue in *Les Jeunes Filles des Saisons (Girls of the Seasons* **[18-15-4]**) by Guy Cambier for D'Arceau-Limoges was initially strong despite the relatively high issue price of $105.00. However, it closed the year still trading at issue.

1975 D'ARCEAU-LIMOGES
NÖEL VITRAIL
"Flight into Egypt
18-15-2.1

The market experienced no severe losses in 1978 and experts generally agreed that no particular significance could be read into the decline of the five Mother's Day and eleven Christmas commemoratives which accounted for sixteen of the twenty steepest declines.

The 1971 Bing & Grøndahl *Mother's Day* **(14-8-3.3)** posted the greatest percentage decrease, 20%, from $15.00 to $12.00. Other issues which suffered significant setbacks were the 1970 and 1971 plates in the Orrefors *Annual Cathedral* series **(76-57-1)** which slumped 13% and

15% respectively and the 1976 Royal Copenhagen *Historical* issue **(14-69-3.2)**, which fell 14%.

A December report on the Franklin Mint by CBS-TV's "60 Minutes" program, which was characterized by a Mint spokesman as "inaccurate and misleading," apparently caused some Mint issues to decline for the first time in twenty months. In on-camera interviews with CBS correspondent Morley Safer, dealers and collectors claimed that the resale value of Franklin Mint's coin and ingot collectibles was reduced to nothing but their silver content.

1972 FRANKLIN MINT
MOTHER'S DAY
"Mother and Child"
84-19-2.1

1977 ARABIA
KALEVALA
"Aino's Fate"
16-5-1.2

Although Franklin Mint collector's plates were not discussed, the 1972 *Mother's Day* issue **(84-19-2.1)** immediately declined 12% and all plates in the *Rockwell Christmas* series **(84-19-1)** were the only Rockwells that did not go up in the year-end trading boom that followed the artist's death.

One new issue which did not generate significant trading was "The Village Smithy" by sculptor Roger Brown, produced by Creative World in a new metal alloy in an edition of 15,000; another disappointment was the "Elvis Presley" plate issued by Amartco in memory of the singer in an edition of 10,000. Despite strong promotion, both plates were still at no better than issue price at the end of the year. Neither issue was Bradex-listed.

The 1978 market also saw its share of notable "firsts." The *Kalevala Annual* **(16-5-1)** by the firm of Arabia in Helsinki became the first Finnish series to be listed on the Bradex and the first collector's plate series by this venerable firm. Official Bradex listing was earned due to the *Kalevala's* impact in Europe where the Bradford Exchange had recently established headquarters in Switzerland to coordinate with subsidiary exchanges in Germany and England. The first issue in the *Kalevala* series, the 1976 "Vainamoinen's Sowing," was quoted at $100.00 by the end of 1978, up 233% from its $30.00 issue price. "Aino's Fate" **(16-5-1.2)**, the 1977 second plate in the series and the first with a regular North American allotment, closed the year up $5.00 from its issue price of $30.00.

Noteworthy for different reasons was "Colleen," the initial issue in Fairmont's *Classical American Beauties* series **(84-14-8)** by Vincent, a California artist known for his idealized nudes. Its subject was advertised as "clad only in the fragrance of roses," making it the first overtly suggestive collector's plate. Planned to begin a series of four plates in editions of 7,500, "Colleen" was still quoted at its $60.00 issue price at year's end.

1978 FAIRMONT
CLASSICAL AMERICAN BEAUTIES
"Colleen"
84-14-8.1

1978 ANNA PERENNA *BYZANTINE TRIPTYCH*

"Gabriel"	"Madonna and Child"	"Michael"
22-3-3.1-1	**22-3-3.1-2**	**22-3-3.1-3**

Another newly Bradex-listed issue was the "Byzantine Triptych" by artists Frank Russell and Gertrude Barrer. Consisting of three plates in a hinged frame, the triptych was the first three-plate issue in market history and carries the hallmark of Anna Perenna, a new firm begun by Klaus Vogt, former president of the Rosenthal sales organization in the United States. The set — "Gabriel" **(22-3-3.1-1)**, "Madonna and Child" **(22-3-3.1-2)**, and "Michael" **(22-3-3.1-3)** — was issued in an edition of 5,000 at $325.00. Two more triptychs are planned to complete the series which is derived from various styles of religious art.

Another two issues introduced by Anna Perenna were by husband-and-wife artists Dr. Irving Burgues and Carol Burgues. Dr. Burgues' plate, "Chun Li at the Pond," was offered in an edition of 5,000 at $100.00 as first in the *Oriental Tranquility* series; Carol Burgues' "June Dream," in an edition of 5,000 at $75.00, opened the *Enchanted Garden* series. Neither was Bradex-listed, and their market performance by year-end was no better than issue despite considerable advance publicity.

The same was true of Royal Doulton's first plate in the *American Tapestries* series by artist C.A. Brown, "Sleigh Bells," which also failed to advance and closed the year trading over-the-counter at its issue price of $70.00.

Also unlisted on the Bradex but watched closely by market analysts was the 1978 River Shore *Della Robbia* annual, first of four issues, hand painted in high-relief and inspired by the fifteenth-century master, André Della Robbia. "Adoration," the initial plate, was issued late in the year at the unusually high price of $550.00 in a relatively large edition of 5,000. If it should generate substantial over-the-counter trading, "Adoration" could encourage other makers to introduce more extremely high-issue-price plates, although it had done nothing by year's end.

1978 RIVER SHORE
DELLA ROBIA ANNUAL
"Adoration"

"The Wise Men," the second issue in a Christmas series, the first from Mettlach, the famous German steinmaker, was issued in an edition of 20,000, of which 6,000 plates were alloted to the American market at the high issue price of $175.00. However, the rest of the edition was offered in Europe at 275 Deutsche Marks (approximately $137.50), which led some European dealers to "bootleg" their plates into the United States and undercut the American issue price. Some American dealers also bought plates directly in Europe for resale in the U.S. at discounted prices, thus further undermining the plate's over-the-counter market position here. The plate closed the year down about 6% at $165.00. It was not Bradex-listed.

In July, the Edwin M. Knowles China Company announced its *Gone With the Wind* series by Raymond Kursár, to begin with "Scarlett" **(84-41-3.1)**, which was featured on the cover of the 1978 *Bradford Book*. However, no plates had been delivered against advance orders by the end of the year. Similar long delays had caused other issues to decline as collector interest fell off, but demand for "Scarlett" remained undiminished at year's end, and the plate was still being ordered at the original issue price of $21.50.

Knowles also added three new issues to its *Wizard of Oz* collection: "If I Only Had a Brain" **(84-41-1.2)**, "If I Only Had a Heart" **(84-41-1.3)**, and "If I Were King" **(84-41-1.4)**. All three issues posted no advances during the year, but they were often traded together among dealers, and market insiders expect complete-set trading once the eight-plate series is finished in 1979.

The first plate in another Knowles series, "The Fourth of July" **(84-41-2.1)** in the *Americana Holidays* collection by Don Spaulding, was disappointing in view of its advance promotion and closed the year still trading at issue price.

1978 D'ARCEAU-LIMOGES
WOMEN OF THE CENTURY
"Hélène, l'Intrepide"
18-15-3.9

1973 ROYAL DOULTON
MOTHER AND CHILD
"Colette and Child"
26-69-2.1

With the issuance of the ninth and tenth plates in the collection, D'Arceau-Limoges' twelve-plate *Women of the Century* series (*Les Femmes du Siècle* [18-15-3]) neared completion. The work of French painter and stage designer François Ganeau, the series is sponsored by the United Nations and was initially available only to private subscribers directly from Limoges. However, various *Women of the Century* issues began appearing in retail shops in 1978 as U.S. dealers bought plates and future options from original subscribers. Early plate editions in the series closed the year strong, at 195% (Plate I, 1976); 131% (Plate II, 1976); and 123% (Plates III-VI, 1976-'77) of their original issue prices, and analysts looked for even sharper gains as more dealers entered this market.

Royal Doulton completed four series in 1978 including *Commedia Dell'Arte* **(26-69-3)** by LeRoy Nieman (which closed the year up 15% to $288.00 for all four plates); Dong Kingman's *Ports of Call* **(26-69-5)**, which also ended after four plates, and the seven-plate *Beswick Christmas* series **(26-69-1)**. All plates in the latter two series were still trading at or near issue price.

The fourth series, however — Edna Hibel's *Mother and Child* collection — was quoted at more than three times the total issue price for all six plates by year's end. The first plate in this series, "Collette and Child," is the landmark issue which introduced Hibel's work to the plate world and set a record for quick appreciation at that time. At the end of 1978 it was trading at $510.00, up more than 1,100% from its $40.00 issue price in 1973.

The 1978 plate, the third, in Haviland Parlon's *Mother's Day* series **(18-32-3)** was cancelled and the future of the series appeared doubtful at year's end.

Although a design by Charlotte Jackson for "The King and His Ladies" plate had been publicized since the fall of 1977, The Calhoun Collectors Society announced at mid-year that her work would not be used and that the artist for all six issues in the *Golden Age of Cinema* series (not Bradex-listed) would instead be Lawrence Whittaker.

"Baby's First Step," a collector's plate attributed to Norman Rockwell, appeared in two different versions — one by Ridgewood (formerly a prominent name and maker of the famous 1974 "Scotty Gets His Tree" for the Rockwell Society of America), and one by Fairmont, a recent entry in the field. Both versions bore the seal of the Norman Rockwell Museum in Philadelphia.

The museum, which claimed to own the artwork copyright, said it originally contracted for the plate to be made by Ridgewood and only had it made by Fairmont after Ridgewood failed to produce by the agreed date, apparently because of the liquidation of Ridgewood's assets. Ridgewood, however, produced 9,900 plates anyway and began distributing them at an issue price of $28.50 in April through Century House,

an affiliated company.

The museum, on the other hand, said it considered the Fairmont version to be the "original" and began distributing it in May at the same $28.50 issue price, calling it the first in a twelve-plate *American Family* series, also in an edition of 9,900.

Still further confusion was added by the fact that neither of the two editions could truly be called Norman Rockwell's work since the original black-and-white sketches done by Rockwell in the 1960s had been colored by another artist, George Malick. Neither could ever be Bradex-listed because they violated the primary rule that there can never be more than one edition of a limited edition.

Plate conventions around the country continued to attract many more thousands of collectors than ever before. In July, more than four thousand people — one-quarter of them dealers — attended the Fourth International Plate Collectors Convention held in South Bend, Indiana.

In September, an overwhelming total of 16,627 collectors jammed the Second Annual World Plate Collectors Fair in New York City.

Chairman of the committee that organized the Fair for the Collector Platemakers Guild was Lee Benson whose death just a week after the Fair closed was a great loss to the plate collecting world. Mr. Benson was a pioneer in the field and founder and chief executive of Creative World and Veneto Flair.

In October, the first American Limited Edition Association (ALEA) Convention and Fair drew nearly two thousand collectors and dealers in Seattle, Washington.

Finally, 1978 will also be remembered as the year in which an early Christmas plate was discovered that may cast a new light on the origin of all collector's plates. Found in a private collection in Germany by Klaus Vogt (who was just beginning his new Anna Perenna, Inc., plate-producing firm), the plate is apparently hand-painted in cobalt-blue underglaze on bas-relief, identified by a Rosenthal backstamp, and — most surprisingly — dated 1907.

Assuming this new 1907 Rosenthal to be authentic and therefore predating the first previously known plate in the Rosenthal Christmas series, a number of factors still seemed to suggest that it did not mark the beginning of that series but was instead an early attempt by Rosenthal to copy the successful Bing & Grøndahl Christmas plates with an issue made in Germany exclusively for the Danish market.

Unlike the early Rosenthal Christmas issues (from 1910) with fairly wide borders and the German word for Christmas, "Weihnachten," the 1907 Rosenthal, like the earliest Bing & Grøndahls, is borderless with its legend in Danish, "Jule-Aften 1907"; the lettering is almost identical to the style used on all Bing & Grøndahl Christmas plates; the subject appears to be an ocean scene even though Bavaria (the home of Rosenthal) is landlocked; and even the stars in the sky are in exactly the same position as those in the 1906 Bing & Grøndahl plate. In total, the composition of the 1907 Rosenthal is strikingly similar to the 1906 Bing & Grøndahl, substituting only a boy in a boat for a boy driving a sleigh.

So a host of unanswered historical questions surrounded the newly discovered 1907 Rosenthal plate. Was it in fact meant to be a prototype for a German-made, Danish-style series? Was the series continued after 1907? If so, where were the subsequent issues for 1908 or 1909? If not, why did Rosenthal feel confident enough to begin its own Christmas series just three years later?

Only one thing seemed certain: The 1907 Rosenthal showed there was more to be discovered, and if other such early editions can be found, collector's plate history will have to be rewritten.

1907 ROSENTHAL
(Untitled)

ARRANGEMENT OF THE LISTINGS

The Bradford Book of Collector's Plates is the official directory of all major issues regularly traded in the market. It is used to locate and identify all plates quickly and accurately. The plates are arranged by:

Country of origin in alphabetical order.

Plate Maker within each country, also in alphabetical order.

Plate Series of each maker in chronological order beginning with the maker's first series.

Individual Plates in each series, also in chronological order beginning with the first plate.

To speed identification, each plate is listed by its Bradex number. *These numbers are in sequence but not consecutive.* The number on the upper outer corner of each page indicates the first plate listed on that page.

THE BRADEX NUMBER

of a plate is made up of four numbers.

(The number used as an example here is that of the 1904 Bing & Grondahl Christmas plate)

14-8-1.10*

COUNTRY	MAKER	SERIES	PLATE
The first number indicates the country of origin. The number **14** is for Denmark. A list of countries with their Bradex numbers is in the Table of Contents on page **5**.	The second number indicates the plate maker. The number **8** is for Bing & Grondahl. A list of makers with their Bradex numbers is in the Table of Contents on page **5**.	The third number indicates the maker's series, listed in chronological order. The number **1** is for Bing & Grondahl's first series, the Christmas series. A list of series by type and name with their Bradex numbers is in the Appendixes on page **A-8**.	The fourth number indicates the individual plate within each series, listed in chronological order. The number **10** is for the tenth plate in the Bing & Grondahl Christmas series, *View of Copenhagen from Fredericksberg Hill*, the 1904. A list of plate titles with their Bradex numbers is in the Appendixes on page **A-8**.

Bradex numbers are indexed by *Maker and Series Types and Names* (in the front of the book) and by *Plate Titles* and *Artists* in the Appendixes. A Glossary of Commonly Used Terms is also provided in the Appendixes.

LOCATION OF OTHER INFORMATION

Information on history and trademarks is included in each maker's listing; artist, medium, plate diameter, hanging provisions, edition limits and numbering appear with each series listing; Bradex number, plate title, artist and issue price are found below each plate in the series. The listings are complete to 1978 issues, except where the maker did not provide information by press time. Typical edition limits given by makers may be defined as follows:

Edition size limited to 10,000 means only 10,000 plates were issued in the edition, and each plate was numbered.

Edition size limited by announced quantity of 10,000 means only 10,000 plates were issued in the edition, and plates were not numbered.

Edition size undisclosed, limited by period of issue means the edition was limited to the number of plates produced during an announced time period.

Edition size undisclosed, limited by year of issue means the edition was limited to the number of plates produced during the year of issue.

Edition size undisclosed means maker provided no information regarding edition size.

*plates issued in sets use an additional successive digit to indicate their identification within the set (see Anna Perenna 22-3-3.1-1).

ARGENTINA
PORCELANA GRANADA
(Rosario)

Since 1972, the Porcelana Granada series of Christmas plates has been made by one of Argentina's largest porcelain factories, Porcelanas Verbano. (The 1971 plate was produced in Cali, Colombia.) Porcelanas Verbano is a recognized producer of dinnerware and hand-painted pieces. The Christmas series, *Pax in Terra*, based on the life of Christ, was begun in 1971 and is to run 15 years.

ARGENTINA
PORCELANA GRANADA
(Rosario)

Pax in Terra (*Peace on Earth*)
Artist: As indicated
Overglaze porcelain decorated in
  cobalt blue
Diameter: 18 centimeters (7 inches)
Pierced foot rim
Edition size: As indicated
Numbered since 1972 without
  certificate

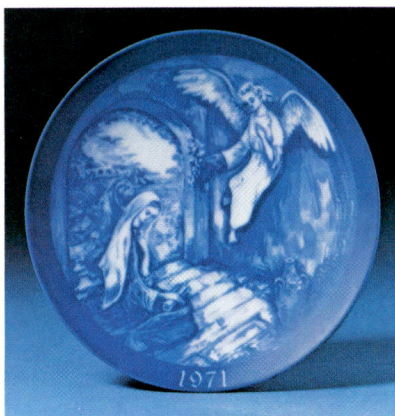

4-61-1.1
1971 *The Annunciation.*
Artist: Tom Fennell, Jr.
Issue price: $12.00. Edition size limited
to announced quantity of 9,300.

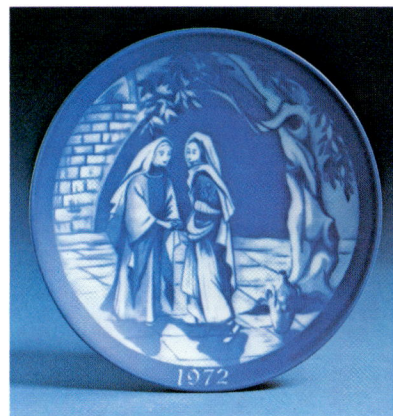

4-61-1.2
1972 *Mary and Elizabeth.*
Artist: Gerry Sparks.
Issue price: $13.00.
Edition size limited to 6,000.

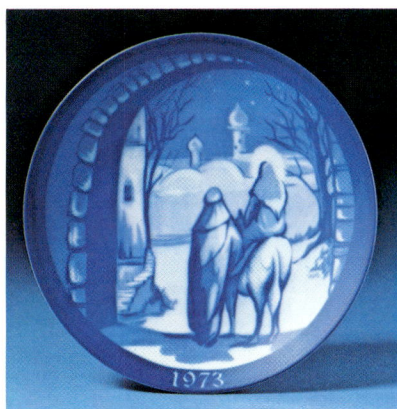

4-61-1.3
1973 *Road to Bethlehem.*
Artist: Gerry Sparks.
Issue price: $14.00.
Edition size limited to 5,000.

4-61-1.4
1974 *No Room at the Inn.*
Artist: Gerry Sparks.
Issue price: $15.00.
Edition size limited to 5,000.

4-61-1.5
1975 *Shepherds in the Field.*
Artist: Gerry Sparks.
Issue price: $16.50.
Edition size limited to 5,000.

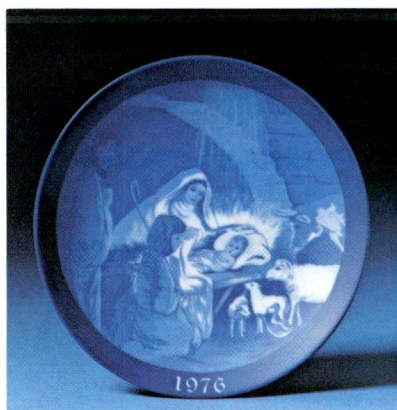

4-61-1.6
1976 *The Nativity.*
Artist: Gerry Sparks.
Issue price: $17.50.
Edition size limited to 5,000.

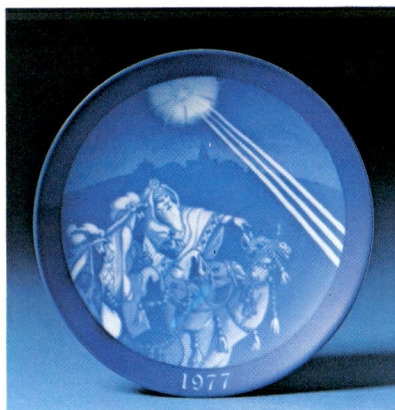

4-61-1.7
1977 *Three Kings.*
Artist: Gerry Sparks.
Issue price: $18.00.
Edition size limited to 5,000.

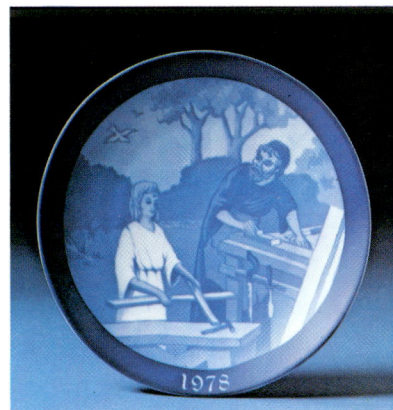

4-61-1.8
1978 *Young Carpenter.*
Artist: Gerry Sparks.
Issue price: $18.00.
Edition size limited to 5,000.

Maker had
no photo at
press time

4-61-1.9
1979 *Calling of Disciples.*
Artist: Gerry Sparks.
Issue price: $19.00.
Edition size limited to 5,000.

KONGELIG HOFLEVERANDOR

COPENHAGEN PORCELAIN
BING & GRØNDAHL
B&G

Bing & Grøndahl, Denmark's second oldest existing porcelain maker (after Royal Copenhagen), was established in 1853 by Frederick Vilhelm Grøndahl and M. H. and J. H. Bing. Grøndahl, a young sculptor previously employed by Royal Copenhagen, supplied the artistic talent while the Bing brothers provided financial backing. Although Grøndahl died before the manufactory's third year of operation, his name was retained in honor of his contribution. Bing & Grøndahl has continued under the leadership of the Bing family for five generations.

The world's first collector's plate, "Behind the Frozen Window," was issued by Bing & Grøndahl in 1895. This began its *Christmas Series* which has been produced each year without interruption despite wars and economic crises. Plates in this series are now the most widely collected of all plates in the market. In 1969 Bing & Grøndahl issued the first Mother's Day plate, "Dog and Puppies."

Besides limited-edition collector's plates, Bing & Grøndahl makes a variety of porcelain articles, including figurines and tableware. Many of their porcelain works can be found in museums around the world and they have achieved the distinction of appointment to the Royal Courts of Denmark, Sweden and Great Britain. This distinction is symbolized by the crown which is part of their trademark.

Christmas Series

Artist: As indicated

True underglaze porcelain hand painted in Copenhagen blue on bas-relief

Diameter: 18 centimeters (7 inches)

Pierced foot rim

Edition size undisclosed, limited by year of issue

Not numbered, without certificate; individually initialed on back by each painter

14-8-1.1
1895 *Behind the Frozen Window.*
Artist: F. A. Hallin.
Issue price: $.50.

14-8-1.2
1896 *New Moon over Snow-covered Trees.*
Artist: F. A. Hallin.
Issue price: $.50.

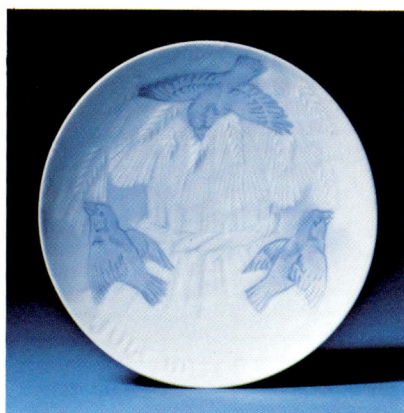

14-8-1.3
1897 *Christmas Meal of the Sparrows.*
Artist: F. A. Hallin.
Issue price: $.75.

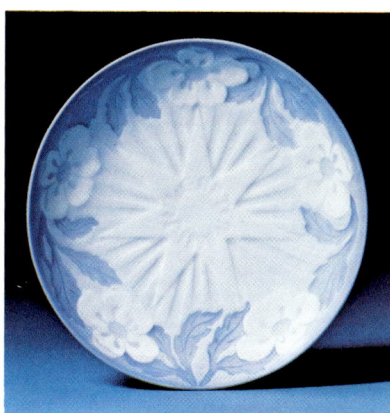

14-8-1.4
1898 *Christmas Roses and Christmas Star.*
Artist: Fanny Garde.
Issue price: $.75.

14-8-1.5
1899 *The Crows Enjoying Christmas.*
Artist: Dahl Jensen.
Issue price: $.75.

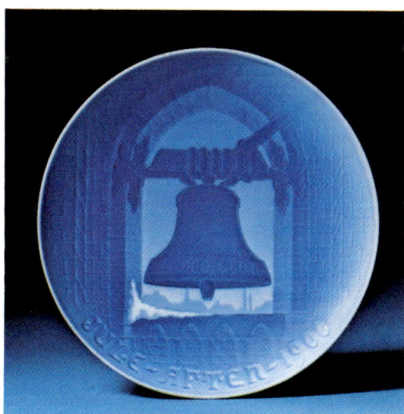

14-8-1.6
1900 *Church Bells Chiming in Christmas.*
Artist: Dahl Jensen.
Issue price: $.75.

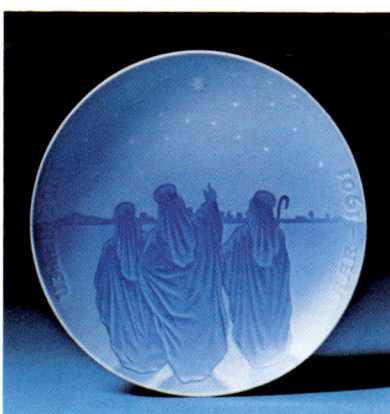

14-8-1.7
1901 *The Three Wise Men from the East.*
Artist: S. Sabra.
Issue price: $1.00.

14-8-1.8
1902 *Interior of a Gothic Church.*
Artist: Dahl Jensen.
Issue price: $1.00.

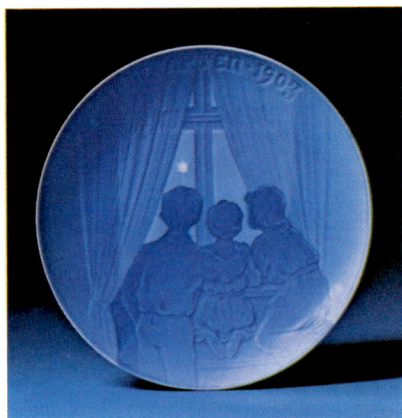

14-8-1.9
1903 *Happy Expectation of Children.*
Artist: Margrethe Hyldahl.
Issue price: $1.00.

14-8-1.10
1904 *View of Copenhagen from Frederiksberg Hill.*
Artist: Cathinka Olsen.
Issue price: $1.00.

14-8-1.11
1905 *Anxiety of the Coming Christmas Night.*
Artist: Dahl Jensen.
Issue price: $1.00.

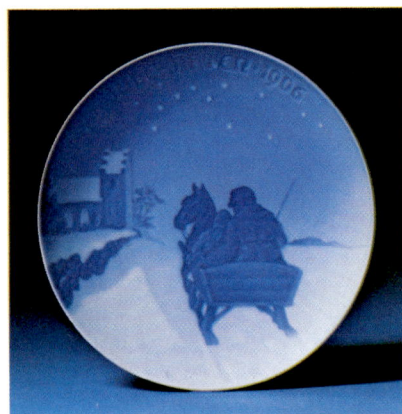

14-8-1.12
1906 *Sleighing to Church on Christmas Eve.*
Artist: Dahl Jensen.
Issue price: $1.00.

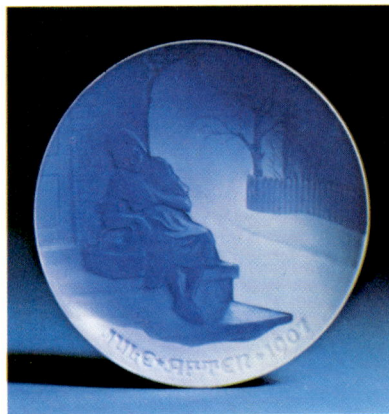

14-8-1.13
1907 *The Little Match Girl.*
Artist: E. Plockross.
Issue price: $1.00.

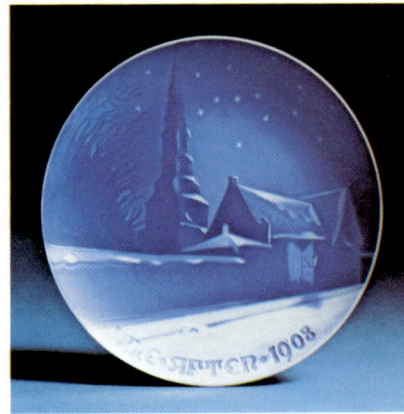

14-8-1.14
1908 *St. Petri Church of Copenhagen.*
Artist: Povl Jorgensen.
Issue price: $1.00.

14-8-1.15
1909 *Happiness over the Yule Tree.*
Artist: Aarestrup.
Issue price: $1.50.

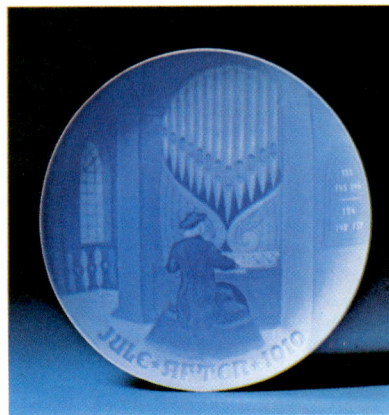

14-8-1.16
1910 *The Old Organist.*
Artist: C. Ersgaard.
Issue price: $1.50.

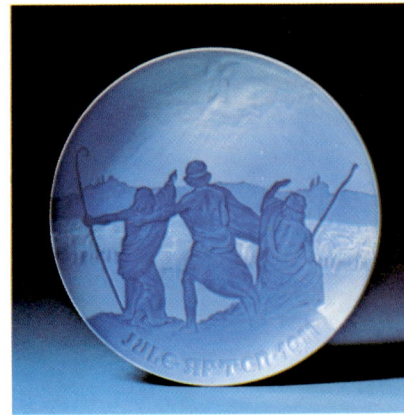

14-8-1.17
1911 *First It Was Sung by Angels to Shepherds in the Fields.*
Artist: H. Moltke.
Issue price: $1.50.

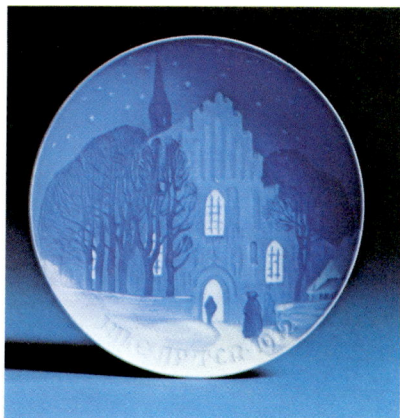

14-8-1.18
1912 *Going to Church on Christmas Eve.*
Artist: Einar Hansen.
Issue price: $1.50.

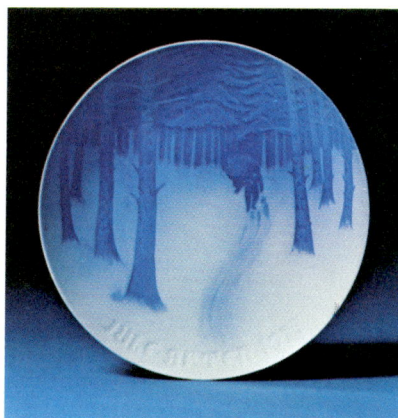

14-8-1.19
1913 *Bringing Home the Yule Tree.*
Artist: Th. Larsen.
Issue price: $1.50.

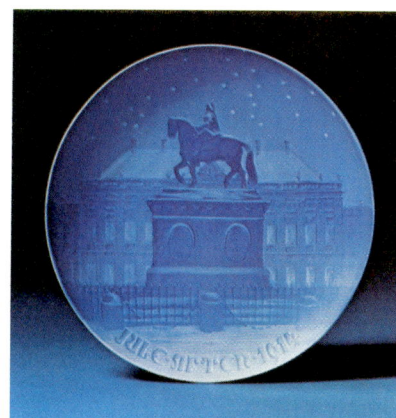

14-8-1.20
1914 *Royal Castle of Amalienborg,
Copenhagen.*
Artist: Th. Larsen.
Issue price: $1.50.

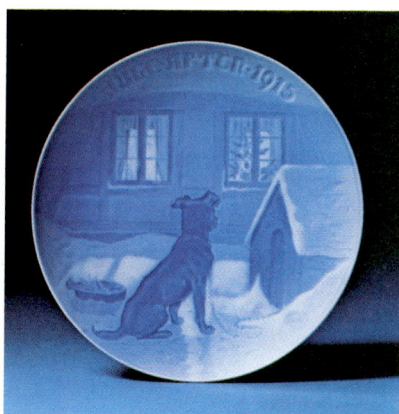

14-8-1.21
1915 *Chained Dog Getting Double Meal
on Christmas Eve.*
Artist: Dahl Jensen.
Issue price: $1.50.

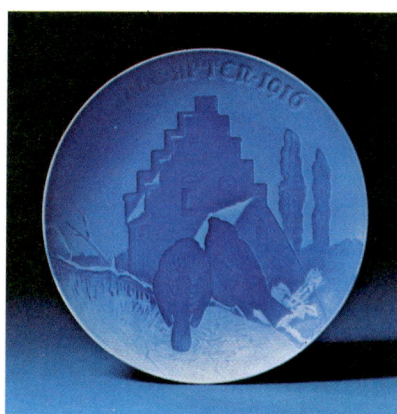

14-8-1.22
1916 *Christmas Prayer of the Sparrows.*
Artist: J. Bloch Jorgensen.
Issue price: $1.50.

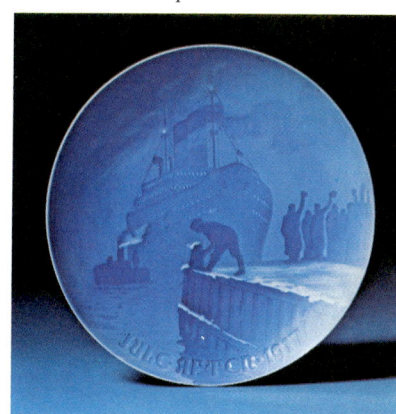

14-8-1.23
1917 *Arrival of the Christmas Boat.*
Artist: Achton Friis.
Issue price: $1.50.

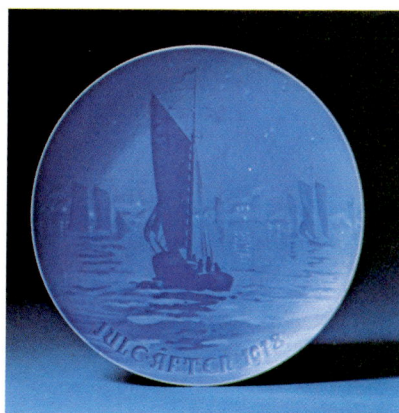

14-8-1.24
1918 *Fishing Boat Returning Home for
Christmas.*
Artist: Achton Friis.
Issue price: $1.50.

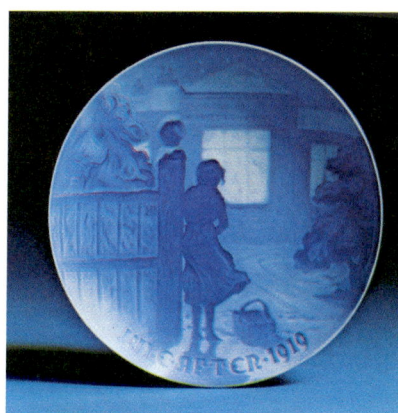

14-8-1.25
1919 *Outside the Lighted Window.*
Artist: Achton Friis.
Issue price: $2.00.

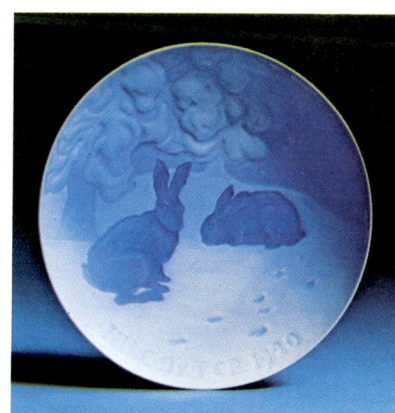

14-8-1.26
1920 *Hare in the Snow.*
Artist: Achton Friis.
Issue price: $2.00.

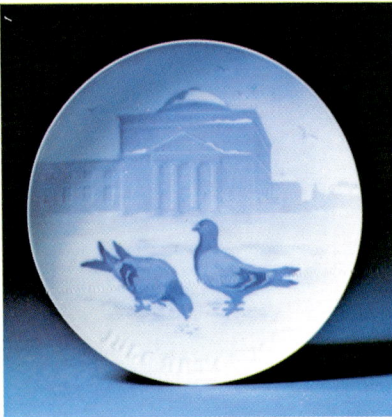

14-8-1.27
1921 *Pigeons in the Castle Court.*
Artist: Achton Friis.
Issue price: $2.00.

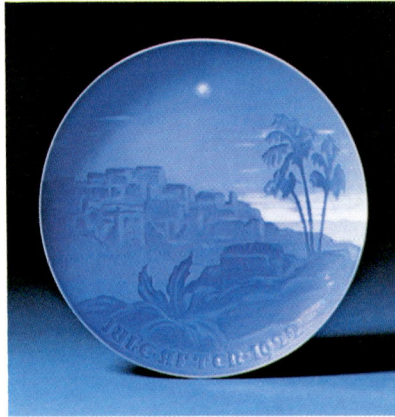

14-8-1.28
1922 *Star of Bethlehem.*
Artist: Achton Friis.
Issue price: $2.00.

14-8-1.29
1923 *Royal Hunting Castle, the Ermitage.*
Artist: Achton Friis.
Issue price: $2.00.

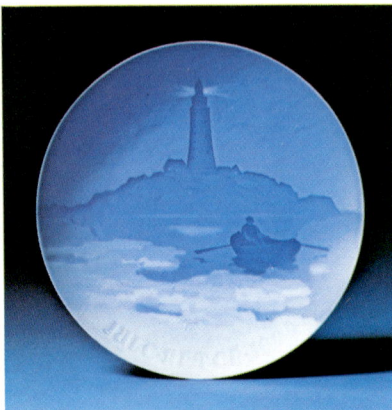

14-8-1.30
1924 *Lighthouse in Danish Waters.*
Artist: Achton Friis.
Issue price: $2.50.

14-8-1.31
1925 *The Child's Christmas.*
Artist: Achton Friis.
Issue price: $2.50.

14-8-1.32
1926 *Churchgoers on Christmas Day.*
Artist: Achton Friis.
Issue price: $2.50.

14-8-1.33
1927 *Skating Couple.*
Artist: Achton Friis.
Issue price: $2.50.

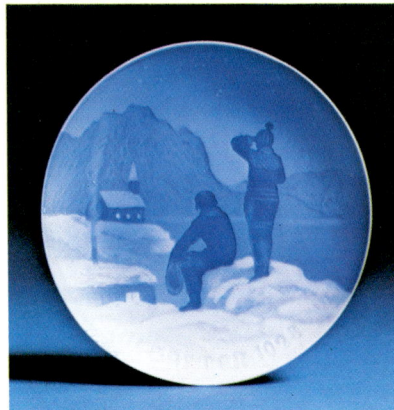

14-8-1.34
1928 *Eskimos Looking at Village Church
in Greenland.*
Artist: Achton Friis.
Issue price: $2.50.

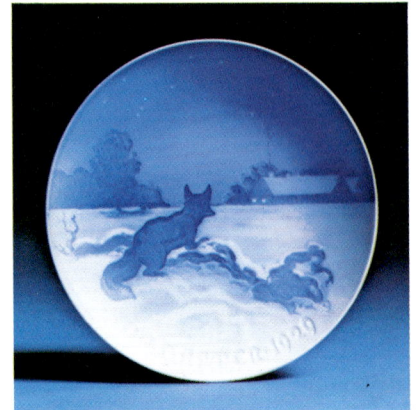

14-8-1.35
1929 *Fox Outside Farm on Christmas Eve.*
Artist: Achton Friis.
Issue price: $2.50.

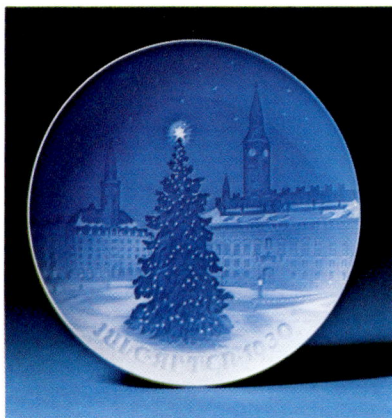

14-8-1.36
1930 *Yule Tree in Town Hall Square of Copenhagen.*
Artist: H. Flugenring.
Issue price: $2.50.

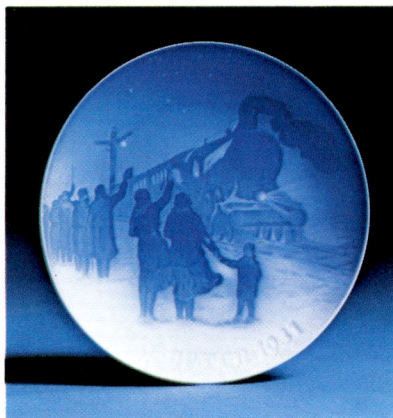

14-8-1.37
1931 *Arrival of the Christmas Train.*
Artist: Achton Friis.
Issue price: $2.50.

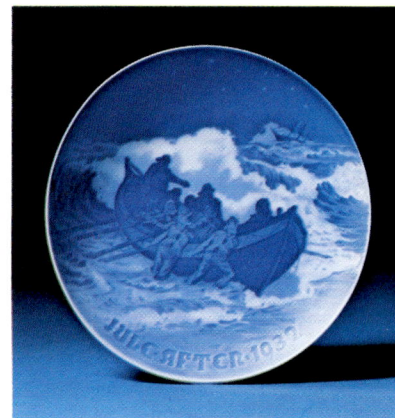

14-8-1.38
1932 *Lifeboat at Work.*
Artist: H. Flugenring.
Issue price: $2.50.

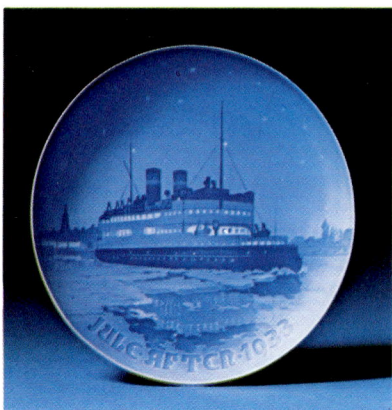

14-8-1.39
1933 *The Korsor-Nyborg Ferry.*
Artist: H. Flugenring.
Issue price: $3.00.

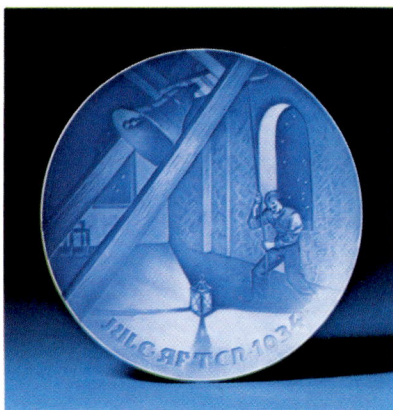

14-8-1.40
1934 *Church Bell in Tower.*
Artist: Immanuel Tjerne.
Issue price: $3.00.

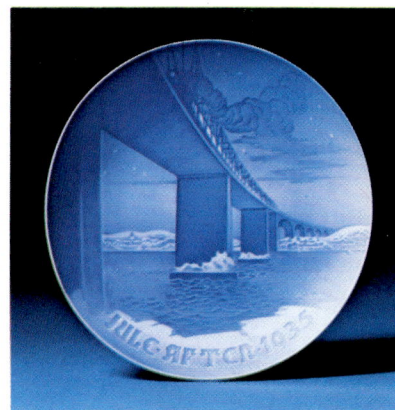

14-8-1.41
1935 *Lillebelt Bridge Connecting Funen with Jutland.*
Artist: Ove Larsen.
Issue price: $3.00.

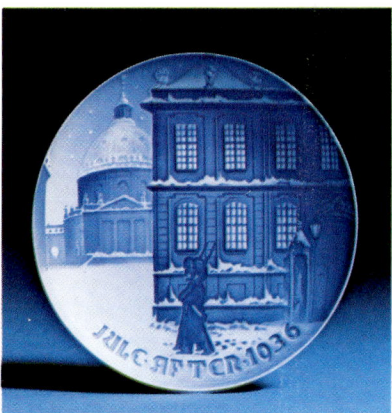

14-8-1.42.
1936 *Royal Guard Outside Amalienborg Castle in Copenhagen.*
Artist: Ove Larsen.
Issue price: $3.00.

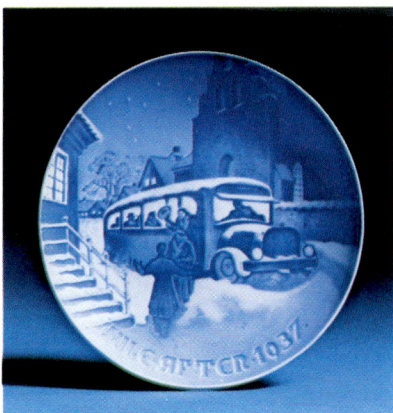

14-8-1.43
1937 *Arrival of Christmas Guests.*
Artist: Ove Larsen.
Issue price: $3.00.

14-8-1.44
1938 *Lighting the Candles.*
Artist: Immanuel Tjerne.
Issue price: $3.00.

14-8-1.45
1939 *Ole Lock-Eye, the Sandman.*
Artist: Immanuel Tjerne.
Issue price: $3.00.

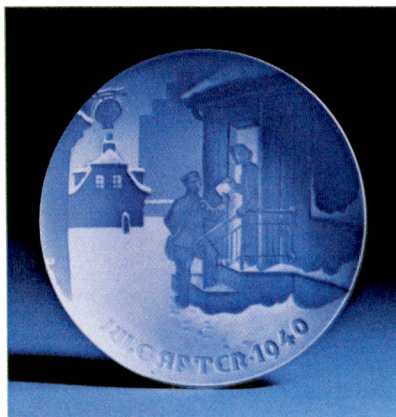

14-8-1.46
1940 *Delivering Christmas Letters.*
Artist: Ove Larsen.
Issue price: $4.00.

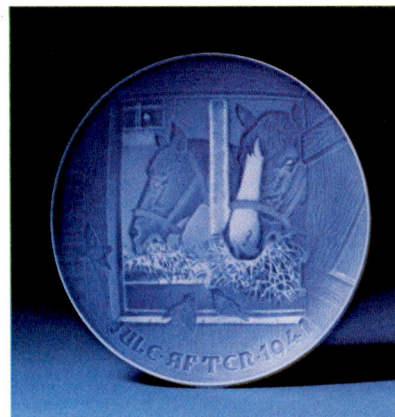

14-8-1.47
1941 *Horses Enjoying Christmas Meal in Stable.*
Artist: Ove Larsen.
Issue price: $4.00.

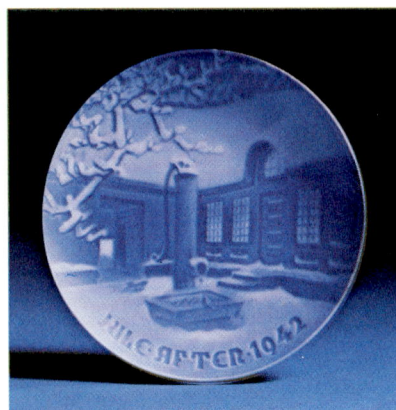

14-8-1.48
1942 *Danish Farm on Christmas Night.*
Artist: Ove Larsen.
Issue price: $4.00.

14-8-1.49
1943 *The Ribe Cathedral.*
Artist: Ove Larsen.
Issue price: $5.00.

14-8-1.50
1944 *Sorgenfri Castle.*
Artist: Ove Larsen.
Issue price: $5.00.

14-8-1.51
1945 *The Old Water Mill.*
Artist: Ove Larsen.
Issue price: $5.00.

14-8-1.52
1946 *Commemoration Cross in Honor
of Danish Sailors Who Lost Their Lives
in World War II.*
Artist: Margrethe Hyldahl.
Issue price: $5.00.

14-8-1.53
1947 *Dybbol Mill.*
Artist: Margrethe Hyldahl.
Issue price: $5.00.

14-8-1.54
1948 *Watchman, Sculpture of Town Hall, Copenhagen.*
Artist: Margrethe Hyldahl.
Issue price: $5.50.

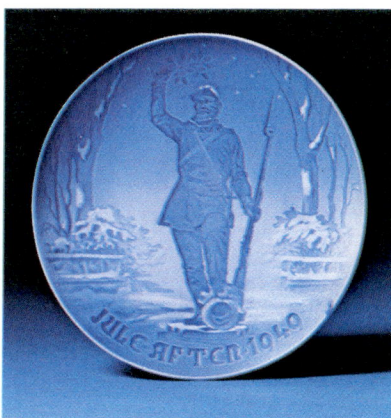

14-8-1.55
1949 *Landsoldaten, 19th Century Danish Soldier.*
Artist: Margrethe Hyldahl.
Issue price: $5.50.

14-8-1.56
1950 *Kronborg Castle at Elsinore.*
Artist: Margrethe Hyldahl.
Issue price: $5.50.

14-8-1.57
1951 *Jens Bang, New Passenger Boat Running Between Copenhagen and Aalborg.*
Artist: Margrethe Hyldahl.
Issue price: $6.00.

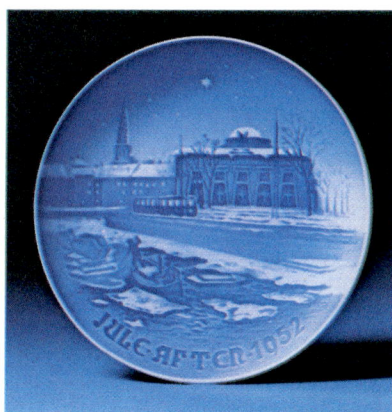

14-8-1.58
1952 *Old Copenhagen Canals at Wintertime with Thorvaldsen Museum in Background.*
Artist: Borge Pramvig.
Issue price: $6.00.

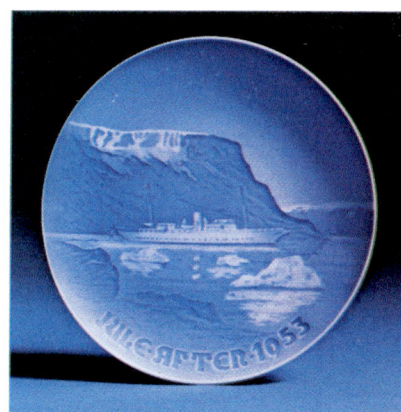

14-8-1.59
1953 *Royal Boat in Greenland Waters.*
Artist: Kjeld Bonfils.
Issue price: $7.00.

14-8-1.60
1954 *Birthplace of Hans Christian Andersen, with Snowman.*
Artist: Borge Pramvig.
Issue price: $7.50.

14-8-1.61
1955 *Kalundborg Church.*
Artist: Kjeld Bonfils.
Issue price: $8.00.

14-8-1.62
1956 *Christmas in Copenhagen.*
Artist: Kjeld Bonfils.
Issue price: $8.50.

14-8-1.63
1957 *Christmas Candles.*
Artist: Kjeld Bonfils.
Issue price: $9.00.

14-8-1.64
1958 *Santa Claus.*
Artist: Kjeld Bonfils.
Issue price: $9.50.

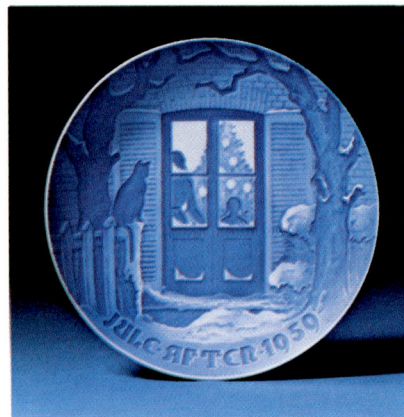

14-8-1.65
1959 *Christmas Eve.*
Artist: Kjeld Bonfils.
Issue price: $10.00.

14-8-1.66
1960 *Danish Village Church.*
Artist: Kjeld Bonfils.
Issue price: $10.00.

14-8-1.67
1961 *Winter Harmony.*
Artist: Kjeld Bonfils.
Issue price: $10.50.

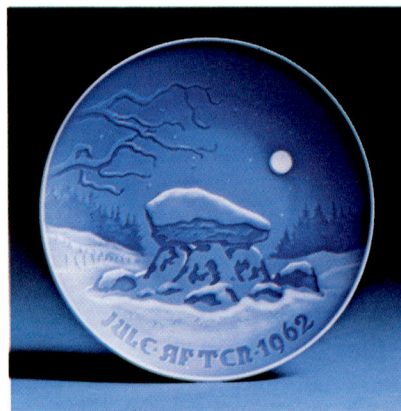

14-8-1.68
1962 *Winter Night.*
Artist: Kjeld Bonfils.
Issue price: $11.00.

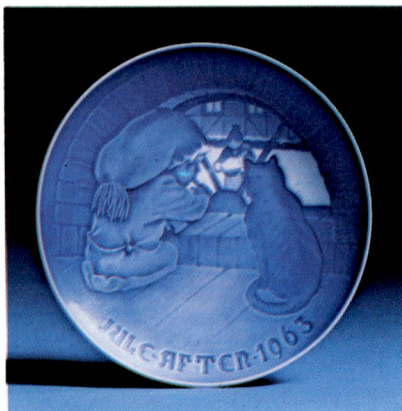

14-8-1.69
1963 *The Christmas Elf.*
Artist: Henry Thelander.
Issue price: $11.00.

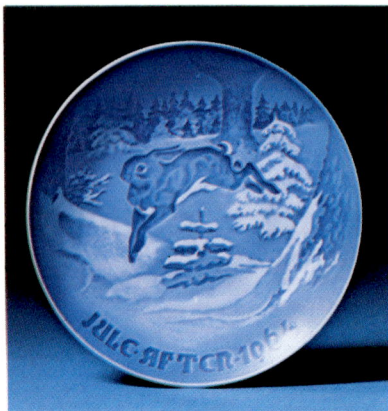

14-8-1.70
1964 *The Fir Tree and Hare.*
Artist: Henry Thelander.
Issue price: $11.50.

14-8-1.71
1965 *Bringing Home the Christmas Tree.*
Artist: Henry Thelander.
Issue price: $12.00.

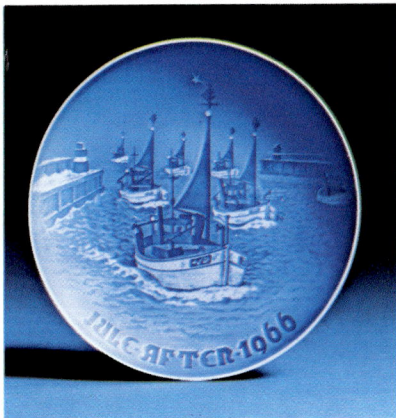

14-8-1.72
1966 *Home for Christmas.*
Artist: Henry Thelander.
Issue price: $12.00.

14-8-1.73
1967 *Sharing the Joy of Christmas.*
Artist: Henry Thelander.
Issue price: $13.00.

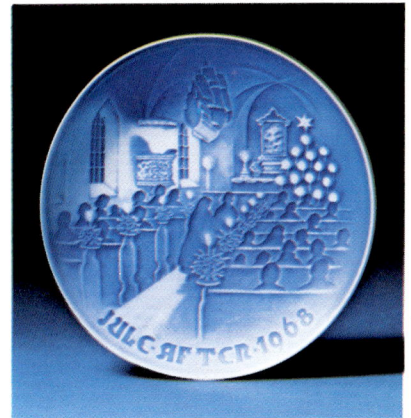

14-8-1.74
1968 *Christmas in Church.*
Artist: Henry Thelander.
Issue price: $14.00.

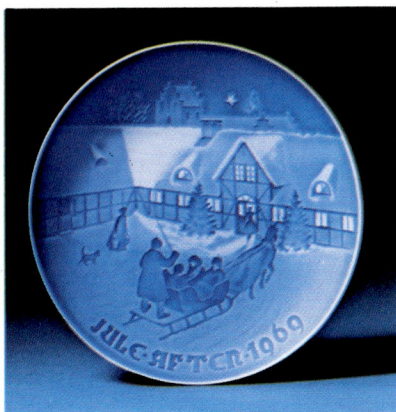

14-8-1.75
1969 *Arrival of Christmas Guests.*
Artist: Henry Thelander.
Issue price: $14.00.

14-8-1.76
1970 *Pheasants in the Snow at Christmas.*
Artist: Henry Thelander.
Issue price: $14.50.

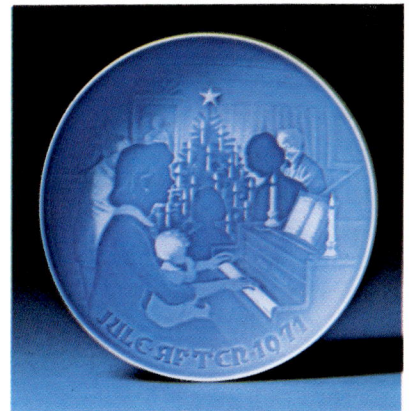

14-8-1.77
1971 *Christmas at Home.*
Artist: Henry Thelander.
Issue price: $15.00.

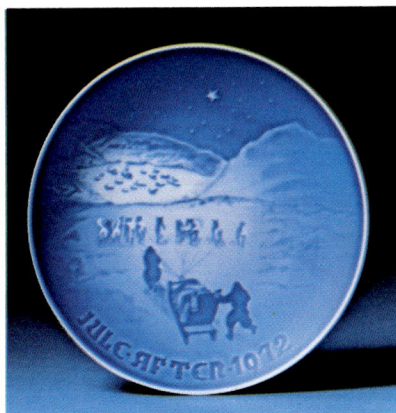

14-8-1.78
1972 *Christmas in Greenland.*
Artist: Henry Thelander.
Issue price: $16.50.

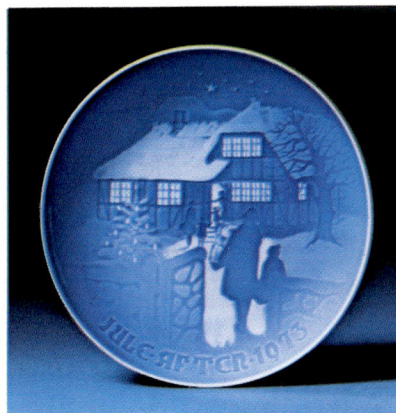

14-8-1.79
1973 *Family Reunion.*
Artist: Henry Thelander.
Issue price: $19.50.

14-8-1.80
1974 *Christmas in the Village.*
Artist: Henry Thelander.
Issue price: $22.00.

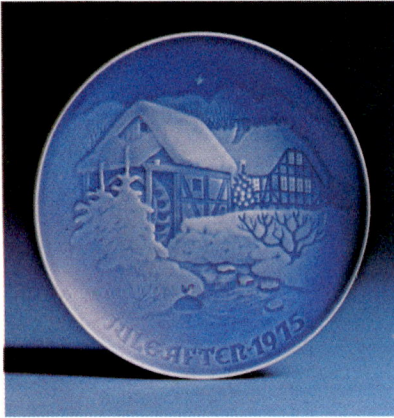

14-8-1.81
1975 *The Old Water Mill.*
Artist: Henry Thelander.
Issue price: $27.50.

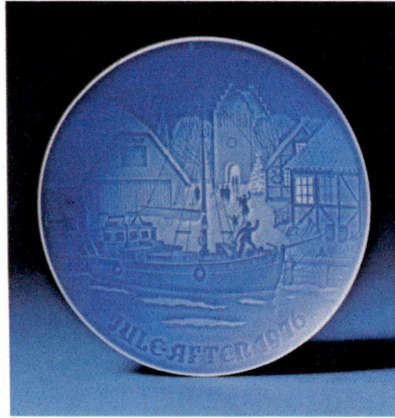

14-8-1.82
1976 *Christmas Welcome.*
Artist: Henry Thelander.
Issue price: $27.50.

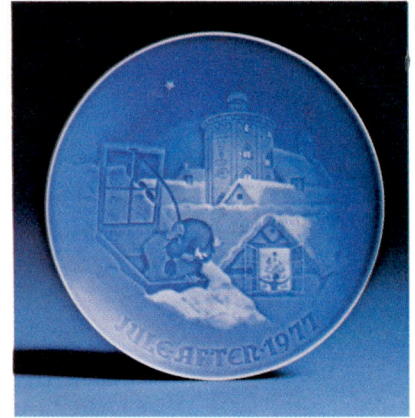

14-8-1.83
1977 *Copenhagen Christmas.*
Artist: Henry Thelander.
Issue price: $29.50.

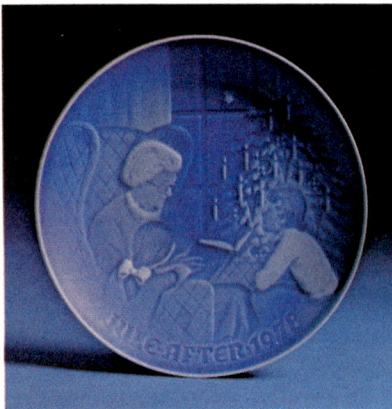

14-8-1.84
1978 *A Christmas Tale.*
Artist: Henry Thelander.
Issue price: $32.00.

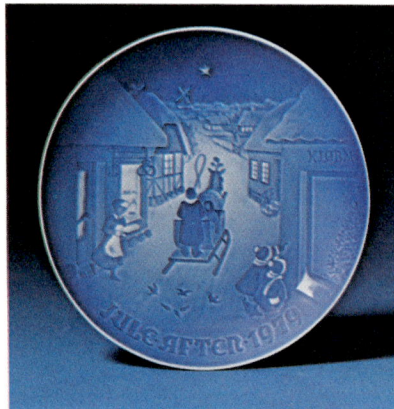

14-8-1.85
1979 *White Christmas.*
Artist: Henry Thelander.
Issue price: $36.50.

Mother's Day Series

Artist: Henry Thelander

True underglaze porcelain hand painted in Copenhagen blue on bas-relief

Diameter: 15.5 centimeters (6 inches)

Pierced foot rim

Edition size undisclosed, limited by year of issue

Not numbered, without certificate; individually initialed on back by each painter

14-8-3.1
1969 *Dog and Puppies.*
Artist: Henry Thelander.
Issue price: $9.75.

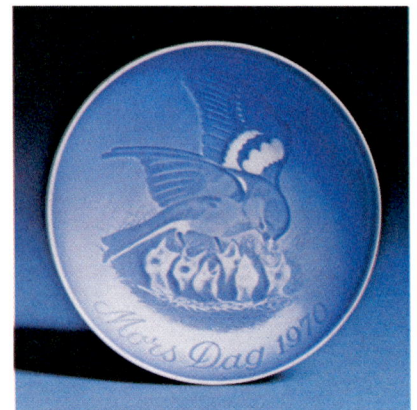

14-8-3.2
1970 *Bird and Chicks.*
Artist: Henry Thelander.
Issue price: $10.00.

14-8-3.3
1971 *Cat and Kitten.*
Artist: Henry Thelander.
Issue price: $11.00.

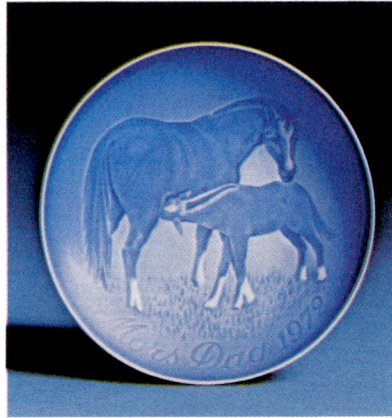

14-8-3.4
1972 *Mare and Foal.*
Artist: Henry Thelander.
Issue price: $12.00.

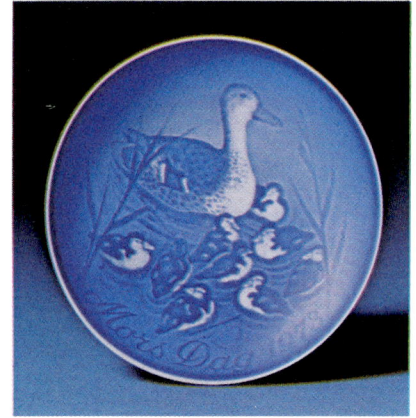

14-8-3.5
1973 *Duck and Ducklings.*
Artist: Henry Thelander.
Issue price: $13.00.

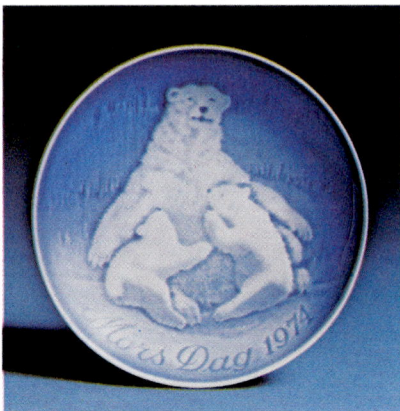

14-8-3.6
1974 *Bear and Cubs.*
Artist: Henry Thelander.
Issue price: $16.50.

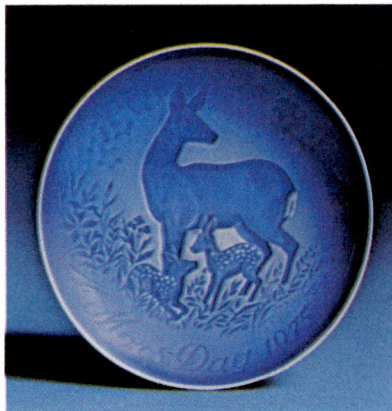

14-8-3.7
1975 *Doe and Fawns.*
Artist: Henry Thelander.
Issue price: $19.50.

14-8-3.8
1976 *Swan Family.*
Artist: Henry Thelander.
Issue price: $22.50.

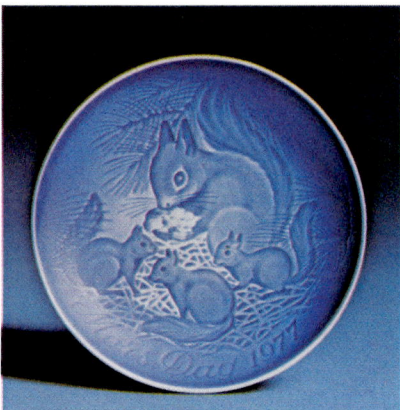

14-8-3.9
1977 *Squirrel and Young.*
Artist: Henry Thelander.
Issue price: $23.50.

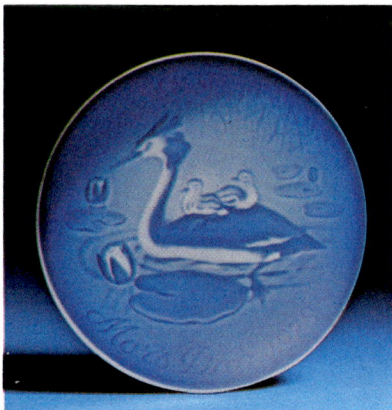

14-8-3.10
1978 *Heron.*
Artist: Henry Thelander.
Issue price: $24.50.

14-8-3.11
1979 *Fox and Cubs.*
Artist: Henry Thelander.
Issue price: $27.50.

Grande Copenhagen plates are produced at the Eslau porcelain factory near Copenhagen. Grande Copenhagen began its *Christmas Series* of plates depicting Danish winter scenes in 1975.

DENMARK
GRANDE COPENHAGEN
(Copenhagen)

Christmas Series
Artist: Undisclosed

True underglaze porcelain hand painted in Copenhagen blue on bas-relief

Diameter: 18.5 centimeters (7¼ inches)

Pierced foot rim

Edition size undisclosed, limited by year of issue

Not numbered, without certificate; individually initialed on back by each painter

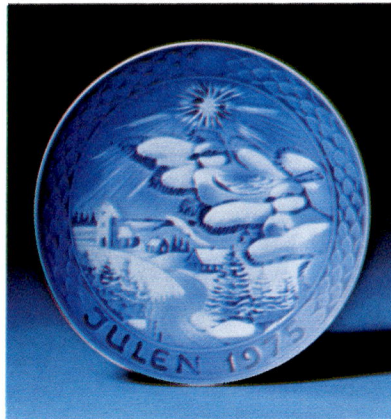

14-26-1.1
1975 *Alone Together*.
Artist: Undisclosed.
Issue price: $24.50.

14-26-1.2
1976 *Christmas Wreath*.
Artist: Undisclosed.
Issue price: $24.50.

14-26-1.3
1977 *Fishwives at Gammelstrand*.
Artist: Undisclosed.
Issue price: $26.50.

14-26-1.4
1978 *Hans Christian Andersen*.
Artist: Undisclosed.
Issue price: $32.50.

Georg Jensen, known primarily for Danish silver, also issued porcelain collector's plates made at a porcelain factory in Eslau near Copenhagen. The *Christmas Series* began in 1972 and terminated in 1976.

DENMARK
GEORG JENSEN
(Copenhagen)

Christmas Series

Artist: Undisclosed

True underglaze porcelain hand painted in Copenhagen blue on bas-relief

Diameter: 18.5 centimeters (7¼ inches)

Pierced foot rim

Edition size undisclosed, limited by year of issue

Not numbered; without certificate

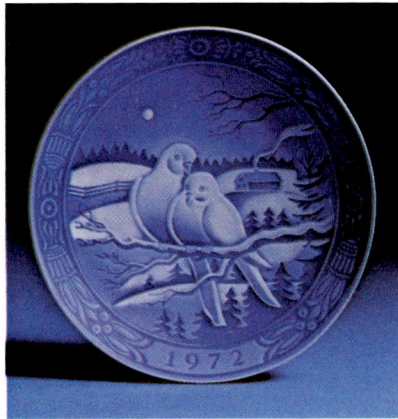

14-38-1.1
1972 *Doves.*
Artist: Undisclosed.
Issue price: $15.00.

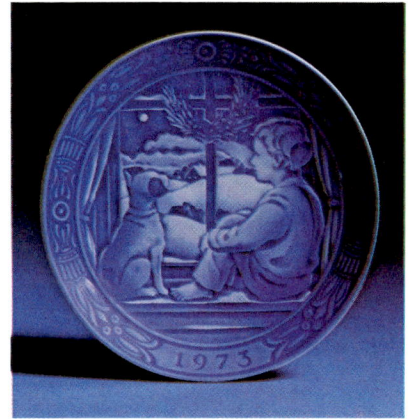

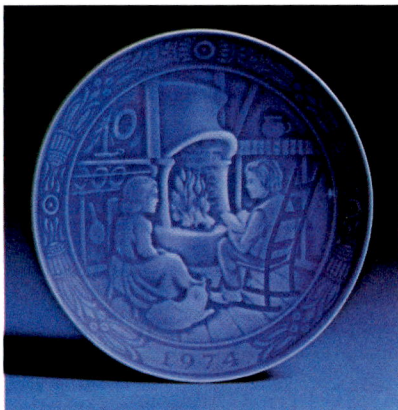

14-38-1.2
1973 *Boy and Dog on Christmas Eve.*
Artist: Undisclosed.
Issue price: $15.00.

14-38-1.3
1974 *Christmas Story.*
Artist: Undisclosed.
Issue price: $17.50.

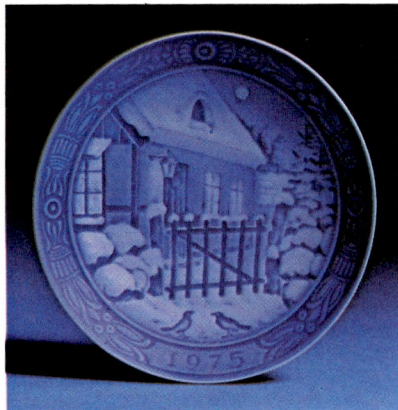

14-38-1.4
1975 *Winter Scene.*
Artist: Undisclosed.
Issue price: $22.50.

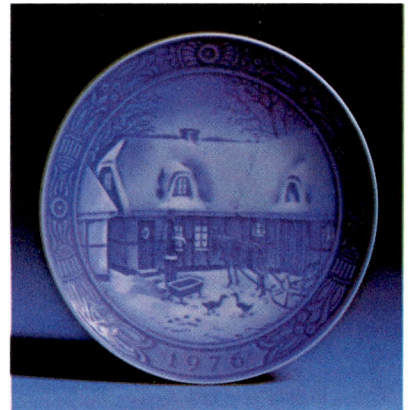

14-38-1.5
1976 *Christmas in the Country.*
Artist: Undisclosed.
Issue price: $22.50.

DÉSIRÉE
DENMARK

Svend Jensen plates are made by the Désirée porcelain factory near Copenhagen and are the result of an association between art consultant Svend Jensen and porcelain expert H. C. Torbal. In 1970 they issued the first limited-edition plates in two Svend Jensen annual collections—a *Christmas Series* based on Hans Christian Andersen fairy tales, and a *Mother's Day Series.*

Christmas Series

Artist: As indicated. Artist's name appears on back

True underglaze porcelain hand painted in Copenhagen blue on bas-relief

Diameter: 18 centimeters (7 inches)

Pierced foot rim

Edition size undisclosed, limited by year of issue

Not numbered, without certificate; individually initialed on back by each painter

14-40-1.1
1970 *Hans Christian Andersen House.*
Artist: Gerhard Sausmark.
Issue price: $14.50.

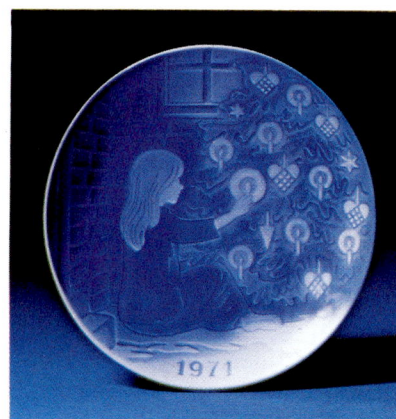

14-40-1.2
1971 *The Little Match Girl.*
Artist: Mads Stage.
Issue price: $15.00.

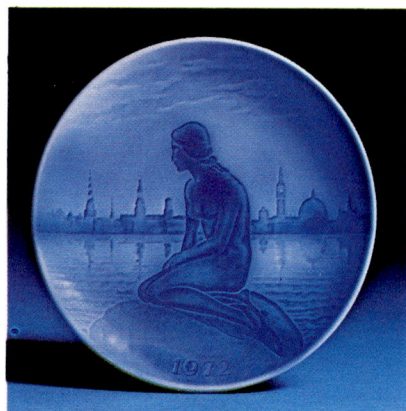

14-40-1.3
1972 *Little Mermaid of Copenhagen.*
Rights from family of Edvard Eriksen, sculptor.
Issue price: $16.50.

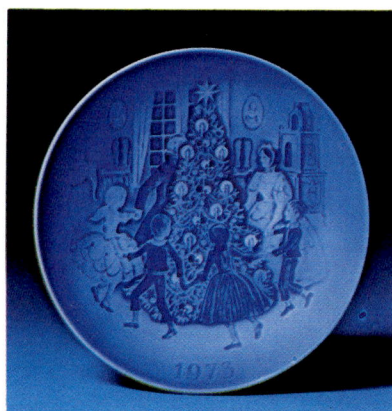

14-40-1.4
1973 *The Fir Tree.*
Artist: Svend Otto.
Issue price: $22.00.

14-40-1.5
1974 *The Chimney Sweep.*
Artist: Svend Otto.
Issue price: $25.00.

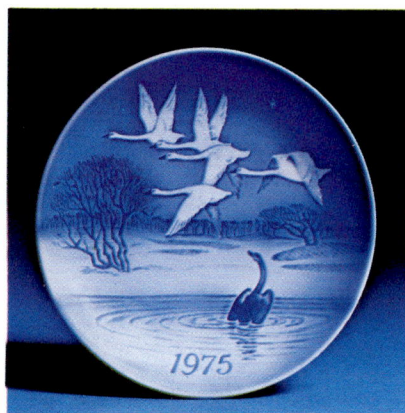

14-40-1.6
1975 *The Ugly Duckling.*
Artist: Svend Otto.
Issue price: $27.50.

14-40-1.7
1976 *The Snow Queen.*
Artist: Mads Stage.
Issue price: $27.50.

14-40-1.8
1977 *The Snowman.*
Artist: Svend Otto.
Issue price: $29.50.

14-40-1.9

DENMARK
SVEND JENSEN
(Ringsted)

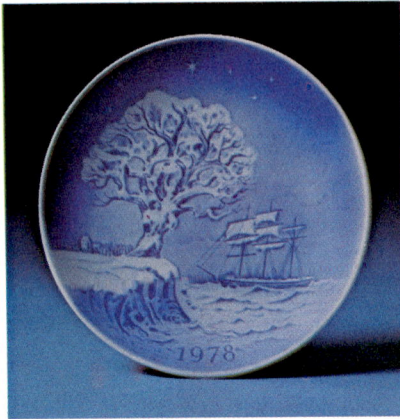

14-40-1.9
1978 *The Last Dream of the Old Oak Tree.*
Artist: Svend Otto.
Issue price: $32.00.

14-40-1.10
1979 *The Old Street Lamp.*
Artist: Svend Otto.
Issue price: $36.50.

Mother's Day Series

Artist: As indicated. Artist's name appears on back

True underglaze porcelain hand painted in Copenhagen blue on bas-relief

Diameter: 18 centimeters (7 inches)

Pierced foot rim

Edition size undisclosed, limited by year of issue

Not numbered with certificate since 1977; individually initialed on back by each painter

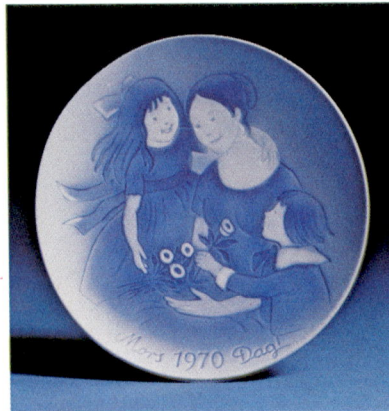

14-40-2.1
1970 *A Bouquet for Mother.*
Artist: Maggi Baaring.
Issue price: $14.50.

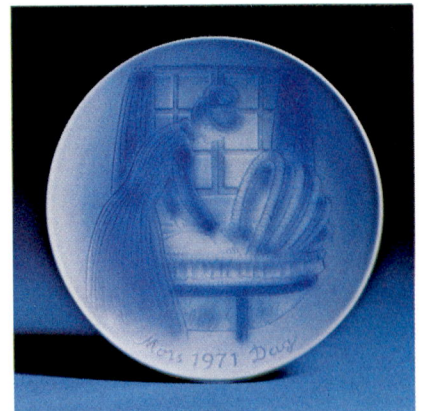

14-40-2.2
1971 *Mother's Love.*
Artist: Nulle Oigaard.
Issue price: $15.00.

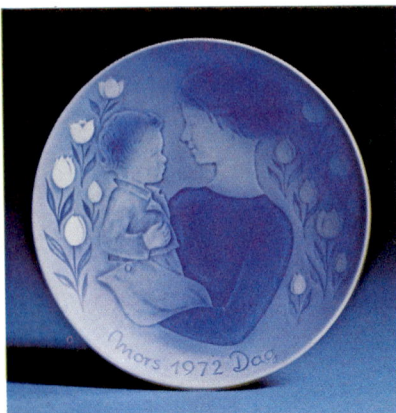

14-40-2.3
1972 *Good Night.*
Artist: Mads Stage.
Issue price: $15.00.

14-40-2.4
1973 *Flowers for Mother.*
Artist: Mads Stage.
Issue price: $20.00.

14-40-2.5
1974 *Daisies for Mother.*
Artist: Mads Stage.
Issue price: $25.00.

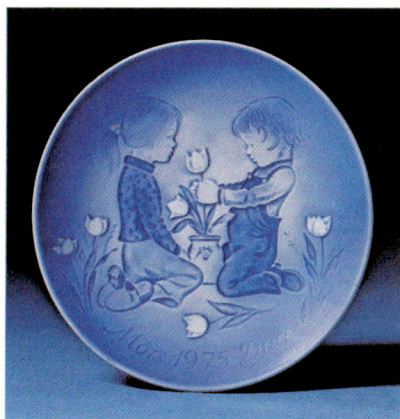

14-40-2.6
1975 *Surprise for Mother.*
Artist: Mads Stage.
Issue price: $27.50.

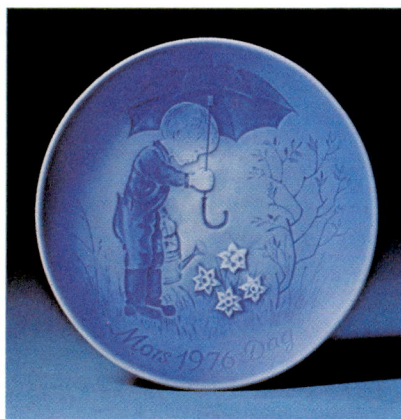

14-40-2.7
1976 *The Complete Gardener.*
Artist: Mads Stage.
Issue price: $27.50.

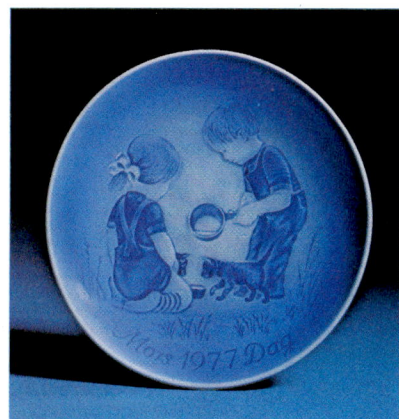

14-40-2.8
1977 *Little Friends.*
Artist: Mads Stage.
Issue price: $29.50.

14-40-2.9
1978 *Dreams.*
Artist: Mads Stage.
Issue price: $32.00.

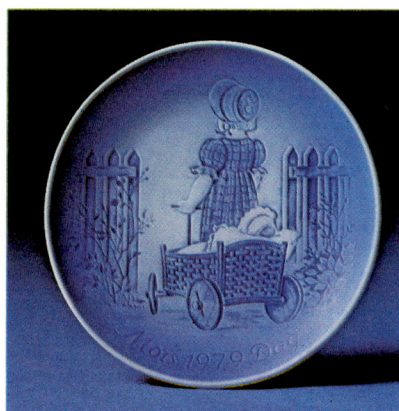

14-40-2.10
1979 *Promenade.*
Artist: Mads Stage.
Issue price: $36.50.

The Royal Copenhagen Porcelain Manufactory, Denmark's oldest existing porcelain maker, was established by Franz Henrich Muller with the support of Denmark's queen dowager, Juliane Marie, in January 1775. Since the 1760s, members of the Danish royal family had been interested in the white hard-paste porcelain made in China, but it was not until 1772 that Muller, a Danish pharmacist and chemist, was able to duplicate the fine porcelain. In 1779 "The Danish Porcelain Factory," as Royal Copenhagen was then called, came under royal control.

The Danish Court controlled the firm from 1779 to 1867, a period in its history that is still symbolized by the crown in its trademark. The three wavy lines under the crown, part of the factory trademark since 1775, pay tribute to Denmark's tradition as a seafaring nation and represent Denmark's three ancient waterways: the Sound, the Great Belt, and the Little Belt. In 1867 the factory was sold and has continued under private ownership. It is still a supplier to the royal court in Denmark.

The first Royal Copenhagen Christmas plate was issued in 1908 and the series has continued every year since then. For the first three years the plates were six inches in diameter. Beginning with the 1911 issue, they were changed to the seven-inch size. From the beginning, the motif for each year's Christmas plate has been selected from suggestions submitted by employees of the Royal Copenhagen factory.

The Royal Copenhagen *Mother's Day Series* was started in 1971 and the *Historical Series* was introduced in 1975 to celebrate the company's own two-hundredth anniversary. Yearly issues of this series commemorate other bicentennial anniversaries.

Christmas Series

Artist: As indicated. Artist's name appears on back since 1955

True underglaze porcelain hand painted in Copenhagen blue on bas-relief

Diameter: 18 centimeters (7 inches)

Pierced foot rim

Edition size unannounced, limited by year of issue

Not numbered, without certificate; individually initialed on back by each painter

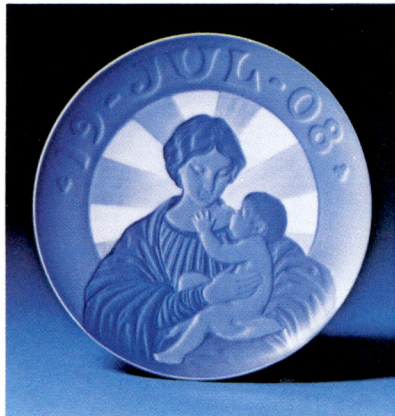

14-69-1.1
1908 *Madonna and Child.*
Artist: Chr. Thomsen.
Diameter: 6 inches.
Issue price: $1.00.

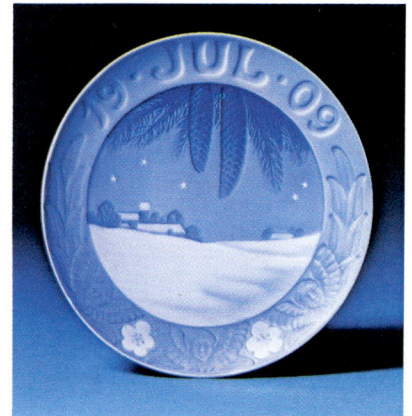

14-69-1.2
1909 *Danish Landscape.*
Artist: St. Ussing.
Diameter: 6 inches.
Issue price: $1.00.

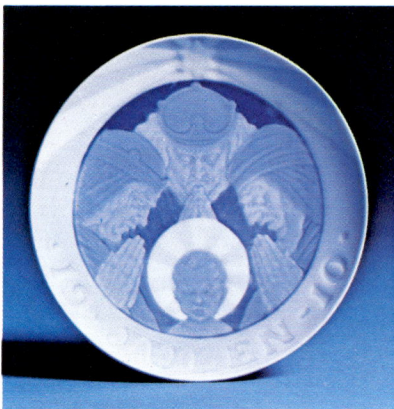

14-69-1.3
1910 *The Magi.*
Artist: Chr. Thomsen.
Diameter: 6 inches.
Issue price: $1.00.

14-69-1.4
1911 *Danish Landscape.*
Artist: Oluf Jensen.
Issue price: $1.00.

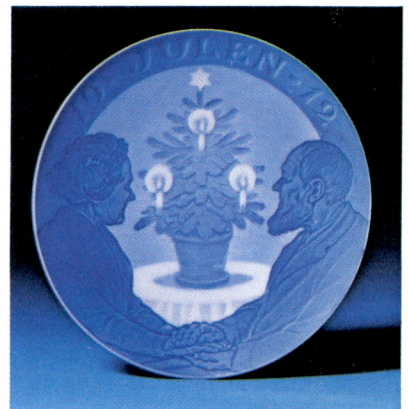

14-69-1.5
1912 *Elderly Couple by Christmas Tree.*
Artist: Chr. Thomsen.
Issue price: $1.00.

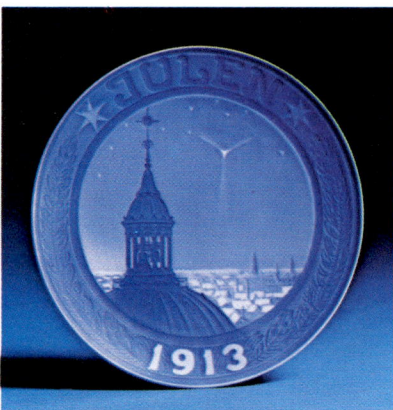

14-69-1.6
1913 *Spire of Frederik's Church, Copenhagen.*
Artist: A. Boesen.
Issue price: $1.50.

14-69-1.7
1914 *Sparrows in Tree at Church of the Holy Spirit, Copenhagen.*
Artist: A. Boesen.
Issue price: $1.50.

14-69-1.8
1915 *Danish Landscape.*
Artist: A. Krog.
Issue price: $1.50.

14-69-1.9
1916 *Shepherd in the Field on Christmas Night.*
Artist: R. Bocher.
Issue price: $1.50.

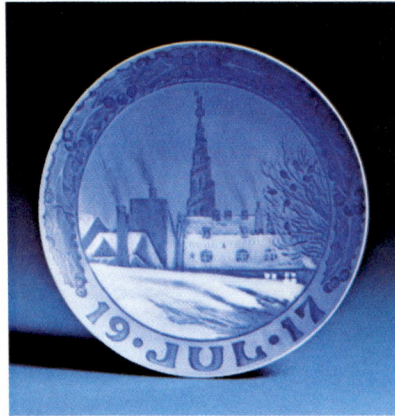

14-69-1.10
1917 *Tower of Our Savior's Church, Copenhagen.*
Artist: Oluf Jensen.
Issue price: $2.00.

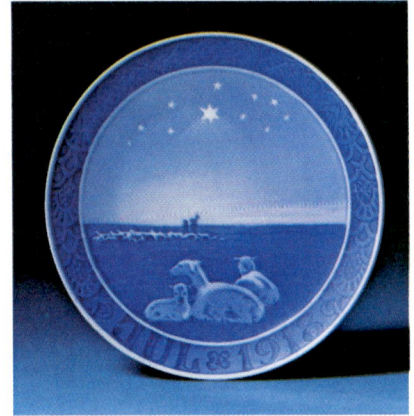

14-69-1.11
1918 *Sheep and Shepherds.*
Artist: Oluf Jensen.
Issue price: $2.00.

14-69-1.12
1919 *In the Park.*
Artist: Oluf Jensen.
Issue price: $2.00.

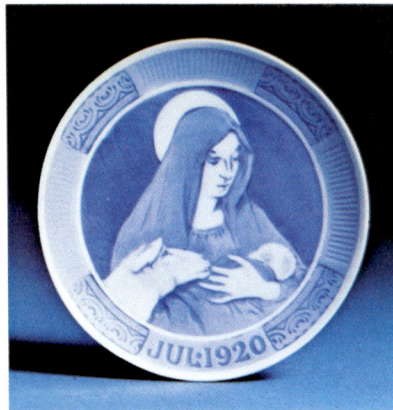

14-69-1.13
1920 *Mary with the Child Jesus.*
Artist: G. Rode.
Issue price: $2.00.

14-69-1.14
1921 *Aabenraa Marketplace.*
Artist: Oluf Jensen.
Issue price: $2.00.

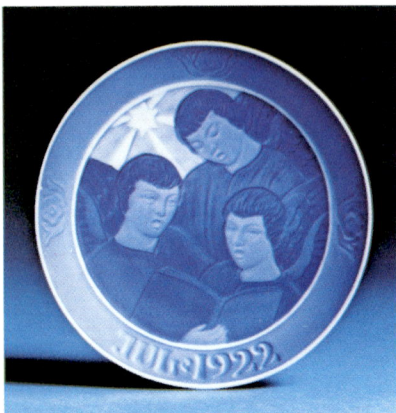

14-69-1.15
1922 *Three Singing Angels.*
Artist: Mrs. Selschou Olsen.
Issue price: $2.00.

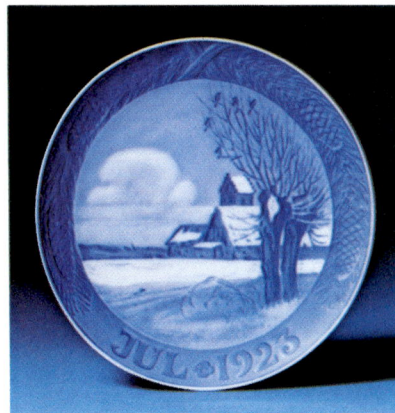

14-69-1.16
1923 *Danish Landscape.*
Artist: Oluf Jensen.
Issue price: $2.00.

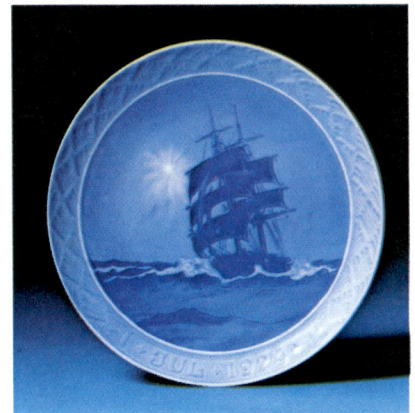

14-69-1.17
1924 *Christmas Star over the Sea and Sailing Ship.*
Artist: Benjamin Olsen.
Issue price: $2.00.

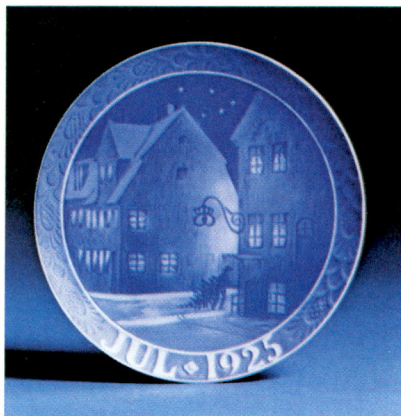

14-69-1.18
1925 *Street Scene from Christianshavn,*
Copenhagen.
Artist: Oluf Jensen.
Issue price: $2.00.

14-69-1.19
1926 *View of Christianshavn Canal,*
Copenhagen.
Artist: R. Bocher.
Issue price: $2.00.

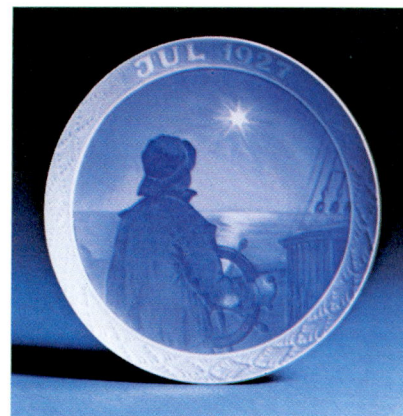

14-69-1.20
1927 *Ship's Boy at the Tiller on Christmas*
Night.
Artist: Benjamin Olsen.
Issue price: $2.00.

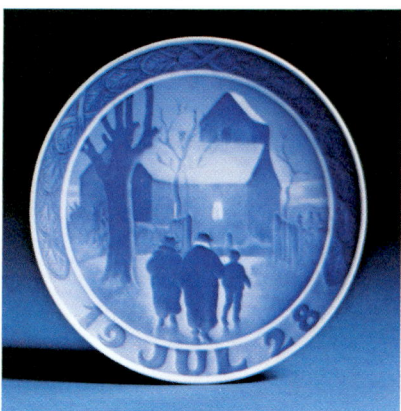

14-69-1.21
1928 *Vicar's Family on Way to Church.*
Artist: G. Rode.
Issue price: $2.00.

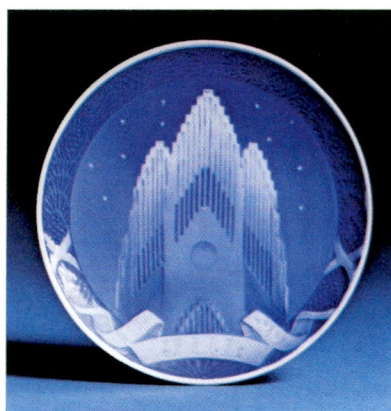

14-69-1.22
1929 *Grundtvig Church, Copenhagen.*
Artist: Oluf Jensen.
Issue price: $2.00.

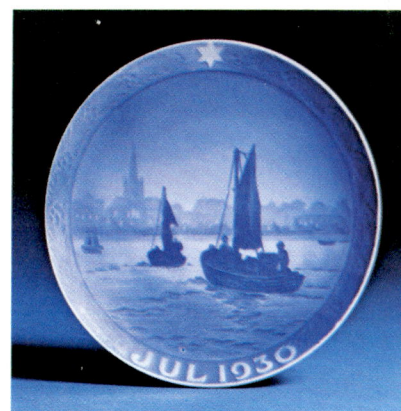

14-69-1.23
1930 *Fishing Boats on the Way to the*
Harbor.
Artist: Benjamin Olsen.
Issue price: $2.50.

14-69-1.24
1931 *Mother and Child.*
Artist: G. Rode.
Issue price: $2.50.

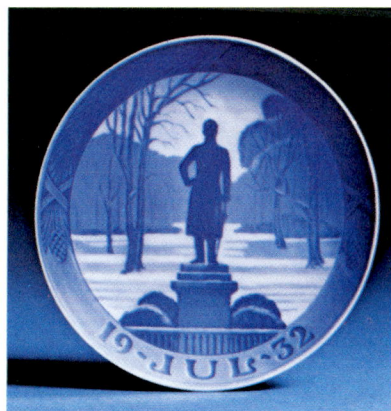

14-69-1.25
1932 *Frederiksberg Gardens with Statue of*
Frederik VI.
Artist: Oluf Jensen.
Issue price: $2.50.

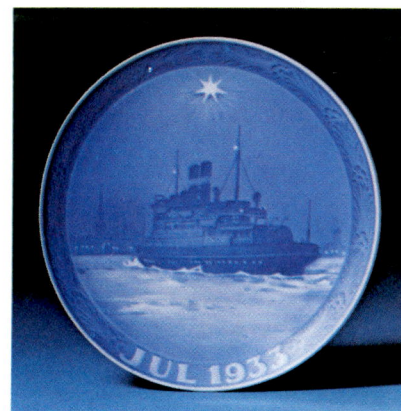

14-69-1.26
1933 *The Great Belt Ferry.*
Artist: Benjamin Olsen.
Issue price: $2.50.

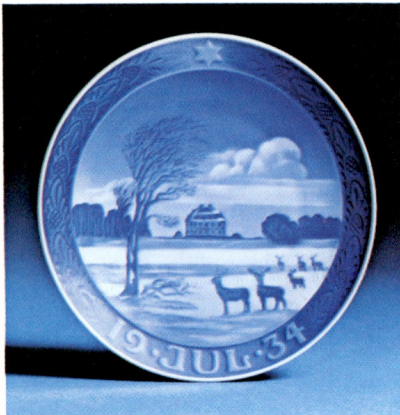

14-69-1.27
1934 *The Hermitage Castle.*
Artist: Oluf Jensen.
Issue price: $2.50.

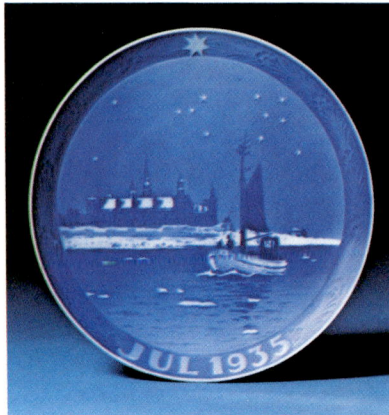

14-69-1.28
1935 *Fishing Boat off Kronborg Castle.*
Artist: Benjamin Olsen.
Issue price: $2.50.

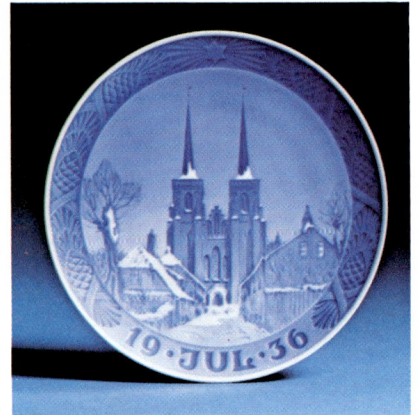

14-69-1.29
1936 *Roskilde Cathedral.*
Artist: R. Bocher.
Issue price: $2.50.

14-69-1.30
1937 *Christmas Scene in Main Street,
Copenhagen.*
Artist: Nils Thorsson.
Issue price: $2.50.

14-69-1.31
1938 *Round Church in Osterlars on
Bornholm.*
Artist: Herne Nielsen.
Issue price: $3.00.

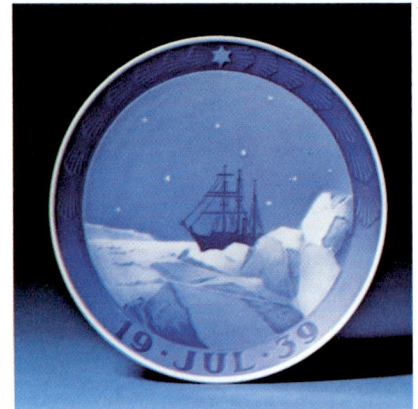

14-69-1.32
1939 *Expeditionary Ship in Pack-ice of
Greenland.*
Artist: Sv. Nic. Nielsen.
Issue price: $3.00.

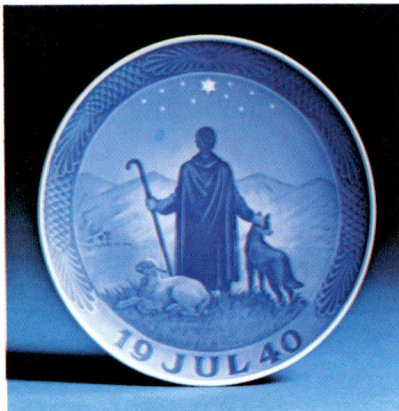

14-69-1.33
1940 *The Good Shepherd.*
Artist: Kai Lange.
Issue price: $3.00.

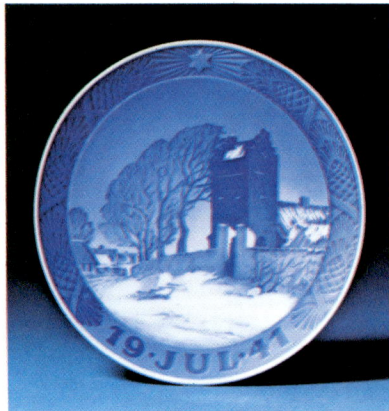

14-69-1.34
1941 *Danish Village Church.*
Artist: Th. Kjolner.
Issue price: $3.00.

14-69-1.35
1942 *Bell Tower of Old Church in Jutland.*
Artist: Nils Thorsson.
Issue price: $4.00.

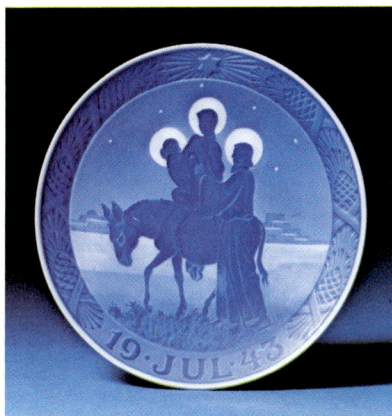

14-69-1.36
1943 *Flight of Holy Family to Egypt.*
Artist: Nils Thorsson.
Issue price: $4.00.

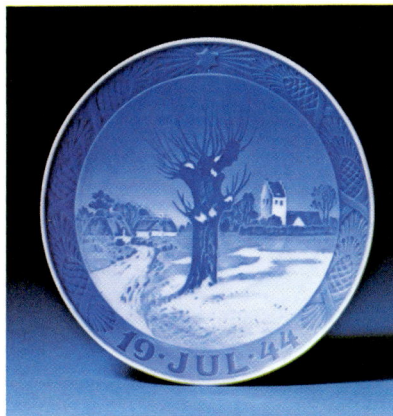

14-69-1.37
1944 *Typical Danish Winter Scene.*
Artist: Viggo Olsen.
Issue price: $4.00.

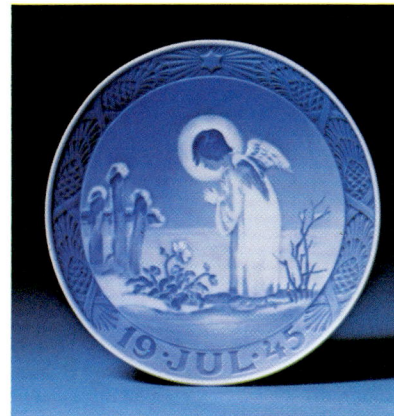

14-69-1.38
1945 *A Peaceful Motif.*
Artist: R. Bocher.
Issue price: $4.00.

14-69-1.39
1946 *Zealand Village Church.*
Artist: Nils Thorsson.
Issue price: $4.00.

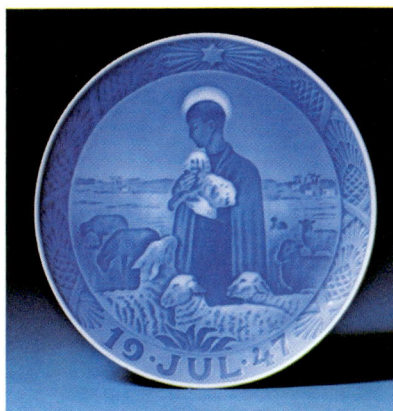

14-69-1.40
1947 *The Good Shepherd.*
Artist: Kai Lange.
Issue price: $4.50.

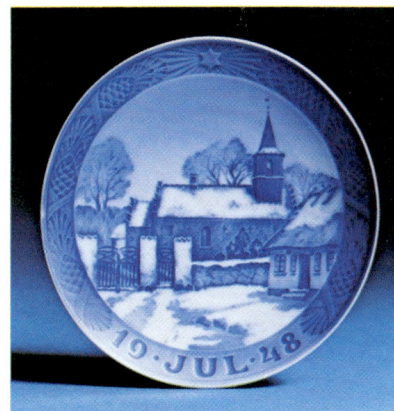

14-69-1.41
1948 *Nodebo Church at Christmastime.*
Artist: Th. Kjolner.
Issue price: $4.50.

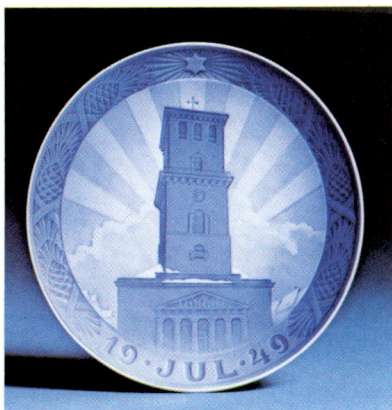

14-69-1.42
1949 *Our Lady's Cathedral, Copenhagen.*
Artist: Hans H. Hansen.
Issue price: $5.00.

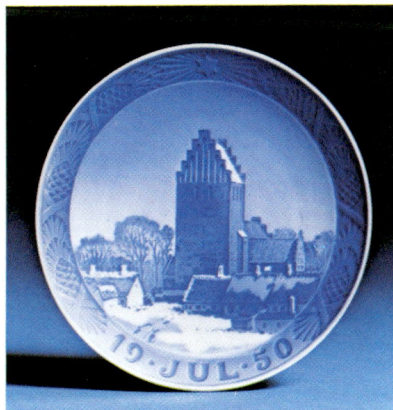

14-69-1.43
1950 *Boeslunde Church, Zealand.*
Artist: Viggo Olsen.
Issue price: $5.00.

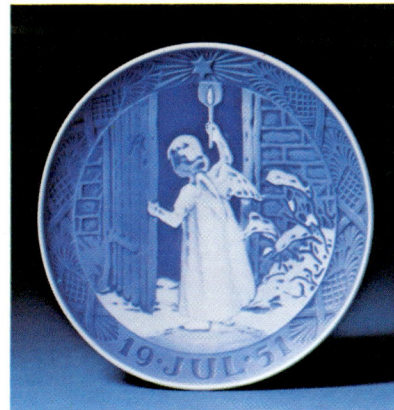

14-69-1.44
1951 *Christmas Angel.*
Artist: R. Bocher.
Issue price: $5.00.

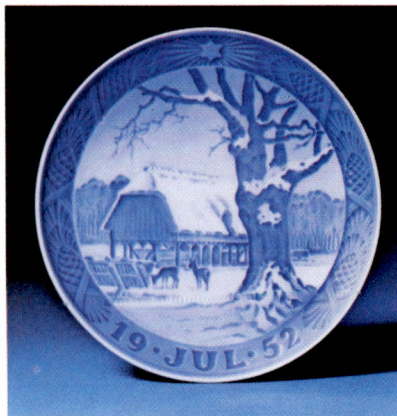

14-69-1.45
1952 *Christmas in the Forest.*
Artist: Kai Lange.
Issue price: $5.00.

14-69-1.46
1953 *Frederiksberg Castle.*
Artist: Th. Kjolner.
Issue price: $6.00.

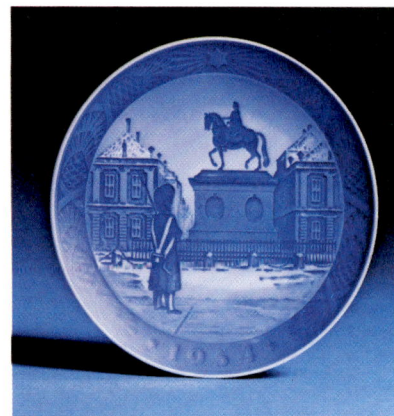

14-69-1.47
1954 *Amalienborg Palace, Copenhagen.*
Artist: Kai Lange.
Issue price: $6.00.

14-69-1.48
1955 *Fano Girl.*
Artist: Kai Lange.
Issue price: $7.00.

14-69-1.49
1956 *Rosenborg Castle, Copenhagen.*
Artist: Kai Lange.
Issue price: $7.00.

14-69-1.50
1957 *The Good Shepherd.*
Artist: Hans H. Hansen.
Issue price: $8.00.

14-69-1.51
1958 *Sunshine over Greenland.*
Artist: Hans H. Hansen.
Issue price: $9.00.

14-69-1.52
1959 *Christmas Night.*
Artist: Hans H. Hansen.
Issue price: $9.00.

14-69-1.53
1960 *The Stag.*
Artist: Hans H. Hansen.
Issue price: $10.00.

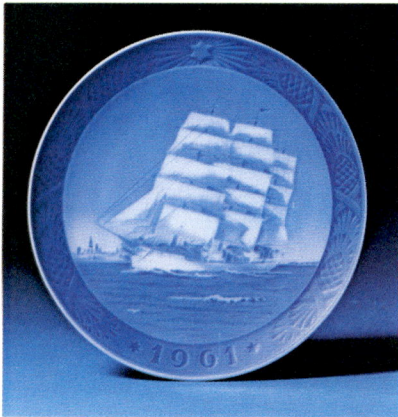

14-69-1.54
1961 *Training Ship Danmark.*
Artist: Kai Lange.
Issue price: $10.00.

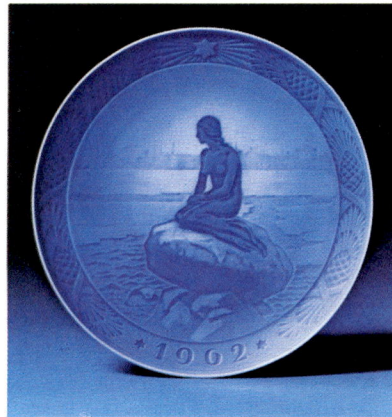

14-69-1.55
1962 *The Little Mermaid at Wintertime.*
Specific artist not named because of
special nature of this motif.
Issue price: $11.00.

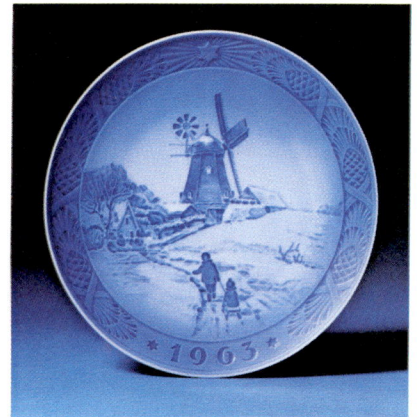

14-69-1.56
1963 *Hojsager Mill.*
Artist: Kai Lange.
Issue price: $11.00.

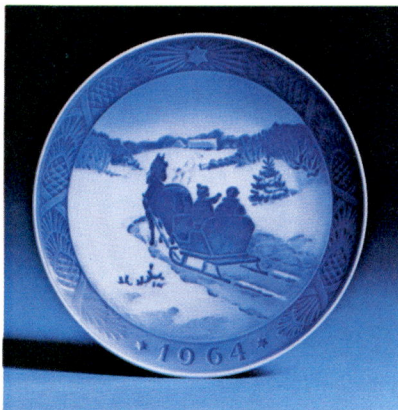

14-69-1.57
1964 *Fetching the Christmas Tree.*
Artist: Kai Lange.
Issue price: $11.00.

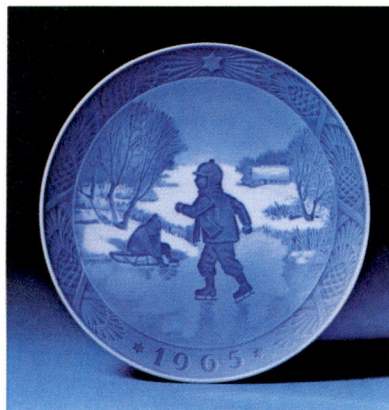

14-69-1.58
1965 *Little Skaters.*
Artist: Kai Lange.
Issue price: $12.00.

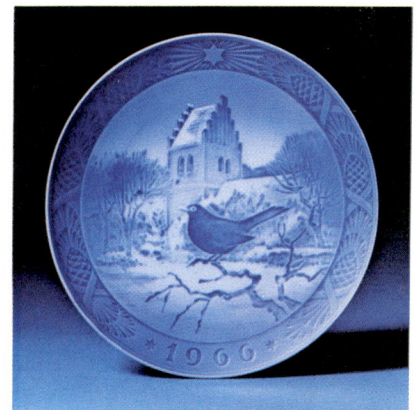

14-69-1.59
1966 *Blackbird at Christmastime.*
Artist: Kai Lange.
Issue price: $12.00.

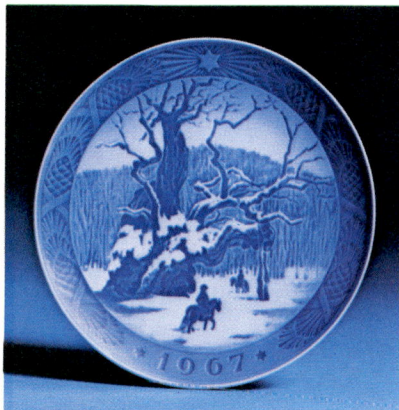

14-69-1.60
1967 *The Royal Oak.*
Artist: Kai Lange.
Issue price: $13.00.

14-69-1.61
1968 *The Last Umiak.*
Artist: Kai Lange.
Issue price: $13.00.

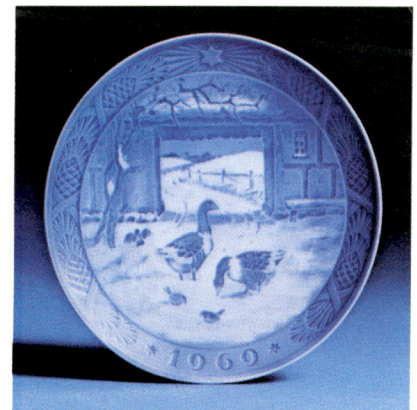

14-69-1.62
1969 *The Old Farmyard.*
Artist: Kai Lange.
Issue price: $14.00.

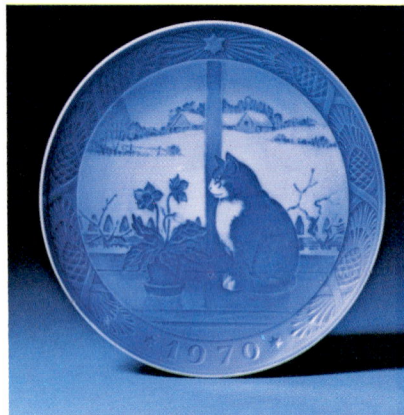

14-69-1.63
1970 *Christmas Rose and Cat.*
Artist: Kai Lange.
Issue price: $14.00.

14-69-1.64
1971 *Hare in Winter.*
Artist: Kai Lange.
Issue price: $15.00.

14-69-1.65
1972 *In the Desert.*
Artist: Kai Lange.
Issue price: $16.00.

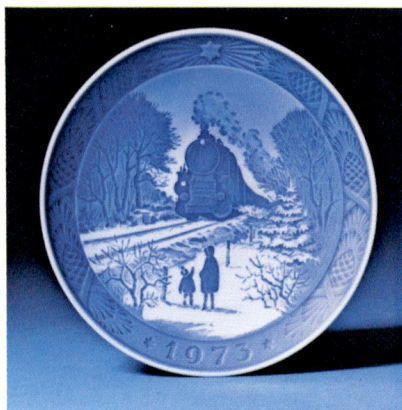

14-69-1.66
1973 *Train Homeward Bound for
Christmas.*
Artist: Kai Lange.
Issue price: $22.00.

14-69-1.67
1974 *Winter Twilight.*
Artist: Kai Lange.
Issue price: $22.00.

14-69-1.68
1975 *Queen's Palace.*
Artist: Kai Lange.
Issue price: $27.50.

14-69-1.69
1976 *Danish Watermill.*
Artist: Kai Lange.
Issue price: $27.50.

14-69-1.70
1977 *Immervad Bridge.*
Artist: Kai Lange.
Issue price: $32.00.

14-69-1.71
1978 *Greenland Scenery.*
Artist: Kai Lange.
Issue price: $35.00.

14-69-1.72
1979 *Choosing the Christmas Tree.*
Artist: Kai Lange.
Issue price $42.50.

Mother's Day Series

Artist: As indicated.

True underglaze porcelain hand painted in Copenhagen blue on bas-relief

Diameter: 16 centimeters (6¼ inches)

Pierced foot rim

Edition size unannounced, limited by year of issue

Not numbered, without certificate; individually initialed on back by each painter

14-69-2.1
1971 *American Mother.*
Artist: Kamma Svensson.
Issue price: $12.50.

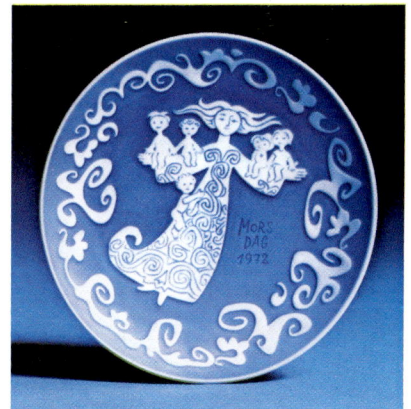

14-69-2.2
1972 *Oriental Mother.*
Artist: Kamma Svensson.
Issue price: $14.00.

14-69-2.3
1973 *Danish Mother.*
Artist: Arne Ungermann.
Issue price: $16.00.

14-69-2.4
1974 *Greenland Mother.*
Artist: Arne Ungermann.
Issue price: $16.50.

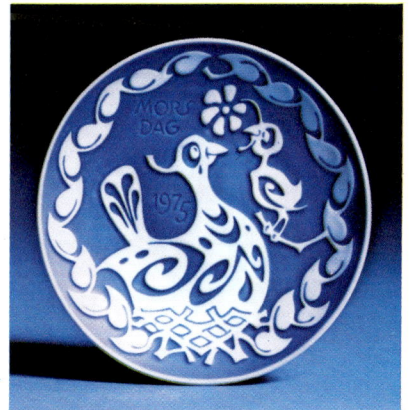

14-69-2.5
1975 *Bird in Nest.*
Artist: Arne Ungermann.
Issue price: $20.00.

14-69-2.6
1976 *Mermaids.*
Artist: Arne Ungermann.
Issue price: $20.00.

14-69-2.7
1977 *The Twins.*
Artist: Arne Ungermann.
Issue price: $24.00.

14-69-2.8
1978 *Mother and Child.*
Artist: Ib Spang Olsen.
Issue price: $26.00.

14-69-2.9
1979 *A Loving Mother.*
Artist: Ib Spang Olsen.
Issue price: $29.50.

Historical Series

Artist: As indicated

True underglaze porcelain hand painted in Copenhagen blue on bas-relief

Diameter: 19 centimeters (7½ inches)

Pierced foot rim

Edition size unannounced, limited by year of issue

Not numbered, without certificate; individually initialed on back by each painter

14-69-3.1
1975 *Royal Copenhagen Bicentennial.*
Artist: Sven Vestergaard.
Issue price: $30.00.

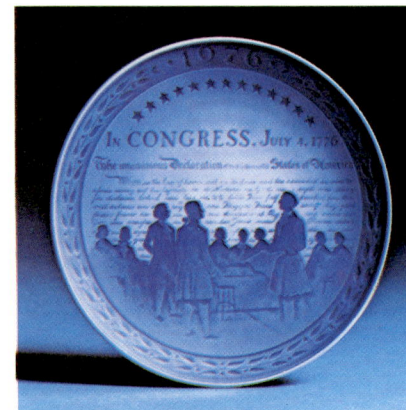

14-69-3.2
1976 *United States Bicentennial.*
Artist: Sven Vestergaard.
Issue price: $35.00.

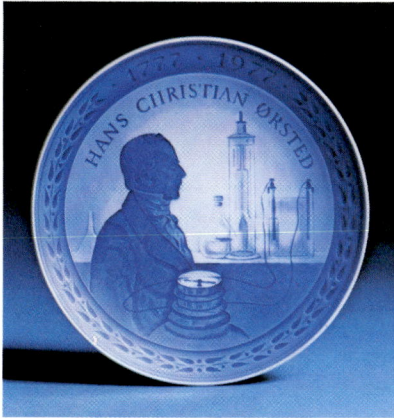

14-69-3.3
1977 *The Discovery of Electro-Magnetism.*
Artist: Sven Vestergaard.
Issue price: $35.00.

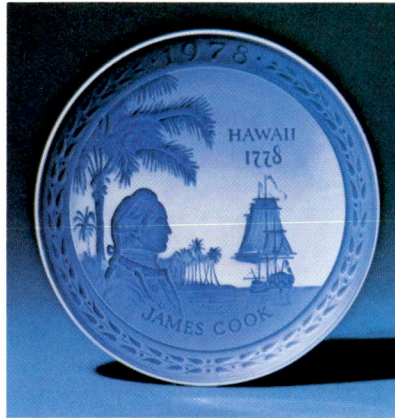

14-69-3.4
1978 *Captain Cook Landing on Hawaii.*
Artist: Sven Vestergaard.
Issue price: $37.50.

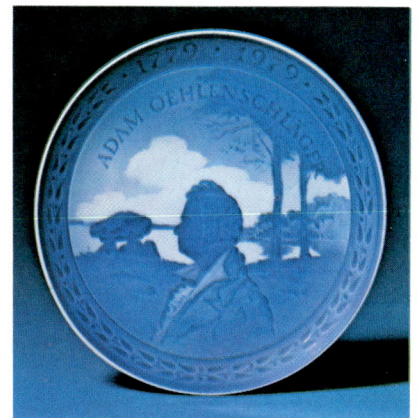

14-69-3.5
1979 *Adam Oehlenschlager.*
Artist: Sven Vestergaard.
Issue price: $42.50.

ARABIA
FINLAND

In 1873 Arabia was founded as a subsidiary of the Swedish firm Rörstrand (see Sweden, RORSTRAND). The factory was located on the outskirts of Helsinki, a site chosen in hopes of supplying the growing markets for ceramics in Finland and the Russian Empire. Early products included dinner services, pitchers, and mugs, almost all based on Rörstrand designs.

In 1884 Arabia was reorganized as a Finnish company, Arabia Aktiefabrik, and developed its own designs from that time on. The company won a gold medal at the Paris World Exhibition in 1900, and is the only pottery producing both household and art ceramics in Finland today.

To celebrate the one-hundredth anniversary of the firm in 1973, Arabia produced a limited-edition anniversary plate. Its success, in turn, led to the introduction in 1976 of an annual limited-edition series based on the Finnish national epic, the *Kalevala*.

FINLAND
ARABIA
(Helsinki)

Kalevala Series
Artist: Raija Uosikkinen
Stoneware
Diameter: 21 centimeters (8 inches square)
Pierced foot rim
Edition size undisclosed
Not numbered, without certificate

16-5-1.1
1976 *Vainamoinen's Sowing.*
Artist: Raija Uosikkinen.
Issue price: $30.00.

16-5-1.2
1977 *Aino's Fate.*
Artist: Raija Uosikkinen.
Issue price: $30.00.

16-5-1.3
1978 *Lemminkainen's Chase.*
Artist: Raija Uosikkinen.
Issue price: $39.00.

16-5-1.4
1979 *Kullervo's Revenge.*
Artist: Raija Uosikkinen.
Issue price: $39.50.

Henri d'Arceau L. et Fils, one of the smaller houses in this famous porcelain center, claims to adhere to the original "Grellet Standard" of 1768 for handcraftsmanship. Today the firm is directed by Gerard Boyer, a descendant of the founder.

The firm was commissioned by L'Association l'Esprit de Lafayette to produce the six-plate bicentennial series *Collection Le Patrimoine de Lafayette (Lafayette Legacy Series)*, 1973-1975, which chronicles the role of the Marquis de Lafayette in America's War of Independence. The D'Arceau-Limoges *Christmas Series, Nöel Vitrail*, begun in 1975, was inspired by the stained-glass windows of the cathedral at Chartres. *Les Femmes du Siècle (Women of the Century)*, a twelve-plate series commissioned by the Chambre Syndicale de la Couture Parisienne, began in 1976. This series, with United Nations recognition, depicts Western women's fashions from 1865 to 1965.

D'Arceau-Limoges introduced *Les Jeunes Filles des Saisons (Girls of the Seasons)* in 1978.

FRANCE
D'ARCEAU-LIMOGES
(Limoges)

Collection *Le Patrimoine de Lafayette* (*The Lafayette Legacy Collection*)

Artist: Andre Restieau. Artist's signature appears on front, initials on back

Overglaze porcelain

Diameter: 21.5 centimeters (8½ inches)

Attached back hanger

Edition size undisclosed, limited by announced period of issue

Numbered with certificate

18-15-1.1
1973 *The Secret Contract.*
Artist: André Restieau.
Issue price: $14.82.

18-15-1.2
1973 *The Landing at North Island.*
Artist: André Restieau.
Issue price: $19.82.

18-15-1.3
1974 *The Meeting at City Tavern.*
Artist: André Restieau.
Issue price: $19.82.

18-15-1.4
1974 *The Battle of Brandywine.*
Artist: André Restieau.
Issue price: $19.82.

18-15-1.5
1975 *The Messages to Franklin.*
Artist: André Restieau.
Issue price: $19.82.

18-15-1.6
1975 *The Siege at Yorktown.*
Artist: André Restieau.
Issue price: $19.82.

Noël Vitrail
(Stained-glass Christmas)

Artist: André Restieau. Artist's signature appears on front, initials on back

Overglaze porcelain

Diameter: 21 centimeters (8¼ inches)

Attached back hanger

Edition size undisclosed, limited by announced period of issue

Numbered with certificate

18-15-2.1
1975 *La Fuite en Egypte.*
(Flight into Egypt)
Artist: André Restieau.
Issue price: $24.32.

18-15-2.2
1976 *Dans la Crèche.*
(In the Manger)
Artist: André Restieau.
Issue price: $24.32.

18-15-2.3
1977 *Le Refus d'Hébergement.*
(No Room at the Inn)
Artist: André Restieau.
Issue price: $24.32.

18-15-2.4
1978 *La Purification.*
(The Purification)
Artist: André Restieau.
Issue price: $26.81.

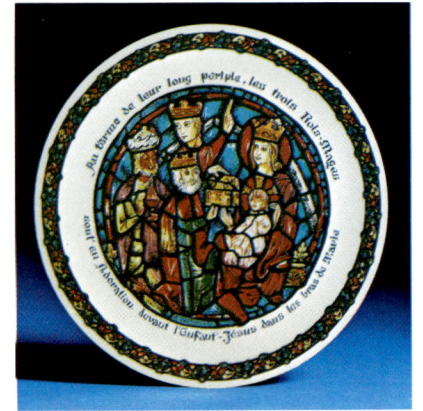

18-15-2.5
1979 *L'Adoration des Rois.*
(The Adoration of Kings)
Artist: André Restieau.
Issue price: $26.81.

Les Femmes du Siècle
(The Women of the Century)

Artist: François Ganeau. Artist's signature appears on front, initials on back

Overglaze porcelain

Diameter: 21.5 centimeters (8½ inches)

Attached back hanger

Edition size undisclosed, limited by announced period of issue

Numbered with certificate

18-15-3.1
1976 *Scarlet en Crinoline.*
Artist: François Ganeau.
Issue price: $14.80.

18-15-3.2
1976 *Sarah en Tournure.*
Artist: François Ganeau.
Issue price: $22.74.

18-15-3.3
1976 *Colette, la Femme Sportive.*
Artist: François Ganeau.
Issue price: $22.74.

18-15-3.4
1976 *Léa, la Femme Fleur.*
Artist: François Ganeau.
Issue price: $22.74.

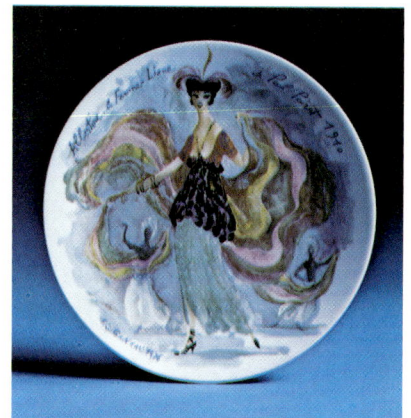

18-15-3.5
1977 *Albertine, la Femme Liane.*
Artist: François Ganeau.
Issue price: $22.74.

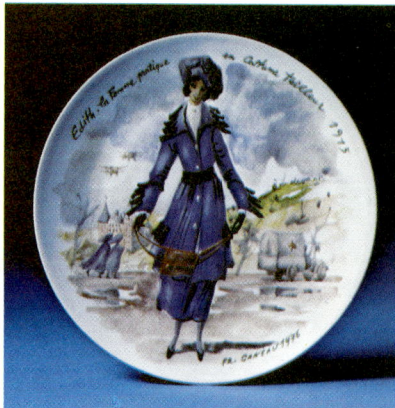

18-15-3.6
1977 *Edith, la Femme Pratique.*
Artist: François Ganeau.
Issue price: $22.74.

18-15-3.7
1977 *Daisy, la Garçonne.*
Artist: François Ganeau.
Issue price: $22.74.

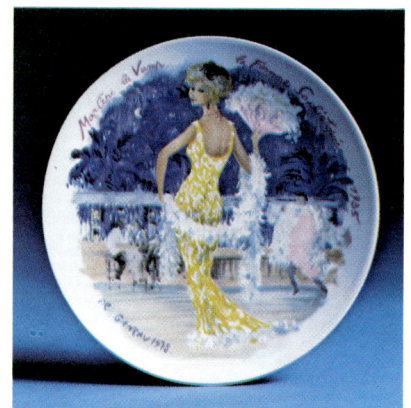

18-15-3.8
1977 *Marlène, la Vamp.*
Artist: François Ganeau.
Issue price: $22.74.

18-15-3.9
1978 *Hélène, l'Intrépide.*
Artist: François Ganeau.
Issue price: $22.74.

18-15-3.10
1978 *Sophie, la Féminité Retrouvée.*
Artist: François Ganeau.
Issue price: $22.74.

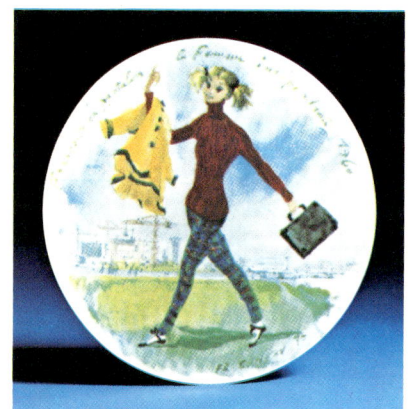

18-15-3.11
1978 *Françoise en Pantalon.*
Artist: François Ganeau.
Issue price: $22.74.

18-15-3.12
1978 *Brigitte en Mini-jupe.*
Artist: François Ganeau.
Issue price: $22.74.

Les Jeunes Filles des Saisons
(The Girls of the Seasons)
Artist: Guy Cambier
Overglaze porcelain
Diameter: 25 centimeters
  (9⅞ inches)
No hanger
Edition size limited to 15,000
Numbered with certificate

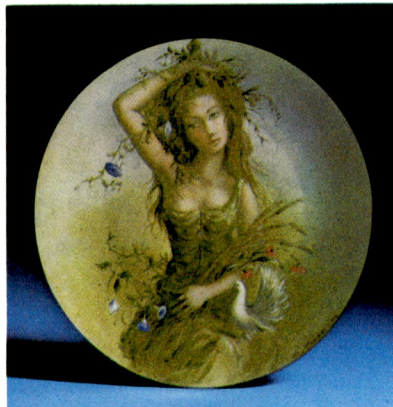

18-15-4.1
1978 *La Jeune Fille d'Eté.*
(Summer Girl)
Artist: Guy Cambier.
Issue price: $105.00.

18-15-4.2
1979 *La Jeune Fille d'Hiver.*
(Winter Girl)
Artist: Guy Cambier.
Issue price: $105.00.

FRANCE
D'ARCEAU – LIMOGES
(Limoges)

The Book of Hours Series
(Les Tres Riches Heures)
Artist: Jean Dutheil
Overglaze porcelain
Diameter: 23 centimeters
    (9¾ inches)
Attached back hanger
Edition size unannounced
Numbered with certificate

18-15-5.1
1979 *Janvier*.
Artist: Jean Dutheil.
Issue price: Not available at press time.

In 1839 David Haviland of New York City became the first American importer of Limoges porcelain made from white kaolin clay. When, in 1842, he realized that French factories would not adjust methods to meet the tastes of his American market, Haviland established his own pottery in Limoges.

In 1892 his son, Theodore, left the firm but remained in Limoges to set up Theodore Haviland & Company for production of porcelain dinnerware and decorative pieces. In the 1930s, Theodore Haviland & Company opened an American Haviland factory to produce tableware; the firm also bought the original Haviland & Company established by David Haviland.

All Haviland collector's plates are produced in Limoges, France. The *Christmas Series*, begun in 1970, is based on the carol "The Twelve Days of Christmas." The five-plate *Bicentennial Series*, introduced in 1972, commemorates events leading to the American Declaration of Independence. In 1973, the *Mother's Day Series* of seven plates, entitled *The French Collection*, was started.

The Twelve Days of Christmas Series

Artist: Remy Hétreau. Artist's signature appears on back

Overglaze porcelain

Diameter: 21.5 centimeters (8⅜ inches)

No hanger

Edition size limited to announced quantity of 30,000

Not numbered; without certificate

18-30-1.1
1970 *A Partridge in a Pear Tree.*
Artist: Remy Hétreau.
Issue price: $25.00.

18-30-1.2
1971 *Two Turtle Doves.*
Artist: Remy Hétreau.
Issue price: $25.00.

18-30-1.3
1972 *Three French Hens.*
Artist: Remy Hétreau.
Issue price: $27.50.

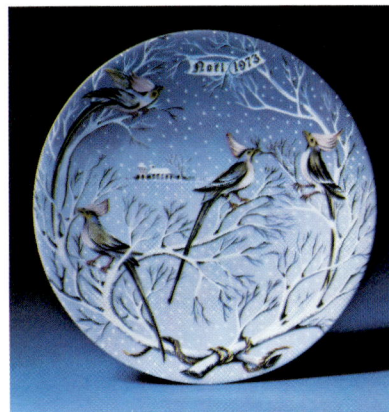

18-30-1.4
1973 *Four Colly Birds.*
Artist: Remy Hétreau.
Issue price: $28.50.

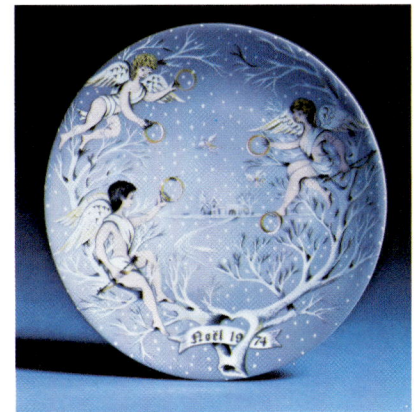

18-30-1.5
1974 *Five Golden Rings.*
Artist: Remy Hétreau.
Issue price: $30.00.

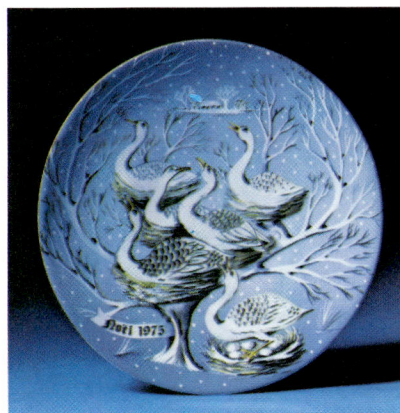

18-30-1.6
1975 *Six Geese A'Laying.*
Artist: Remy Hétreau.
Issue price: $32.50.

18-30-1.7
1976 *Seven Swans A'Swimming.*
Artist: Remy Hétreau.
Issue price: $38.00.

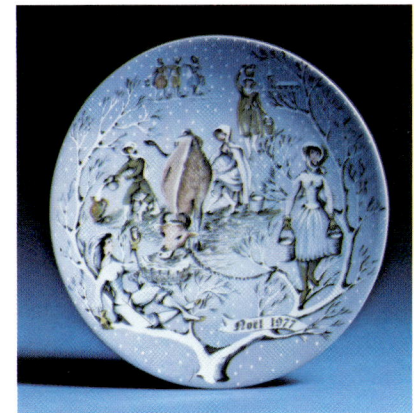

18-30-1.8
1977 *Eight Maids A'Milking.*
Artist: Remy Hétreau.
Issue price: $40.00.

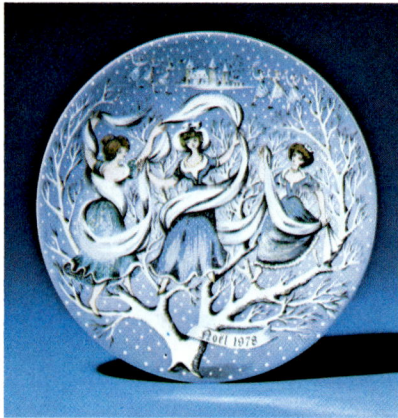

18-30-1.9
1978 *Nine Ladies Dancing.*
Artist: Remy Hétreau.
Issue price: $45.00.

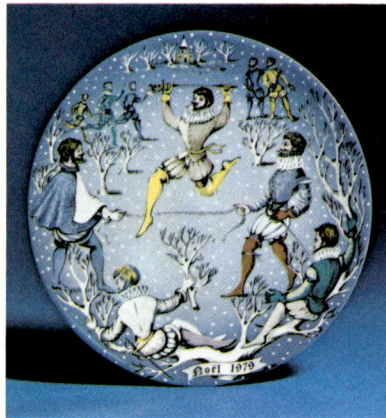

18-30-1.10
1979 *Ten Lords A' Leaping.*
Artist: Remy Hétreau.
Issue price: $50.00.

Bicentennial Series

Artist: Remy Hétreau. Artist's
  signature appears on back
Overglaze porcelain
Diameter: 25 centimeters
  (9¾ inches)
No hanger
Edition size limited to announced
  quantity of 10,000
Not numbered; without certificate

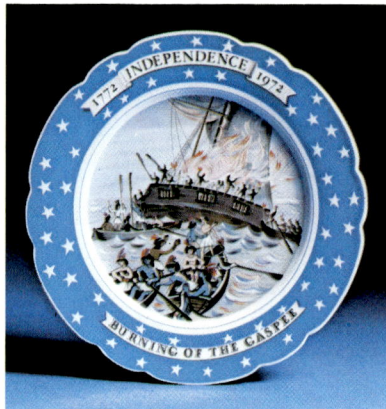

18-30-2.1
1972 *Burning of the Gaspee.*
Artist: Remy Hétreau.
Issue price: $39.95.

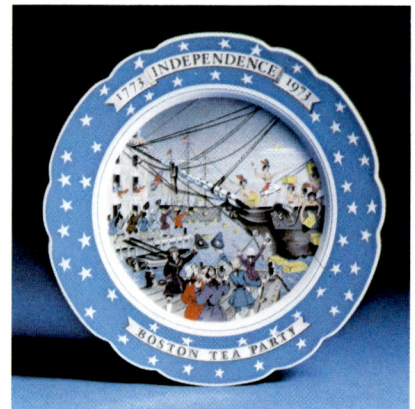

18-30-2.2
1973 *Boston Tea Party.*
Artist: Remy Hétreau.
Issue price: $39.95.

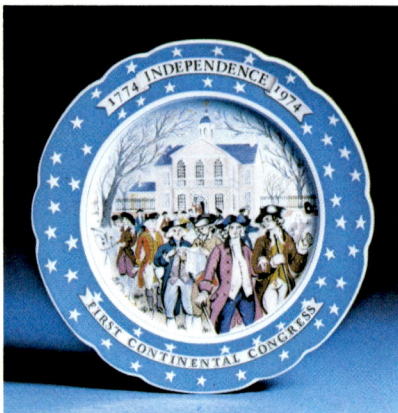

18-30-2.3
1974 *First Continental Congress.*
Artist: Remy Hétreau.
Issue price: $39.95.

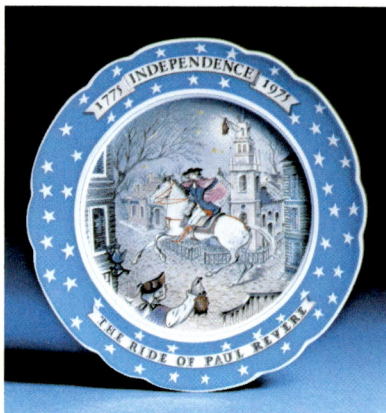

18-30-2.4
1975 *Ride of Paul Revere.*
Artist: Remy Hétreau.
Issue price: $40.00.

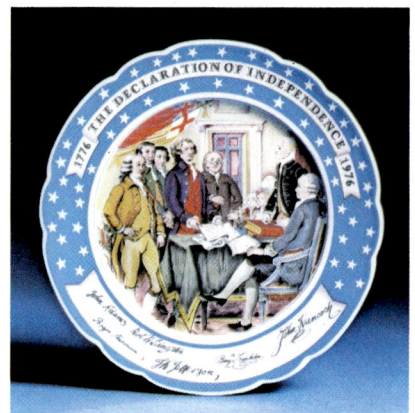

18-30-2.5
1976 *The Declaration of Independence.*
Artist: Remy Hétreau.
Issue price: $48.00.

The French Collection

Artist: Remy Hétreau. Artist's
signature appears on front
Overglaze porcelain
Diameter: 21 centimeters
(8¼ inches)
No hanger
Edition size limited to 10,000
Numbered without certificate

18-30-3.1
1973 *Breakfast.*
Artist: Remy Hétreau.
Issue price: $29.95.

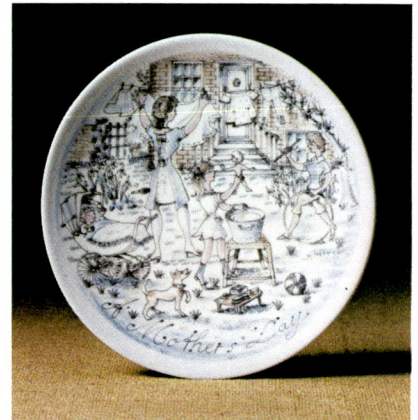

18-30-3.2
1974 *The Wash.*
Artist: Remy Hétreau.
Issue price: $29.95.

18-30-3.3
1975 *In the Park.*
Artist: Remy Hétreau.
Issue price: $30.00.

18-30-3.4
1976 *To Market.*
Artist: Remy Hétreau.
Issue price: $38.00.

18-30-3.5
1977 *A Wash Before Dinner.*
Artist: Remy Hétreau.
Issue price: $38.00.

18-30-3.6
1978 *An Evening at Home.*
Artist: Remy Hétreau.
Issue price: $40.00.

18-30-3.7
1979 *Happy Mother's Day.*
Artist: Remy Hétreau.
Issue price: $45.00.

1001 Arabian Nights
Artist: Liliane Tellier
Porcelain
Diameter: 24 centimeters
 (9¼ inches)
No hanger
Edition size unannounced
Numbered with certificate

18-30-4.1
1979 *The Magic Horse.*
Artist: Liliane Tellier.
Issue price: $54.50.

Haviland Parlon is a chapter in the intricate Haviland porcelain story. In 1853 Robert Haviland left New York City to work for his brother David Haviland in Limoges (see France, HAVILAND). In 1870 Robert's son, Charles Field Haviland, established a porcelain factory in Limoges also, using "Ch. Field Haviland" as his trade name. After he retired in 1881, the firm was known by several different names until 1942, when Robert Haviland (Robert's great-grandson) purchased it. The firm is now known as Robert Haviland & C. Parlon but retains the "Ch. Field Haviland" trademark.

The *Tapestry I Series,* begun in 1971 reproduced six scenes from the French medieval tapestries, *The Hunt of the Unicorn,* now hanging in the Cloisters of the Metropolitan Museum of Art, New York City. The *Christmas Series* of famous Renaissance Madonnas began in 1972, and the *Mother's Day Series,* in 1975. A second tapestry series of six plates called *The Lady and the Unicorn* began in 1977 and reproduces scenes from tapestries hanging in the Cluny Museum in Paris.

Tapestry I Series
Reproduced from French medieval tapestries
Overglaze porcelain
Diameter: 25.5 centimeters
  (10 inches)
No hanger
Edition size limited to announced quantity of 10,000
Not numbered; without certificate

18-32-1.1
1971 *The Unicorn in Captivity.*
Artist: Unknown.
Issue price: $35.00.

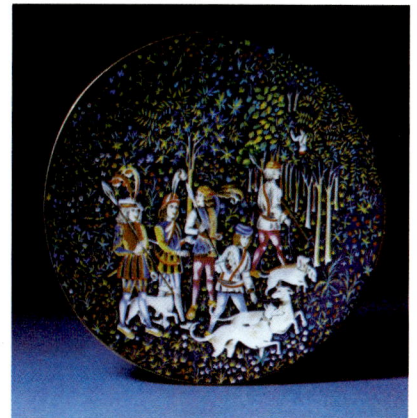

18-32-1.2
1972 *Start of the Hunt.*
Artist: Unknown.
Issue price: $35.00.

18-32-1.3
1973 *Chase of the Unicorn.*
Artist: Unknown.
Issue price: $35.00.

18-32-1.4
1974 *End of the Hunt.*
Artist: Unknown.
Issue price: $37.50.

18-32-1.5
1975 *The Unicorn Surrounded.*
Artist: Unknown.
Issue price: $40.00.

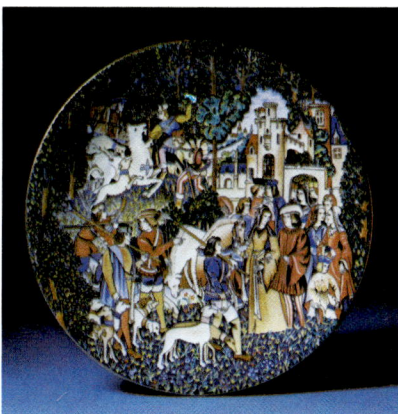

18-32-1.6
1976 *The Unicorn Is Brought to the Castle.*
Artist: Unknown.
Issue price: $42.50.

Christmas Series

Artist: As indicated
Overglaze porcelain
Diameter: 25.5 centimeters
  (10 inches)
No hanger
Edition size: As indicated
Numbered without certificate

18-32-2.1
1972 *Madonna and Child.*
Artist: Rafael.
Issue price: $35.00.
Edition size limited to 5,000.

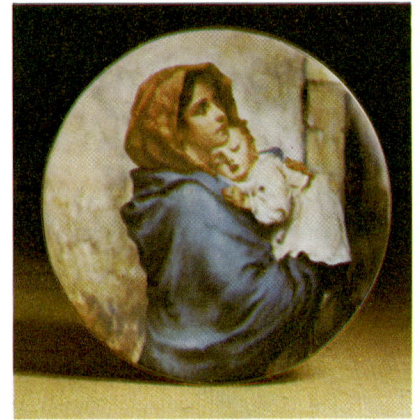

18-32-2.2
1973 *Madonnina.*
Artist: Feruzzi.
Issue price: $40.00.
Edition size limited to 5,000.

18-32-2.3
1974 *Cowper Madonna and Child.*
Artist: Rafael.
Issue price: $42.50.
Edition size limited to 5,000.

18-32-2.4
1975 *Madonna and Child.*
Artist: Murillo.
Issue price: $42.50.
Edition size limited to 7,500.

18-32-2.5
1976 *Madonna and Child.*
Artist: Botticelli.
Issue price: $45.00.
Edition size limited to 7,000.

18-32-2.6
1977 *Madonna and Child.*
Artist: Bellini.
Issue price: $48.00.
Edition size limited to 7,500.

18-32-2.7
1978 *Madonna and Child.*
Artist: Fra Filippo Lippi.
Issue price: $48.00.
Edition size limited to 7,500.

FRANCE
HAVILAND PARLON
(Limoges)

Mother's Day Series
Artist: Marian Carlsen
Overglaze porcelain
Diameter: 19.5 centimeters
 (7¾ inches)
No hanger
Edition size: As indicated
Not numbered; without certificate

18-32-3.1
1975 *Laura and Child.*
Artist: Marian Carlsen.
Issue price: $37.50. Edition size limited
to announced quantity of 15,000.

18-32-3.2
1976 *Pinky and Baby.*
Artist: Marian Carlsen.
Issue price: $42.50. Edition size limited
to announced quantity of 15,000.

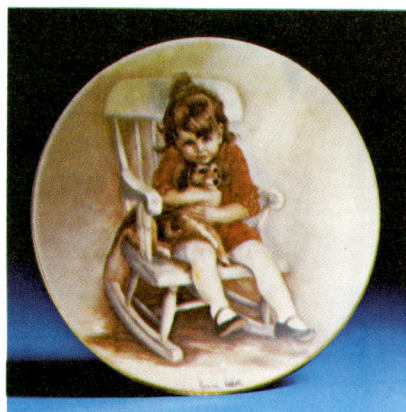

18-32-3.3
1977 *Amy and Snoopy.*
Artist: Marian Carlsen.
Issue price: $45.00. Edition size limited
to announced quantity of 10,000.

Lady and the Unicorn Series
Reproduced from French medieval
 tapestries
Overglaze porcelain
Diameter: 25.5 centimeters
 (10 inches)
No hanger
Edition size limited to announced
 quantity of 20,000
Not numbered; without certificate

18-32-4.1
1977 *To My Only Desire.*
Artist: Unknown.
Issue price: $45.00.

18-32-4.2
1978 *Sight.*
Artist: Unknown.
Issue price: $45.00.

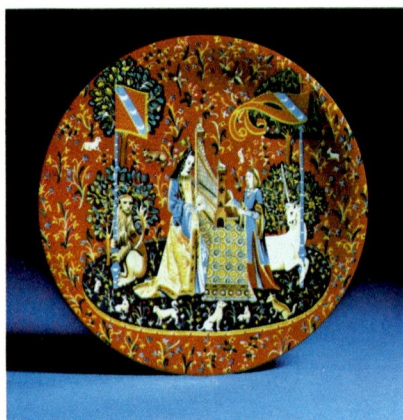

18-32-4.3
1979 *Sound*.
Artist: Unknown.
Issue price: $47.50.

René Lalique, founder of the firm that bears his name, began his career as a goldsmith and jeweler in the late nineteenth century. His clients included such notables as Sarah Bernhardt and the dealers Cartier and Boucheron.

In 1902 his interests turned to glassmaking and he acquired a small glassworks at Clairfontaine, France. In 1909 he opened a glass factory near Paris where he produced bottles for the leading Parisian *parfumiers*, and in 1918 he opened the present Lalique factory in Alsace. Here he began to produce glass items in the Art Deco style. His designs, usually created in pressed lead crystal, are noted for the frosted and satin effects of the glass. Until his death in 1945, Lalique produced numerous commercial glass objects such as perfume bottles, vases, and figurines.

Upon Rene's death in 1945, his son Marc—himself a noted artist—inherited the firm and served as its president until his death in 1977.

The firm is headed by Marc's daughter, Marie-Claude. As Lalique's chief designer, it was she who designed the *Annual Series* of Lalique crystal collector's plates which began in 1965.

Annual Series

Artist: Marie-Claude Lalique

Full lead crystal with incised designs

Diameter: 21.5 centimeters (8½ inches)

No hanger

Edition size: As indicated. Announced between 5,000 and 8,000 from 1967 to 1975

Not numbered, without certificate; engraved "Lalique-France" on back

18-46-1.1
1965 *Deux Oiseaux.*
Artist: Marie-Claude Lalique.
Issue price: $25.00. Limited by announced edition size of 2,000.

18-46-1.2
1966 *Dreamrose.*
Artist: Marie-Claude Lalique.
Issue price: $25.00. Limited by announced edition size of 5,000.

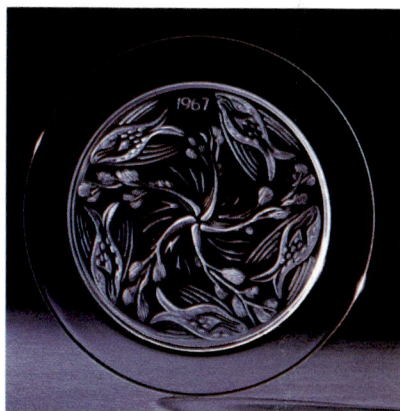

18-46-1.3
1967 *Fish Ballet.*
Artist: Marie-Claude Lalique.
Issue price: $25.00.

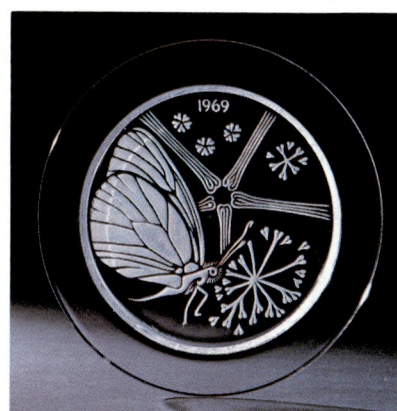

18-46-1.4
1968 *Gazelle Fantaisie.*
Artist: Marie-Claude Lalique.
Issue price: $25.00.

18-46-1.5
1969 *Papillon.*
Artist: Marie-Claude Lalique.
Issue price: $30.00.

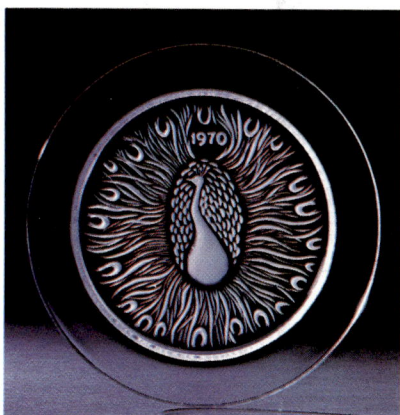

18-46-1.6
1970 *Peacock.*
Artist: Marie-Claude Lalique.
Issue price: $30.00.

18-46-1.7
1971 *Hibou.*
Artist: Marie-Claude Lalique.
Issue price: $35.00.

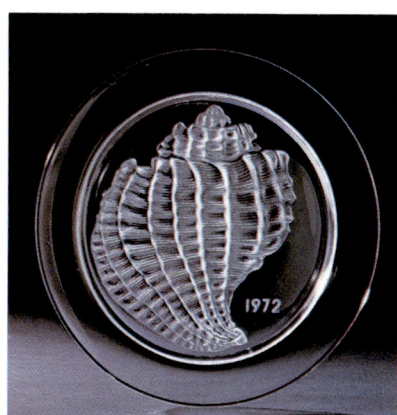

18-46-1.8
1972 *Coquillage.*
Artist: Marie-Claude Lalique.
Issue price: $40.00.

18-46-1.9
1973 *Jayling.*
Artist: Marie-Claude Lalique.
Issue price: $42.50.

18-46-1.10
1974 *Silver Pennies.*
Artist: Marie-Claude Lalique.
Issue price: $47.50.

18-46-1.11
1975 *Fish Duet.*
Artist: Marie-Claude Lalique.
Issue price: $50.00. Limited by
announced edition size of 8,000.

18-46-1.12
1976 *Eagle.*
Artist: Marie-Claude Lalique.
Issue price: $60.00.

The porcelain house of Limoges-Turgot traces its heritage to A.-R.-J. Turgot, Baron de l'Aulne, Louis XVI's administrator for the province of which Limoges was the capital. When kaolin clay, the key ingredient in true hard-fire porcelain, was discovered in 1768 at the nearby town of Saint-Yrieix, it was largely due to Turgot's efforts that the Limoges porcelain industry was established and achieved world renown.

Les Enfants de Durand, Durand's Children Collection, by the late artist Paul Durand, began in 1978 and is the first proprietary issue by Limoges-Turgot.

(Limoges)

Les Enfants de Durand
(Durand's Children Series)

Artist: Paul Durand
Overglaze porcelain
Diameter: 20.5 centimeters
   (8 inches)
Attached back hanger
Edition size undisclosed, limited
   by year of issue
Numbered with certificate

18-52-1.1
1978 *Marie-Ange.*
Artist: Paul Durand.
Issue price: $36.40.

18-52-1.2
1979 *Emilie et Philippe.*
Artist: Paul Durand.
Issue price: $36.40.

GERMANY
ANNA PERENNA, INC.
(Stuttgart)

Named for Anna Perenna, the ancient Roman goddess associated with health, abundance and the rebirth of spring, Anna Perenna, Inc. was founded in 1977 by Klaus D. Vogt who continues as its president. With offices in Stuttgart and New York, the company serves as the exclusive American importer and distributor of limited-edition jewelry and custom-made items by Rosenthal and as the only American importer of KPM plates.

The *Byzantine Triptych*, first issue in a triptych series based on the portable altar-pieces of the Middle Ages, was issued in 1979 and is a three-plate set which reinterprets ancient Byzantine religious motifs. Artwork is by the husband-and-wife team of Frank Russell and Gertrude Barrer.

ANNA PERENNA

(Stuttgart)

The Byzantine Triptych

Artist: Frank Russell and Gertrude Barrer

Hard-paste porcelain with wood frame

Diameter: plates one and three, 22 centimeters (8½ inches); plate two, 25 centimeters (9¾ inches); overall triptych, 89 centimeters x 46 centimeters (35 inches x 18 inches)

Attached back hanger

Edition size limited to 5,000

Individually hand-numbered with certificate

22-3-3.1-1
1979 *Gabriel.*
Artist: Frank Russell and
Gertrude Barrer.
Issue price: $325.00 the set.

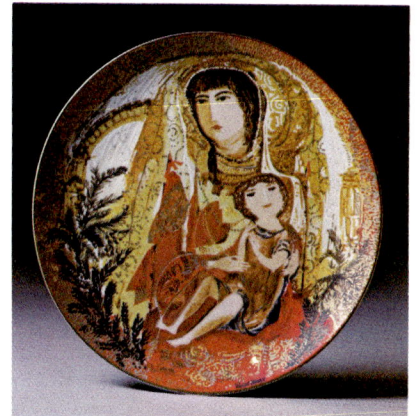

22-3-3.1-2
1979 *Madonna and Child.*

22-3-3.1-3
1979 *Michael.*

The Bareuther & Company porcelain factory began to produce dinnerware, vases, and giftware in 1867. The small shop was established with a porcelain kiln and an annular brick kiln by sculptor Johann Matthaeus Ries. In 1884 Ries's son sold the shop to Oskar Bareuther who continued to produce fine tableware.

To observe the one-hundredth anniversary of the factory in 1967, Bareuther began a series of limited-edition Christmas plates. A *Father's Day Series*, depicting the great castles of Germany, was started in 1969. Bareuther's *Thanksgiving Series*, showing American Thanksgiving scenes, began in 1971.

BAREUTHER

(Waldsassen)

Christmas Series

Artist: Hans Mueller except 1971

Underglaze porcelain decorated in
cobalt blue

Diameter: 20.5 centimeters
(8 inches)

Edition size limited to announced
quantity of 10,000

Pierced foot rim

Not numbered; without certificate

22-6-1.1
1967 *Stiftskirche.*
Artist: Hans Mueller.
Issue price: $12.00.

22-6-1.2
1968 *Kappl.*
Artist: Hans Mueller.
Issue price: $12.00.

22-6-1.3
1969 *Christkindlesmarkt.*
Artist: Hans Mueller.
Issue price: $12.00.

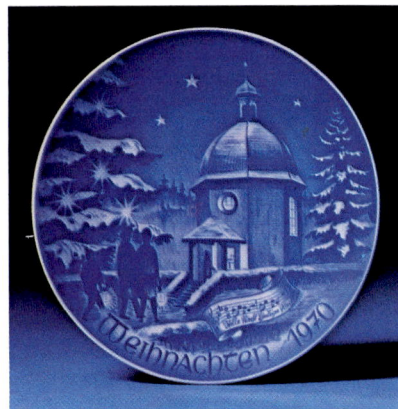

22-6-1.4
1970 *Chapel in Oberndorf.*
Artist: Hans Mueller.
Issue price: $12.50.

22-6-1.5
1971 *Toys for Sale.*
From drawing by Ludwig Richter.
Issue price: $12.75.

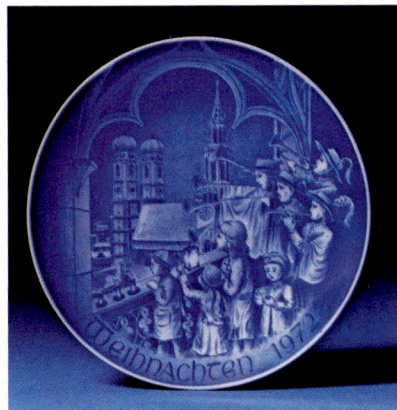

22-6-1.6
1972 *Christmas in Munich.*
Artist: Hans Mueller.
Issue price: $14.50.

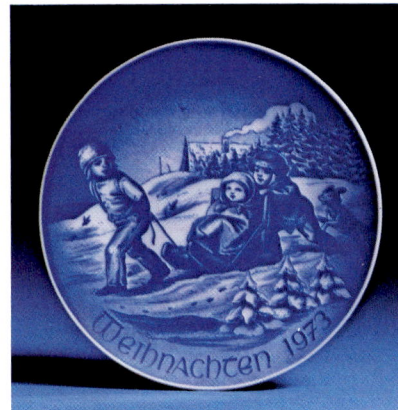

22-6-1.7
1973 *Christmas Sleigh Ride.*
Artist: Hans Mueller.
Issue price: $15.00.

22-6-1.8
1974 *Church in the Black Forest.*
Artist: Hans Mueller.
Issue price: $19.00.

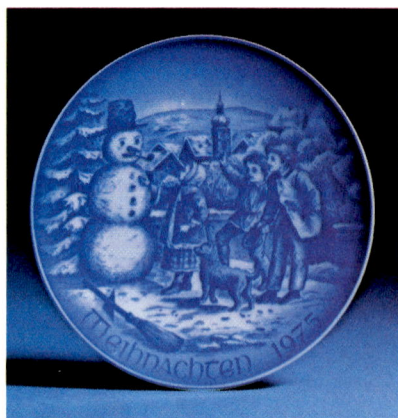

22-6-1.9
1975 *Snowman.*
Artist: Hans Mueller.
Issue price: $21.50.

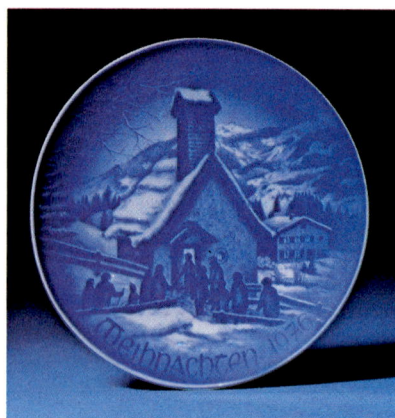

22-6-1.10
1976 *Chapel in the Hills.*
Artist: Hans Mueller.
Issue price: $23.50.

22-6-1.11
1977 *Story Time.*
Artist: Hans Mueller.
Issue price: $24.50.

22-6-1.12
1978 *Mittenwald.*
Artist: Hans Mueller.
Issue price: $27.50.

22-6-1.13
1979 *Winter Day.*
Artist: Hans Mueller.
Issue price: $35.00.

Father's Day Series
Artist: Hans Mueller
Underglaze porcelain decorated in
    cobalt blue
Diameter: 20.5 centimeters
    (8 inches)
Edition size limited to announced
    quantity of 2,500
Pierced foot rim
Not numbered; without certificate

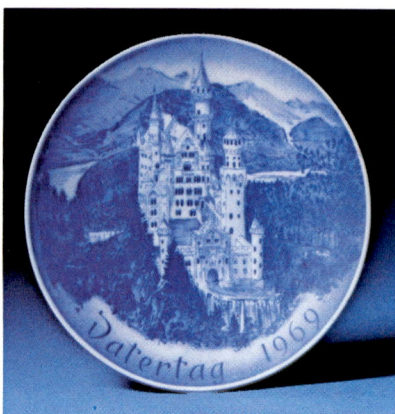

22-6-2.1
1969 *Castle Neuschwanstein.*
Artist: Hans Mueller.
Issue price: $10.50.

22-6-2.2
1970 *Castle Pfalz.*
Artist: Hans Mueller.
Issue price: $12.50.

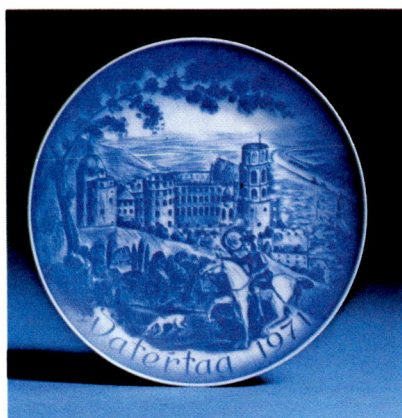

22-6-2.3
1971 *Castle Heidelberg.*
Artist: Hans Mueller.
Issue price: $12.75.

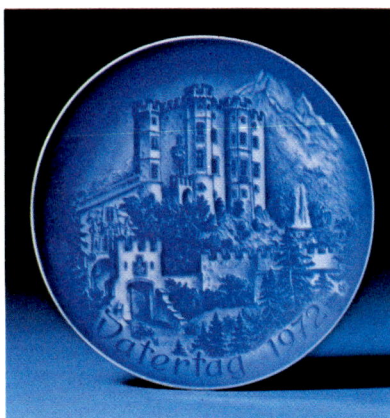

22-6-2.4
1972 *Castle Hohenschwangau.*
Artist: Hans Mueller.
Issue price: $14.50.

22-6-2.5
1973 *Castle Katz.*
Artist: Hans Mueller.
Issue price: $15.00.

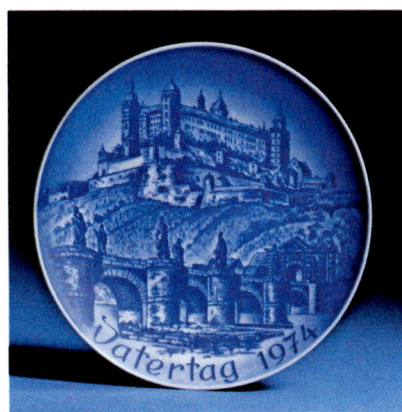

22-6-2.6
1974 *Wurzburg Castle.*
Artist: Hans Mueller.
Issue price: $19.00.

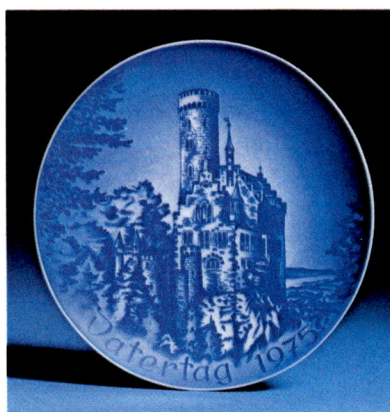

22-6-2.7
1975 *Castle Lichtenstein.*
Artist: Hans Mueller.
Issue price: $21.50.

22-6-2.8
1976 *Castle Hohenzollern.*
Artist: Hans Mueller.
Issue price: $23.50.

22-6-2.9
1977 *Castle Eltz.*
Artist: Hans Mueller.
Issue price: $24.50.

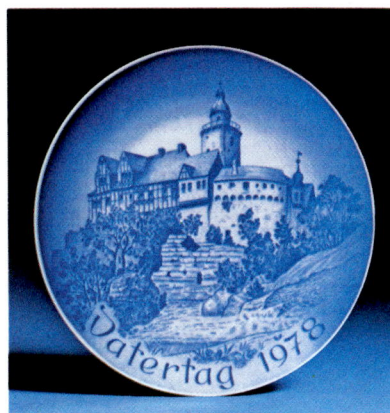

22-6-2.10
1978 *Castle Falkenstein.*
Artist: Hans Mueller.
Issue price: $27.50.

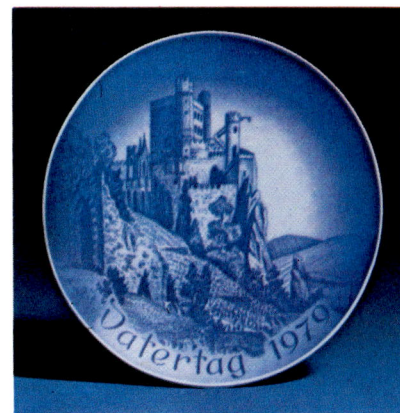

22-6-2.11
1979 *Castle Rheinstein.*
Artist: Hans Mueller.
Issue price: $35.00.

Thanksgiving Series

Artist: As indicated

Underglaze porcelain decorated in cobalt blue

Diameter: 20.5 centimeters (8 inches)

Edition size limited to announced quantity of 2,500

Pierced foot rim

Not numbered; without certificate

22-6-4.1
1971 *First Thanksgiving.*
Artist: Kurt C. Bielefeld.
Issue price: $13.50.

22-6-4.2
1972 *Harvest.*
Artist: Kurt C. Bielefeld.
Issue price: $14.50.

22-6-4.3
1973 *Country Road in Autumn.*
Artist: Kurt C. Bielefeld.
Issue price: $15.00.

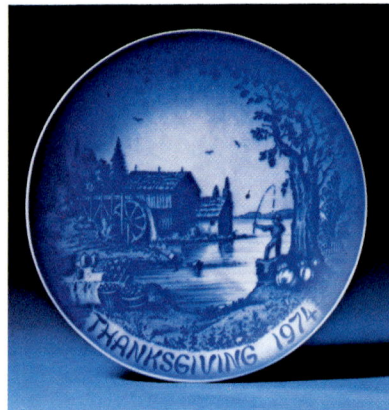

22-6-4.4
1974 *Old Mill.*
Artist: Kurt C. Bielefeld.
Issue price: $19.00.

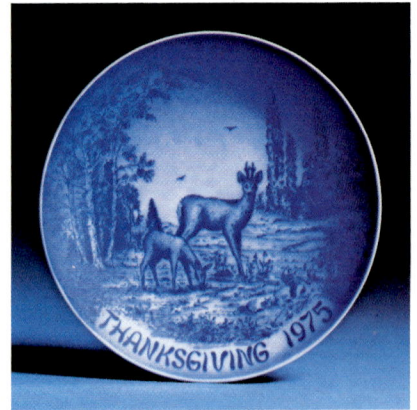

22-6-4.5
1975 *Wild Deer in Forest.*
Artist: Kurt C. Bielefeld.
Issue price: $21.50.

22-6-4.6
1976 *Thanksgiving on the Farm.*
Artist: Hans Mueller.
Issue price: $23.50.

22-6-4.7
1977 *Horses.*
Artist: Hans Mueller.
Issue price: $24.50.

22-6-4.8
1978 *Apple Harvest.*
Artist: Hans Mueller.
Issue price: $27.50.

GERMANY
BAREUTHER
(Waldsassen)

22-6-4.9
1979 *Noontime.*
Artist: Hans Mueller.
Issue price: $35.00.

Berlin Design's limited-edition plates, mugs, and other collectibles are manufactured by the Kaiser Porcelain Company (see Germany, KAISER), and are identified by the distinctive bear and crown symbol of the city of Berlin.

The *Christmas Series*, introduced in 1970, depicts Yule festivities in German towns. The *Mother's Day Series* of animal mothers and their young began in 1971.

Christmas Series

Artist: Undisclosed
Underglaze porcelain decorated in
   cobalt blue
Diameter: 19.5 centimeters
   (7¾ inches)
Edition size: As indicated
Pierced foot rim
Not numbered; without certificate

22-8-1.1
1970 *Christmas in Bernkastel.*
Artist: Undisclosed.
Issue price: $14.50. Edition size limited
to announced quantity of 4,000 .

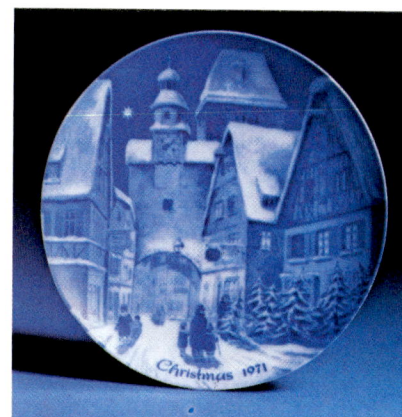

22-8-1.2
1971 *Christmas in Rothenburg on Tauber.*
Artist: Undisclosed.
Issue price: $14.50. Edition size limited
to announced quantity of 20,000.

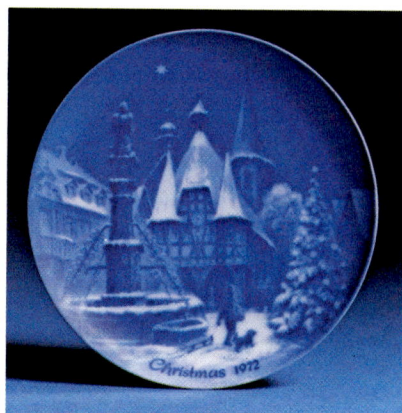

22-8-1.3
1972 *Christmas in Michelstadt.*
Artist: Undisclosed.
Issue price: $15.00. Edition size limited
to announced quantity of 20,000.

22-8-1.4
1973 *Christmas in Wendelstein.*
Artist: Undisclosed.
Issue price: $20.00. Edition size limited
to announced quantity of 20,000.

22-8-1.5
1974 *Christmas in Bremen.*
Artist: Undisclosed.
Issue price: $25.00. Edition size limited
to announced quantity of 20,000.

22-8-1.6
1975 *Christmas in Dortland.*
Artist: Undisclosed.
Issue price: $30.00. Edition size limited
to announced quantity of 20,000.

22-8-1.7
1976 *Christmas Eve in Augsburg.*
Artist: Undisclosed.
Issue price: $32.00. Edition size limited
to announced quantity of 20,000.

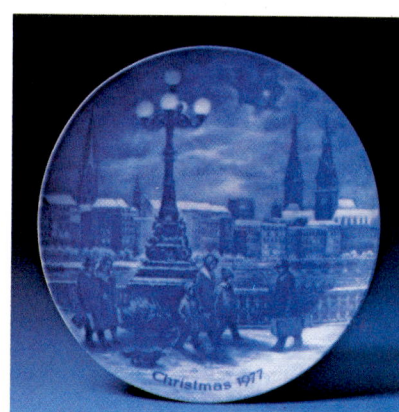

22-8-1.8
1977 *Christmas Eve in Hamburg.*
Artist: Undisclosed.
Issue price: $32.00. Edition size limited
to announced quantity of 20,000.

22-8-1.9
1978 *Christmas Market at the Berlin Cathedral.*
Artist: Undisclosed.
Issue price: $36.00. Edition size limited to announced quantity of 20,000.

22-8-1.10
1979 *Christmas Eve in Greetsiel.*
Artist: Undisclosed.
Issue price: $47.50. Edition size limited to announced quantity of 20,000.

Mother's Day Series

Artist: Undisclosed
Underglaze porcelain decorated in cobalt blue
Diameter: 19.5 centimeters
(7¾ inches)
Edition size: As indicated
Pierced foot rim
Not numbered; without certificate

22-8-3.1
1971 *Grey Poodles.*
Artist: Undisclosed.
Issue price: $14.50. Edition size limited to announced quantity of 20,000.

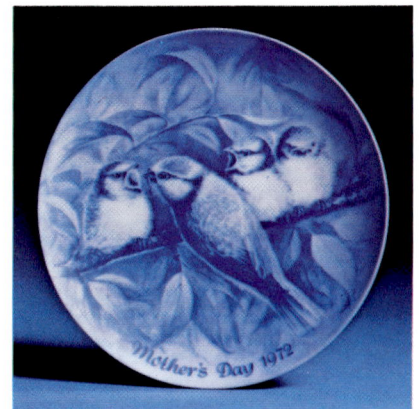

22-8-3.2
1972 *Fledglings.*
Artist: Undisclosed.
Issue price: $15.00. Edition size limited to announced quantity of 10,000.

22-8-3.3
1973 *Duck Family.*
Artist: Undisclosed.
Issue price: $16.50. Edition size limited to announced quantity of 6,000.

22-8-3.4
1974 *Squirrels.*
Artist: Undisclosed.
Issue price: $22.50. Edition size limited to announced quantity of 6,000.

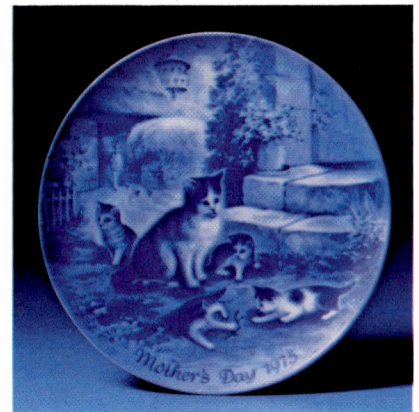

22-8-3.5
1975 *Cats.*
Artist: Undisclosed.
Issue price: $30.00. Edition size limited to announced quantity of 6,000.

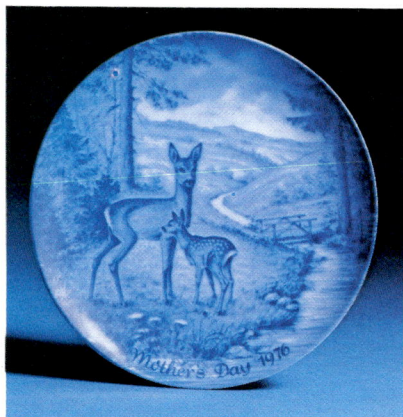

22-8-3.6
1976 *A Doe and Her Fawn.*
Artist: Undisclosed.
Issue price: $32.00. Edition size limited
to announced quantity of 6,000.

22-8-3.7
1977 *Storks.*
Artist: Undisclosed.
Issue price: $32.00. Edition size limited
to announced quantity of 6,000.

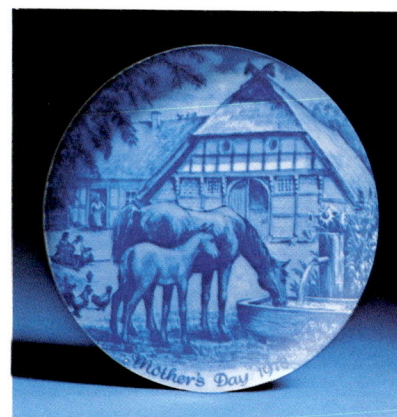

22-8-3.8
1978 *Mare with Foal.*
Artist: Undisclosed.
Issue price: $36.00. Edition size limited
to announced quantity of 6,000.

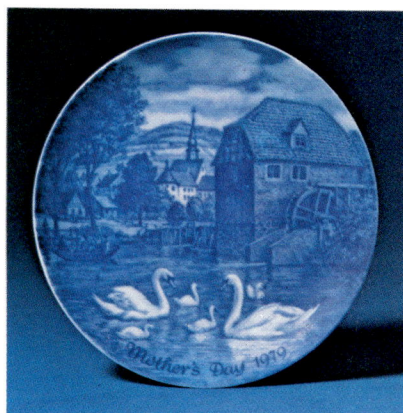

22-8-3.9
1979 *Swans and Cygnets.*
Artist: Undisclosed.
Issue price: $47.50. Edition size limited
to announced quality of 6,000.

Böttger Porzellan traces its heritage to the experiments of Jòhann Friedrich Böttger in the early years of the eighteenth century. An alchemist working under the patronage of Friedrich August I, "The Strong," of Saxony, Böttger was seeking to transmute base metals into gold when by chance he became the first European to discover the secret of making true hard-paste porcelain.

Although fully vitrified porcelain had been made in the Orient for centuries, Europeans had not been able to duplicate its properties. In 1709, however, Böttger made two important discoveries: first, that an intense controlled heat is necessary to vitrify the clay; and second, that the vital ingredient in white porcelain is kaolin clay.

The material produced so impressed August I that he commanded a factory to be built in 1710, thus assuring Böttger's fame as "the father of European porcelain."

Böttger Porzellan began its limited-edition Hedi Keller *Christmas Series* in 1979.

Hedi Keller Christmas Series

Artist: Hedi Keller
Porcelain
Diameter: 25 centimeters
(9½ inches)
Attached back hanger
Edition size unannounced
Numbered with certificate

22-9-1.1
1979 *The Adoration.*
Artist: Hedi Keller.
Issue price: Not available at press time.

*At press time this was the name of the manufacturer given; however Miss Keller said another Bavarian manufacturer may be named as the maker when the plate is produced.

Kirke Platten

Danish Church plates, formerly called Roskilde Church plates, are produced by a division of Bareuther & Company (see Germany, BAREUTHER). The *Church Series*, started in 1968, is of famous Danish churches.

GERMANY
DANISH CHURCH
(Waldsassen)

Church Series
Artist: Undisclosed
Underglaze porcelain decorated in
  cobalt blue
Diameter: 19.5 centimeters
  (7¾ inches)
Edition size undisclosed, limited
  by year of issue
Pierced foot rim
Not numbered; without certificate

22-13-1.1
1968 *Roskilde Cathedral.*
Artist: Undisclosed.
Issue price: $12.00.

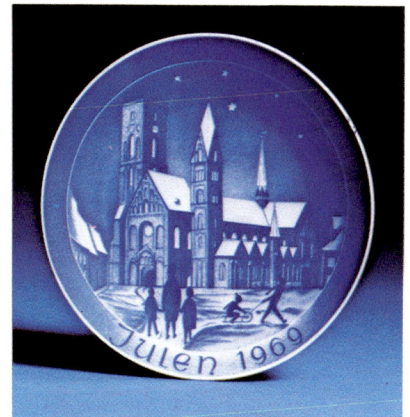

22-13-1.2
1969 *Ribe Cathedral.*
Artist: Undisclosed.
Issue price: $13.00.

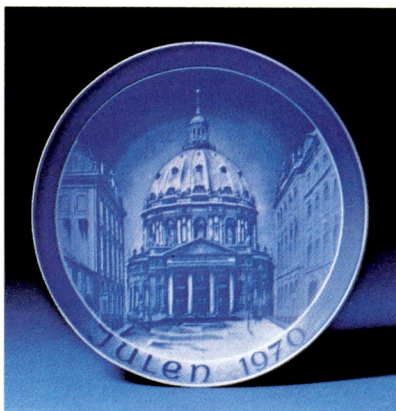

22-13-1.3
1970 *Marmor Church.*
Artist: Undisclosed.
Issue price: $13.00.

22-13-1.4
1971 *Ejby Church.*
Artist: Undisclosed.
Issue price: $13.00.

22-13-1.5
1972 *Kalundborg Church.*
Artist: Undisclosed.
Issue price: $13.00.

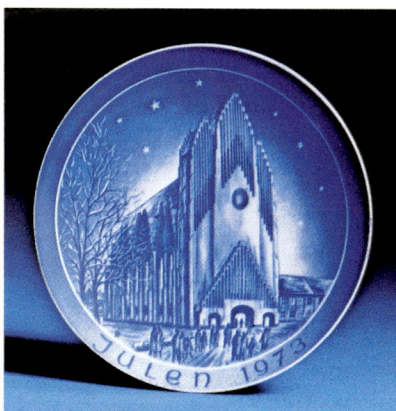

22-13-1.6
1973 *Grundtvig Church.*
Artist: Undisclosed.
Issue price: $15.00.

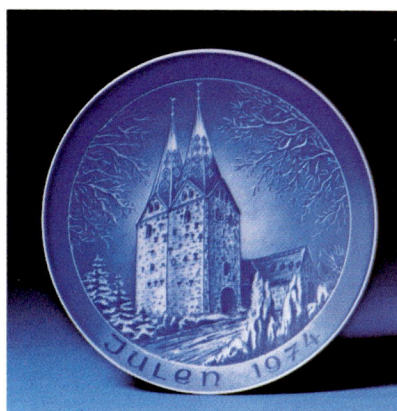

22-13-1.7
1974 *Broager Church.*
Artist: Undisclosed.
Issue price: $15.00.

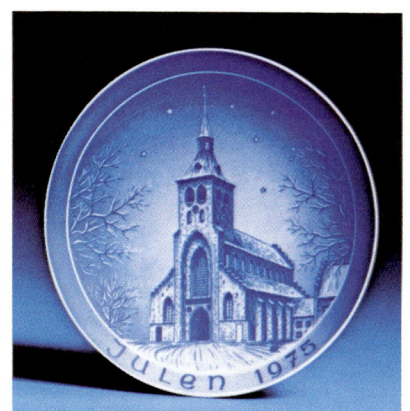

22-13-1.8
1975 *Sct. Knuds Church.*
Artist: Undisclosed.
Issue price: $18.00.

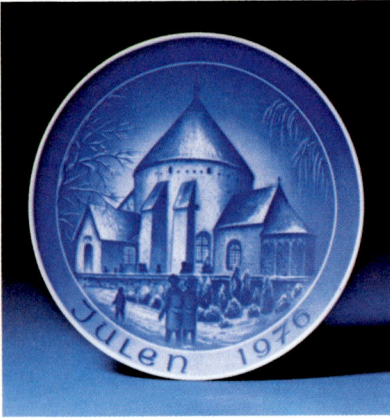

22-13-1.9
1976 *Osterlars Church.*
Artist: Undisclosed.
Issue price: $22.00.

22-13-1.10
1977 *Budolfi Church.*
Artist: Undisclosed.
Issue price: $15.95.

22-13-1.11
1978 *Haderslev Cathedral.*
Artist: Undisclosed.
Issue price: $19.95.

Maker had
no photo at
press time

22-13-1.12
1979 *Holmes Copenhagen.*
Artist: Undisclosed.
Issue price: $15.30.

Plates with the Dresden trademark are produced by the Porzellanzfabrik Tirschenreuth, established in the Dresden-Meissen area in 1838.

Dresden introduced its *Christmas Series* in 1971 and its *Mother's Day Series* in 1972. Both series ended in 1977.

DRESDEN

(Upper Palatinate)

Christmas Series

Artist: Hans Waldheimer

Underglaze porcelain centers
  decorated in cobalt blue,
  white baroque rims in relief
  trimmed with matte gold edges

Diameter: 19 centimeters
  (7½ inches)

Edition size: As indicated

Attached back hanger

Not numbered; without certificate

22-15-1.1
1971 *Shepherd Scene.*
Artist: Hans Waldheimer.
Issue price: $14.50. Edition size limited
to announced quantity of 3,500.

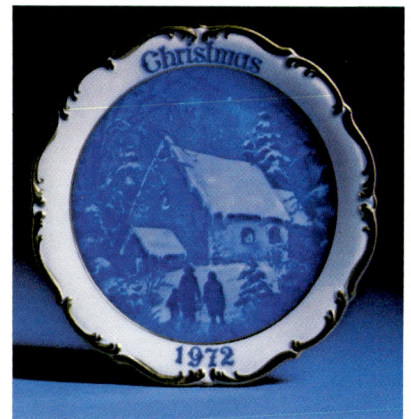

22-15-1.2
1972 *Niklas Church.*
Artist: Hans Waldheimer.
Issue price: $18.00. Edition size limited
to announced quantity of 6,000.

22-15-1.3
1973 *Schwanstein Church.*
Artist: Hans Waldheimer.
Issue price: $18.00. Edition size limited
to announced quantity of 6,000.

22-15-1.4
1974 *Village Scene.*
Artist: Hans Waldheimer.
Issue price: $20.00. Edition size limited
to announced quantity of 5,000.

22-15-1.5
1975 *Rothenberg Scene.*
Artist: Hans Waldheimer.
Issue price: $24.00. Edition size limited
to announced quantity of 5,000.

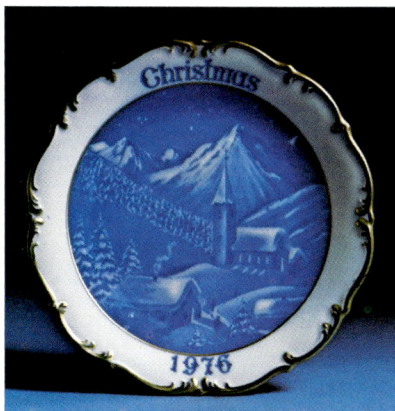

22-15-1.6
1976 *Bavarian Village Church.*
Artist: Hans Waldheimer.
Issue price: $26.00. Edition size limited
to announced quantity of 5,000.

22-15-1.7
1977 *Old Mill in the Hexenloch Valley.*
Artist: Hans Waldheimer.
Issue price: $28.00. Edition size limited
to announced quantity of 5,000.

Mother's Day Series

Artist: Hans Waldheimer

Underglaze porcelain centers
  decorated in cobalt blue,
  white baroque rims in relief,
  trimmed with matte gold edges

Diameter: 19 centimeters
  (7½ inches)

Edition size: As indicated

Attached back hanger

Not numbered; without certificate

22-15-2.1
1972 *Doe and Fawns.*
Artist: Hans Waldheimer.
Issue price: $15.00. Edition size limited
to announced quantity of 8,000.

22-15-2.2
1973 *Mare and Colt.*
Artist: Hans Waldheimer.
Issue price: $16.00. Edition size limited
to announced quantity of 6,000.

22-15-2.3
1974 *Tiger and Cub.*
Artist: Hans Waldheimer.
Issue price: $20.00. Edition size limited
to announced quantity of 5,000.

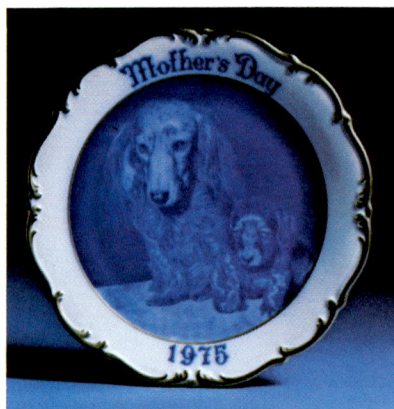

22-15-2.4
1975 *Dachshund Family.*
Artist: Hans Waldheimer.
Issue price: $24.00. Edition size limited
to announced quantity of 5,000.

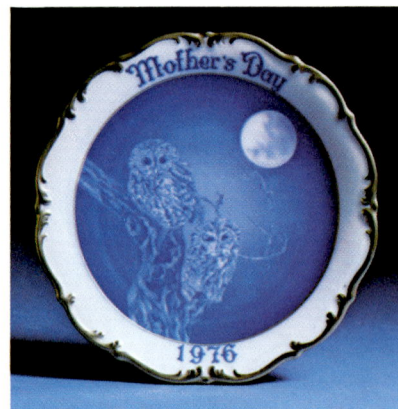

22-15-2.5
1976 *Mother Owl and Young.*
Artist: Hans Waldheimer.
Issue price: $26.00. Edition size limited
to announced quantity of 5,000.

22-15-2.6
1977 *Chamois.*
Artist: Hans Waldheimer.
Issue price: $28.00. Edition size limited
to announced quantity of 5,000.

Fürstenberg, West Germany's oldest existing porcelain factory, was established in 1747 in the fourteenth-century castle of Fürstenberg by order of Duke Karl I of Brunswick. He decreed that each piece of porcelain be initialed with a blue *F* which was later surmounted by a crown.

The factory, privately owned since 1859, presently occupies a modern plant on the grounds of Fürstenberg Castle and produces tableware, vases, and other decorative accessories as well as figurines and plaques.

The Fürstenberg collector's plates began with a *Christmas Series* introduced in 1971. A second *Deluxe Christmas Series* began the same year. They were followed in 1972 by a *Mother's Day Series*. All series have ended.

GERMANY
FURSTENBERG
(Hoxter)

Christmas Series
Artist: As indicated
Underglaze porcelain decorated in cobalt blue
Diameter: 19 centimeters
   (7½ inches)
Attached back hanger
Edition size: As indicated
Not numbered;without certificate

22-23-1.1
1971 *Rabbits*.
Artist: Walter Schoen.
Issue price: $15.00. Edition size limited to announced quantity of 8,500.

22-23-1.2
1972 *Snowy Village*.
Artist: Walter Schoen.
Issue price: $15.00. Edition size limited to announced quantity of 6,000.

22-23-1.3
1973 *Christmas Eve*.
Artist: Walter Schoen.
Issue price: $18.00. Edition size limited to announced quantity of 5,000.

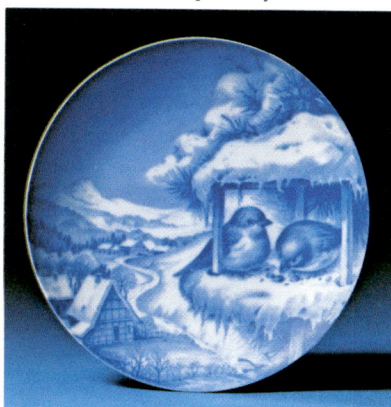

22-23-1.4
1974 *Sparrows*.
Artist: Walter Schoen.
Issue price: $20.00. Edition size limited to announced quantity of 4,000.

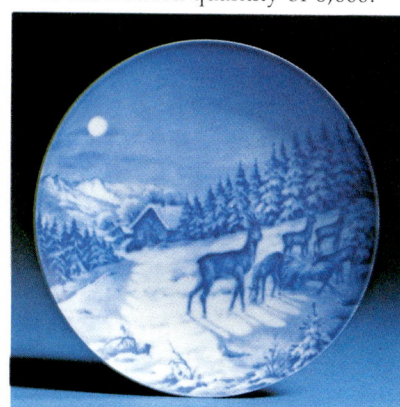

22-23-1.5
1975 *Deer Family*.
Artist: Walter Schoen.
Issue price: $24.00. Edition size limited to announced quantity of 4,000.

22-23-1.6
1976 *Winter Birds Feeding from Pine Cones*.
Artist: I. Gahries.
Issue price: $25.00. Edition size limited to announced quantity of 4,000.

Deluxe Christmas Series

Artist: Eva Grossberg. Artist's
  signature appears on back

Overglaze porcelain decorated in
  various colors with cobalt blue
  border trimmed in 18k gold

Diameter: 24 centimeters
  (9½ inches)

No hanger

Edition size: As indicated

Numbered without certificate

22-23-2.1
1971 *Three Wise Men.*
Artist: Eva Grossberg.
Issue price: $45.00.
Edition size limited to 1,500.

22-23-2.2
1972 *Holy Family and Angel.*
Artist: Eva Grossberg.
Issue price: $45.00.
Edition size limited to 2,000.

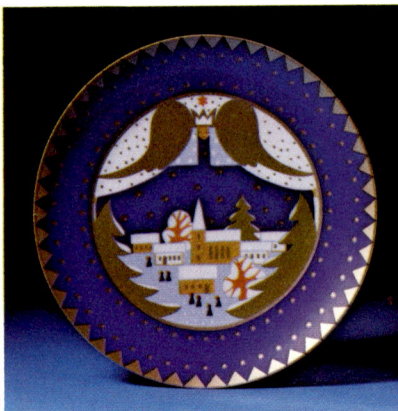

22-23-2.3
1973 *Christmas Eve.*
Artist: Eva Grossberg.
Issue price: $60.00.
Edition size limited to 2,000.

Mother's Day Series

Artist: As indicated

Underglaze porcelain decorated in
  cobalt blue

Diameter: 19 centimeters
  (7½ inches)

Attached back hanger

Edition size: As indicated

Not numbered; without certificate

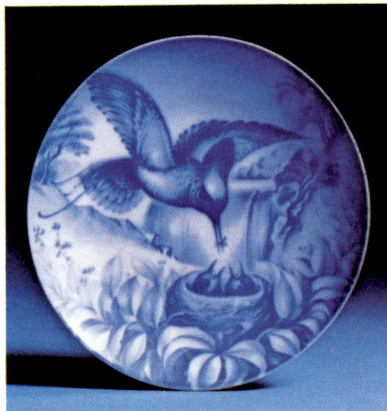

22-23-4.1
1972 *Hummingbird.*
Artist: Undisclosed.
Issue price: $15.00. Edition size limited
to announced quantity of 7,500.

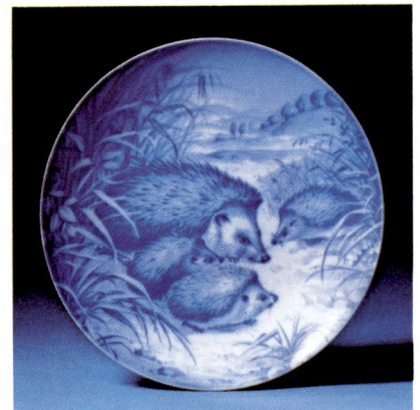

22-23-4.2
1973 *Hedgehogs.*
Artist: Undisclosed.
Issue price: $16.00. Edition size limited
to announced quantity of 5,000.

22-23-4.3
1974 *Doe with Fawn.*
Artist: Undisclosed.
Issue price: $20.00. Edition size limited
to announced quantity of 4,000.

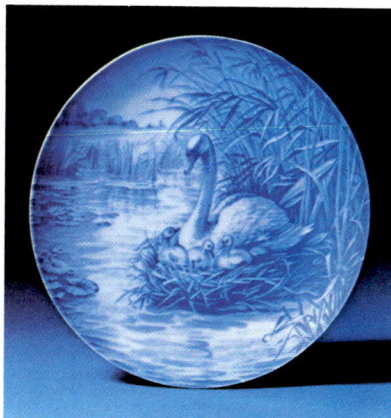

22-23-4.4
1975 *Swan Family.*
Artist: Undisclosed.
Issue price: $24.00. Edition size limited
to announced quantity of 4,000.

22-23-4.5
1976 *Koala Bear and Young.*
Artist: I. Gahries. Issue price: $25.00.
Edition size limited to announced
quantity of 4,000.

Goebel

W. Goebel Porzellanfabrik was established in 1871 in Oeslau by Franz Deleff Goebel and his son William. Headed by Wilhelm Goebel, who represents the fifth generation of the founding family, Goebel produces handcrafted figurines, plates, dinnerware, and gift items.

In 1935 Goebel introduced the famous M. I. Hummel figurines based on sketches by Sister Maria Innocentia Hummel who had joined the Franciscan convent at Siessen the previous year. In 1971, to celebrate the one-hundredth anniversary of the firm, Goebel inaugurated an annual series of limited-edition plates with the M. I. Hummel designs.

The *Hummel Anniversary Series* began in 1975, with a new plate to be issued every five years. Other Goebel plate series include the *Wildlife Series*, which began in 1974, and a *Mother's Series* started in 1975.

Hummel Annual Series
Artist: Sister M. I. Hummel.
  Artist's signature appears on
  front
Stoneware with hand-painted
  bas-relief
Diameter: 19 centimeters
  (7½ inches)
Pierced foot rim
Edition size undisclosed, limited
  by year of issue
Not numbered; without certificate

22-27-1.1
1971 *Heavenly Angel.*
Artist: Sister M. I. Hummel.
Issue price: $25.00.

22-27-1.2
1972 *Hear Ye, Hear Ye.*
Artist: Sister M. I. Hummel.
Issue price: $30.00.

22-27-1.3
1973 *Globe Trotter.*
Artist: Sister M. I. Hummel.
Issue price: $32.50.

22-27-1.4
1974 *Goose Girl.*
Artist: Sister M. I. Hummel.
Issue price: $40.00.

22-27-1.5
1975 *Ride into Christmas.*
Artist: Sister M. I. Hummel.
Issue price: $50.00.

22-27-1.6
1976 *Apple Tree Girl.*
Artist: Sister M. I. Hummel.
Issue price: $50.00.

22-27-1.7
1977 *Apple Tree Boy.*
Artist: Sister M. I. Hummel.
Issue price: $50.00.

22-27-1.8
1978 *Happy Pastime.*
Artist: Sister M. I. Hummel.
Issue price: $65.00.

22-27-1.9
1979 *Singing Lesson*.
Artist: Sister M. I. Hummel.
Issue price: $90.00.

Wildlife Series

Artist: Undisclosed
Stoneware with hand-painted
   bas-relief
Diameter: 19 centimeters
   (7½ inches)
Pierced foot rim
Edition size undisclosed, limited
   by year of issue
Not numbered; without certificate

22-27-2.1
1974 *Robin*.
Artist: Undisclosed.
Issue price: $45.00.

22-27-2.2
1975 *Blue Titmouse*.
Artist: Undisclosed.
Issue price: $50.00.

22-27-2.3
1976 *Barn Owl*.
Artist: Undisclosed.
Issue price: $50.00.

22-27-2.4
1977 *Bullfinch*.
Artist: Undisclosed.
Issue price: $50.00.

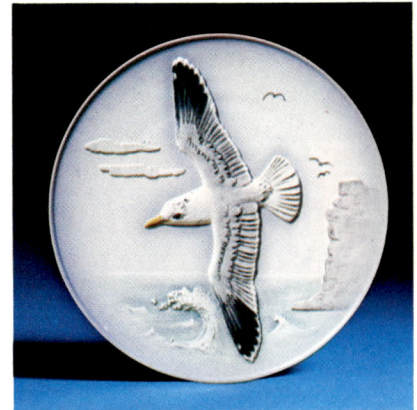

22-27-2.5
1978 *Sea Gull*.
Artist: Undisclosed.
Issue price: $55.00.

Hummel Anniversary Series

Artist: Sister M. I. Hummel.
   Artist's signature appears on
   front

Stoneware with hand-painted
   bas-relief

Diameter: 25.5 centimeters
   (10 inches)

Pierced foot rim

Edition size undisclosed, limited
   by year of issue

Not numbered; without certificate

22-27-3.1
1975 *Stormy Weather.*
Artist: Sister M. I. Hummel.
Issue price: $100.00.

Mothers Series

Artist: Gerhard Bochmann

Stoneware with hand-painted
   bas-relief

Diameter: 19 centimeters
   (7½ inches)

Pierced foot rim

Edition size undisclosed, limited
   by year of issue for plates
   through 1978, other years as
   indicated

22-27-4.1
1975 *Rabbits.*
Artist: Gerhard Bochmann.
Issue price: $45.00.

22-27-4.2
1976 *Cats.*
Artist: Gerhard Bochmann.
Issue price: $45.00.

22-27-4.3
1977 *Panda Bear with Baby.*
Artist: Gerhard Bochmann.
Issue price: $45.00.

22-27-4.4
1978 *Doe and Fawn.*
Artist: Gerhard Bochmann.
Issue price: $50.00.

22-27-4.5
1979 *Long Eared Owl.*
Artist: Gerhard Bochmann.
Issue price: $65.00. Edition size limited
to announced quantity of 10,000.

22-30-0.0

Founded in 1976, Hibel Studio specializes in porcelain figurines, lithographs on porcelain and limited-edition collector's plates. All artwork is approved by Edna Hibel, and plates are made by Kaiser Porcelain (see Germany, KAISER).

Hibel Studio began its first series of collector's plates, *The David Series*, in 1979. The four-plate series is based on the biblical story of King David with artwork by Edna Hibel.

GERMANY
HIBEL STUDIO
(Staffelstein)

David Series
Artist: Edna Hibel
Porcelain
Diameter: 26 centimeters
  (10⅛ inches)
Pierced foot rim
Edition size limited to 5,000
Numbered with certificate

22-30-1.1
1979 *The Wedding of David and
Bathsheba.*
Artist: Edna Hibel.
Issue price: $250.00. Edition size limited to announced quantity of 5,000.

KAISER

The history of Kaiser porcelain began in 1872 when porcelain painter August Alboth set up his own workshop in Coburg. When he retired in 1899, his son Ernst moved the pottery to Bavaria. Marriage united the Alboth and Kaiser families in 1922, resulting in the ALKA trademark—a combination of the first two letters of both names.

In 1938 the firm purchased the old Bavarian pottery of Silbermann Brothers, which had been awarded a royal diploma in 1882 for its "magnificent" cobalt blue underglaze. The company opened its modern factory in Staffelstein in 1953 and in 1970 the trademark was changed to Kaiser Porcelain.

Long a producer of porcelain dinner and coffee sets and figurines, Kaiser introduced its first series of limited-edition plates, the *Christmas Series,* in 1970 which ended in 1978. The *Mother's Day Series* began in 1971, and to observe the company's own centennial, the *Anniversary Series* began a year later.

Christmas Series

Artist: As indicated

Underglaze porcelain decorated in cobalt blue

Diameter: 19 centimeters (7½ inches)

Pierced foot rim

Edition size undisclosed, limited by year of issue except 1974

Not numbered; without certificate

22-42-1.1
1970 *Waiting for Santa Claus.*
Artist: Toni Schoener.
Issue price: $12.50.

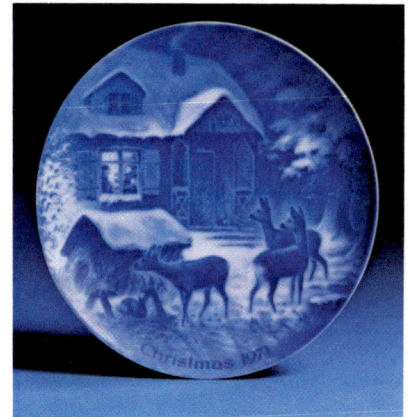

22-42-1.2
1971 *Silent Night.*
Artist: Kurt Bauer.
Issue price: $13.50.

22-42-1.3
1972 *Welcome Home.*
Artist: Kurt Bauer.
Issue price: $16.50.

22-42-1.4
1973 *Holy Night.*
Artist: Toni Schoener.
Issue price: $18.00.

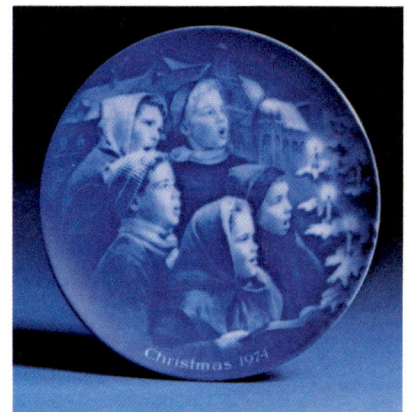

22-42-1.5
1974 *Christmas Carolers.*
Artist: Kurt Bauer.
Issue price: $25.00. Edition size limited to announced quantity of 8,000.

22-42-1.6
1975 *Bringing Home the Christmas Tree.*
Artist: Joann Northcott.
Issue price: $25.00.

22-42-1.7
1976 *Christ the Saviour Is Born.*
Artist: Carlo Maratta.
Issue price: $25.00.

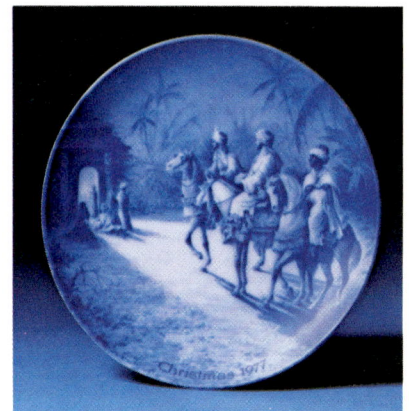

22-42-1.8
1977 *The Three Kings.*
Artist: Toni Schoener.
Issue price: $25.00.

22-42-1.9
1978 *Shepherds in the Fields.*
Artist: Toni Schoener.
Issue price: $30.00.

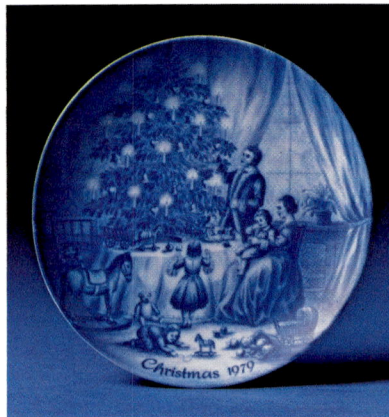

22-42-1.10
1979 *Christmas Eve.*
Artist: H. Blum.
Issue price: $32.00.

Mother's Day Series
Artist: Toni Schoener
Underglaze porcelain decorated in
  cobalt blue
Diameter: 19 centimeters
  (7½ inches)
Pierced foot rim
Edition size undisclosed, limited
  by year of issue except 1974
Not numbered; without certificate

22-42-2.1
1971 *Mare and Foal.*
Artist: Toni Schoener.
Issue price: $13.00.

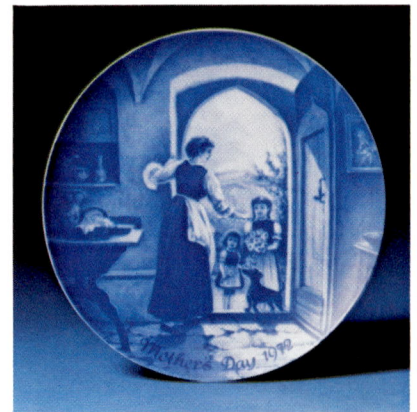

22-42-2.2
1972 *Flowers for Mother.*
Artist: Toni Schoener.
Issue price: $16.50.

22-42-2.3
1973 *Cats.*
Artist: Toni Schoener.
Issue price: $17.00.

22-42-2.4
1974 *Fox.*
Artist: Toni Schoener.
Issue price: $22.00. Edition size limited
to announced quantity of 7,000.

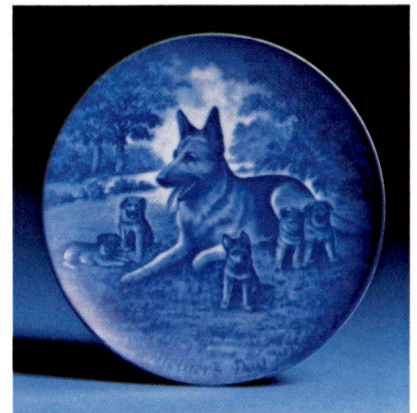

22-42-2.5
1975 *German Shepherd.*
Artist: Toni Schoener.
Issue price: $25.00.

22-42-2.6
1976 *Swan and Cygnets.*
Artist: Toni Schoener.
Issue price: $25.00.

22-42-2.7
1977 *Mother Rabbit and Young.*
Artist: Toni Schoener.
Issue price: $25.00.

22-42-2.8
1978 *Hen and Chicks.*
Artist: Toni Schoener.
Issue price: $30.00.

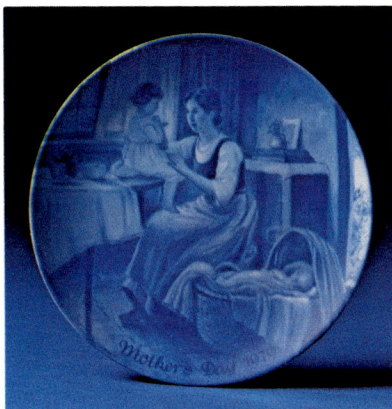

22-42-2.9
1979 *A Mother's Devotion.*
Artist: Nori Peter.
Issue price: $32.00.

Anniversary Series

Artist: Toni Schoener
Underglaze porcelain decorated in cobalt blue
Diameter: 19 centimeters (7½ inches)
Pierced foot rim
Edition size undisclosed, limited by year of issue except 1974 and 1975
Not numbered; without certificate

22-42-3.1
1972 *Love Birds.*
Artist: Toni Schoener.
Issue price: $16.50.

22-42-3.2
1973 *In the Park.*
Artist: Toni Schoener.
Issue price: $18.00.

22-42-3.3
1974 *Canoeing down River.*
Artist: Toni Schoener.
Issue price: $22.00. Edition size limited
to announced quantity of 7,000.

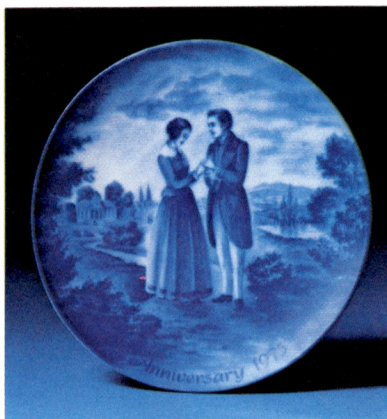

22-42-3.4
1975 *Tender Moment.*
Artist: Toni Schoener.
Issue price: $25.00. Edition size limited
to announced quantity of 7,000.

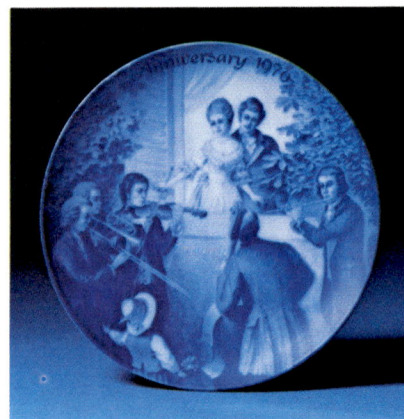

22-42-3.5
1976 *Serenade for Lovers.*
Artist: Toni Schoener.
Issue price: $25.00.

22-42-3.6
1977 *A Simple Gift.*
Artist: Toni Schoener.
Issue price: $25.00.

22-42-3.7
1978 *Viking Toast.*
Artist: Toni Schoener.
Issue price: $30.00.

22-42-3.8
1979 *Romantic Interlude.*
Artist: H. Blum.
Issue price: $32.00.

Lindner

The Lindner porcelain factory was established by Ernst Lindner in the 1930s in Kueps, Bavaria. Collector's plates by Lihs-Lindner were the product of collaboration between Lindner and Helmut H. Lihs of Long Beach, California. Lihs provided motifs and sketches which were finished by Lindner's artist, Josef Neubauer. Lindner also produces bells, vases and various porcelain items.

The *Christmas Series* started in 1972; the *Easter Series* began in 1973; and the *Playmates Series* was started in 1976. In 1978 Lihs-Lindner introduced a second Christmas series, *A Child's Christmas*.

GERMANY
LIHS-LINDNER
(Kueps)

Christmas Series
Artist: Josef Neubauer
Overglaze porcelain decorated in
 cobalt blue and 24k gold
Diameter: 19 centimeters
 (7½ inches)
Pierced foot rim
Edition size: As indicated
Numbered; with certificate
 since 1976

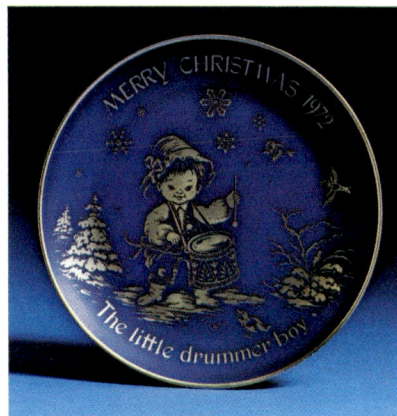

22-47-1.1
1972 *Little Drummer Boy.*
Artist: Josef Neubauer.
Issue price: $25.00.
Edition size limited to 6,000.

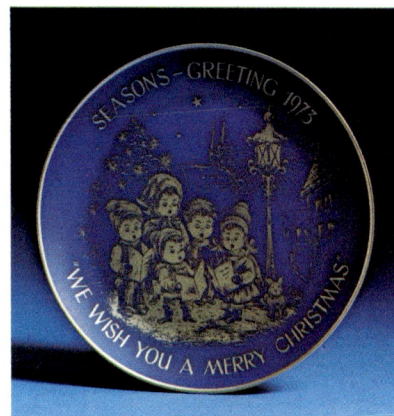

22-47-1.2
1973 *The Little Carolers.*
Artist: Josef Neubauer.
Issue price: $25.00.
Edition size limited to 6,000.

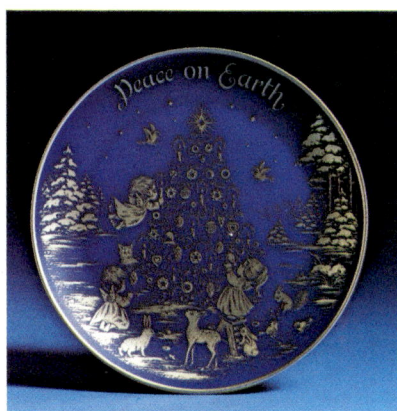

22-47-1.3
1974 *Peace on Earth.*
Artist: Josef Neubauer.
Issue price: $25.00.
Edition size limited to 6,000.

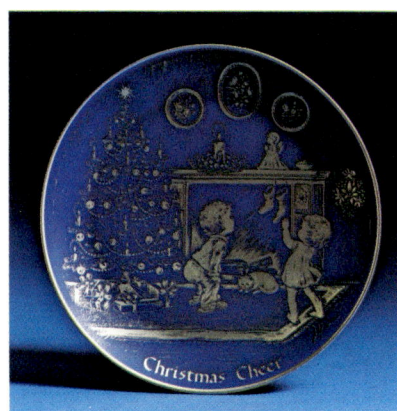

22-47-1.4
1975 *Christmas Cheer.*
Artist: Josef Neubauer.
Issue price: $30.00.
Edition size limited to 6,000.

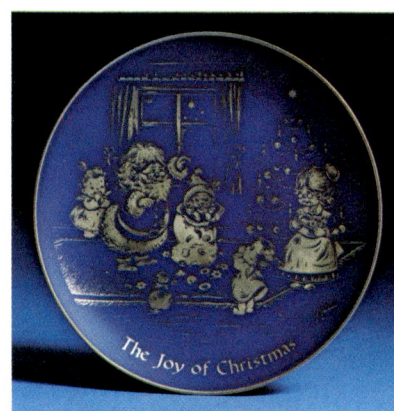

22-47-1.5
1976 *The Joy of Christmas.*
Artist: Josef Neubauer.
Issue price: $30.00.
Edition size undisclosed.

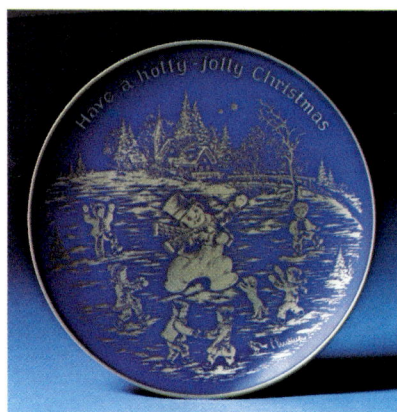

22-47-1.6
1977 *Have a Holly-Jolly Christmas.*
Artist: Josef Neubauer.
Issue price: $30.00.
Edition size undisclosed.

Easter Series
Artist: Josef Neubauer
Overglaze porcelain decorated in cobalt blue and 24k gold
Diameter: 19 centimeters
(7½ inches)
Pierced foot rim
Edition size limited to 1,500
Numbered without certificate

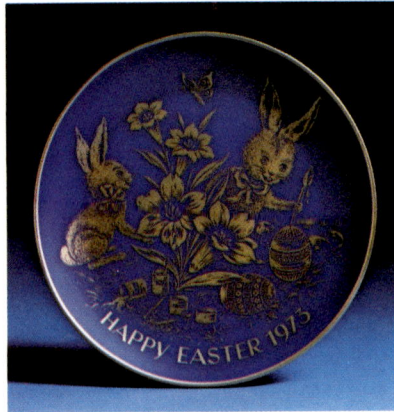

22-47-3.1
1973 *Happy Easter.*
Artist: Josef Neubauer.
Issue price: $25.00.

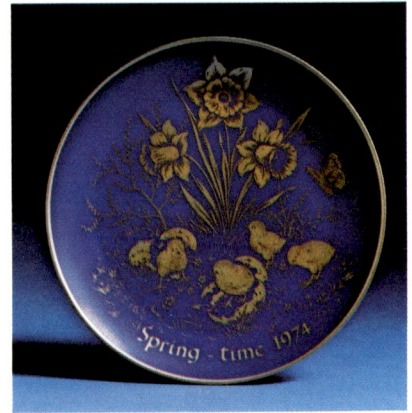

22-47-3.2
1974 *Spring-time.*
Artist: Josef Neubauer.
Issue price: $25.00.

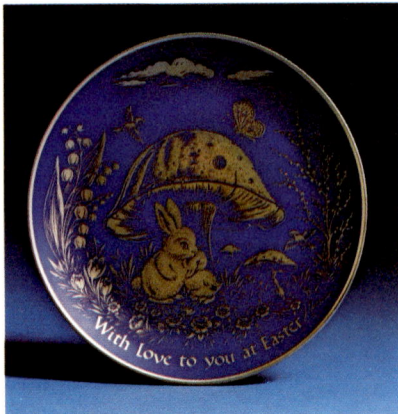

22-47-3.3
1975 *With Love to You at Easter.*
Artist: Josef Neubauer.
Issue price: $28.00.

Playmate Series
Artist: Louise Forbes. Artist's signature appears on front
Overglaze porcelain decorated in cobalt blue and 24k gold
Diameter: 19 centimeters
(7½ inches)
Pierced foot rim
Edition size limited to 5,000
Numbered without certificate

22-47-4.1
1976 *Timmy and His Best Pal.*
Artist: Louise Forbes.
Issue price: $45.00.

22-47-4.2
1977 *Heidi and Her Friend.*
Artist: Louise Forbes.
Issue price: $45.00.

LIHS-LINDNER

(Kueps)

A Child's Christmas Series

Artist: H. Ferner

Overglaze porcelain decorated in
    cobalt blue and 24K gold

Diameter: 20 centimeters
    (7¾ inches)

Attached back hanger

Edition size limited to 5,000

Numbered with certificate

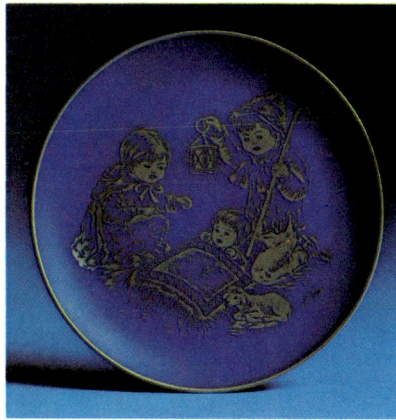

22-47-5.1
1978 *Holy Night.*
Artist: H. Ferner.
Issue price: $40.00.

studio-linie

Philip Rosenthal began his business in 1879 in the town of Selb in Bavaria. He initially purchased "white ware" from various porcelain manufacturers in Selb (including Hutschenreuther) and painted it with his own designs.

In 1895 he established his own factory in Kronach where he produced fine porcelain signed *Rosenthal* on the back, making him one of the first porcelain makers to use his name rather than a symbol. Philip died in 1937 and the business was taken over by his son, Philip Jr. who still heads the firm.

Rosenthal's *Traditional Christmas Series* began in 1910. From 1969 to 1971 some of these earlier plates were reissued in small quantities (no more than 500 per reissue). Reissued plates, regardless of the year depicted, have a post-1957 backstamp and their foot rims are not pierced. After 1971, the firm discontinued the practice of reissuing plates from previous years, and each Rosenthal collector's plate is now produced only during its current year. The *Traditional* Christmas plates now qualify as limited editions. Since 1975, plates in this series bear Rosenthal's Classic Rose Collection backstamp.

In 1971 Rosenthal began the first of its Studio-Linie collections with the *Wiinblad Christmas Series*. These plates carry intricate modern designs partially hand painted in as many as eighteen colors and are embellished with platinum and 18k gold. A second Wiinblad series was begun in 1976 entitled the *Fantasies and Fables Series* and also carries the Rosenthal Studio-Linie backstamp. *The Nobility of Children Series* and the *Oriental Gold Series* were also begun in 1976 and carry Rosenthal's Classic Rose Collection backstamp.

GERMANY
ROSENTHAL

(Selb, Rothbühl, Selb-Plössberg, München, Kronach, Amberg,
Bad Soden, Neusorg)

Traditional Christmas Series

Artist: As indicated. Artist's name
appears on back
Overglaze porcelain
Diameter: 21.5 centimeters
(8½ inches)
Pierced foot rim until 1971,
attached back hanger thereafter
Edition size: Undisclosed
Not numbered; without certificate

22-69-1.1
1910 *Winter Peace.*
Artist: Jul Guldbrandson.
Issue price: Unknown.

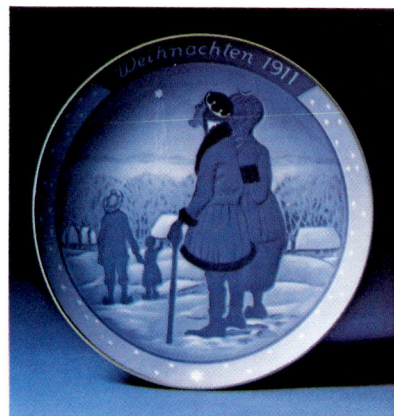

22-69-1.2
1911 *The Three Wise Men.*
Artist: Heinrich Vogoler.
Issue price: Unknown.

22-69-1.3
1912 *Stardust.*
Artist: Paul Rieth.
Issue price: Unknown.

22-69-1.4
1913 *Christmas Lights.*
Artist: Julius Dietz.
Issue price: Unknown.

22-69-1.5
1914 *Christmas Song.*
Artist: Prof. L. V. Zumbusch.
Issue price: Unknown.

22-69-1.6
1915 *Walking to Church.*
Artist: Jul V. Guldbrandson.
Issue price: Unknown.

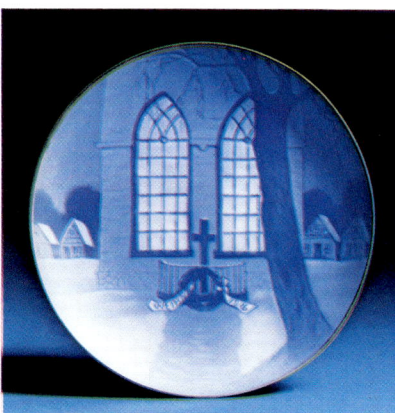

22-69-1.7
1916 *Christmas During War.*
Artist: Jul V. Guldbrandson.
Issue price: Unknown.

22-69-1.8
1917 *Angel of Peace.*
Artist: Moere.
Issue price: Unknown.

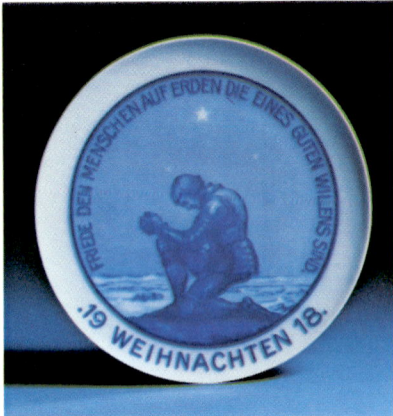

22-69-1.9
1918 *Peace on Earth.*
Artist: Pfeifer.
Issue price: Unknown.

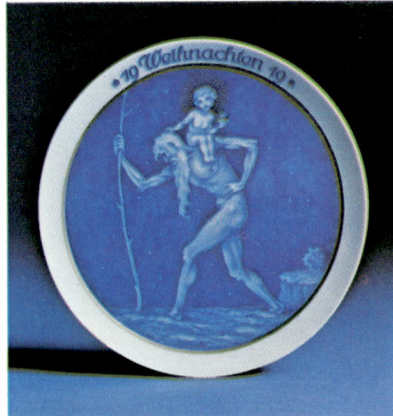

22-69-1.10
1919 *St. Christopher with the Christ Child.*
Artist: Dr. W. Schertel.
Issue price: Unknown.

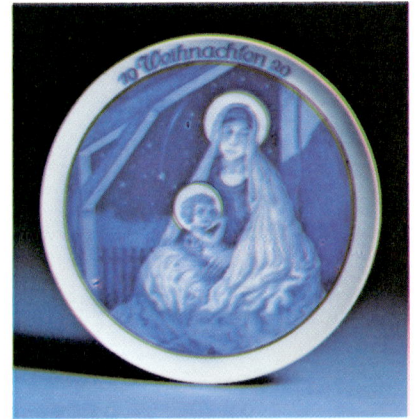

22-69-1.11
1920 *The Manger in Bethlehem.*
Artist: Dr. W. Schertel.
Issue price: Unknown.

22-69-1.12
1921 *Christmas in the Mountains.*
Artist: Jupp Wiertz.
Issue price: Unknown.

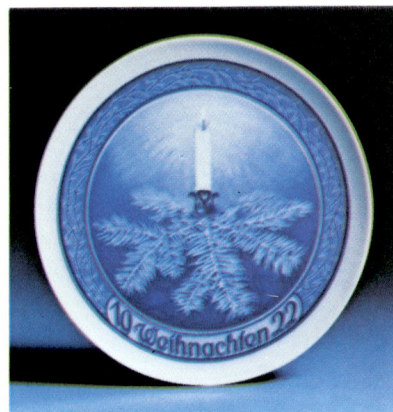

22-69-1.13
1922 *Advent Branch.*
Artist: F. Nicolai.
Issue price: Unknown.

22-69-1.14
1923 *Children in the Winter Wood.*
Artist: Ernst Hofer.
Issue price: Unknown.

22-69-1.15
1924 *Deer in the Woods.*
Artist: Theo Karner.
Issue price: Unknown.

22-69-1.16
1925 *The Three Wise Men.*
Artist: Tauschek.
Issue price: Unknown.

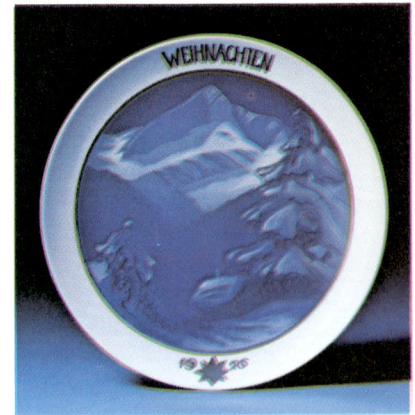

22-69-1.17
1926 *Christmas in the Mountains.*
Artist: Theo Schmutz-Baudess.
Issue price: Unknown.

22-69-1.18
1927 *Station on the Way.*
Artist: Theo Schmutz-Baudess.
Issue price: Unknown.

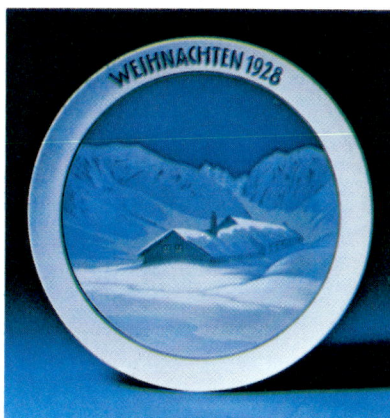

22-69-1.19
1928 *Chalet Christmas.*
Artist: Heinrich Fink.
Issue price: Unknown.

22-69-1,20
1929 *Christmas in the Alps.*
Artist: Heinrich Fink.
Issue price: Unknown.

22-69-1.21
1930 *Group of Deer Under the Pines.*
Artist: Theo Karner.
Issue price: Unknown.

22-69-1.22
1931 *Path of the Magi.*
Artist: Heinrich Fink.
Issue price: Unknown.

22-69-1.23
1932 *Christ Child.*
Artist: Otto Koch.
Issue price: Unknown.

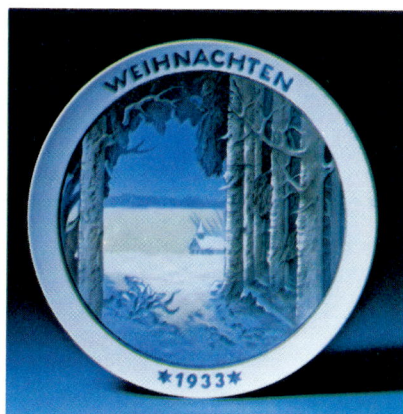

22-69-1.24
1933 *Through the Night to Light.*
Artist: Hans Schiffner.
Issue price: Unknown.

22-69-1.25
1934 *Christmas Peace.*
Artist: Heinrich Fink.
Issue price: Unknown.

22-69-1.26
1935 *Christmas by the Sea.*
Artist: Heinrich Fink.
Issue price: Unknown.

22-69-1.27
1936 *Nurnberg Angel.*
Artist: Heinrich Fink.
Issue price: Unknown.

22-69-1.28
1937 *Berchtesgaden.*
Artist: Heinrich Fink.
Issue price: Unknown.

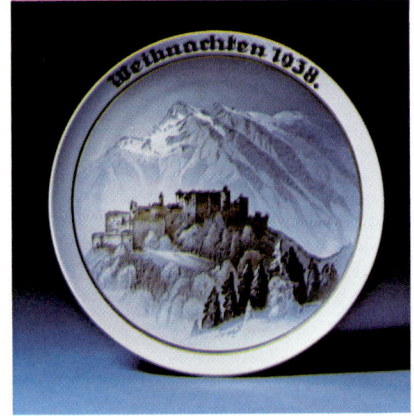

22-69-1.29
1938 *Christmas in the Alps.*
Artist: Heinrich Fink.
Issue price: Unknown.

22-69-1.30
1939 *Schneekoppe Mountain.*
Artist: Heinrich Fink.
Issue price: Unknown.

22-69-1.31
1940 *Marien Church in Danzig.*
Artist: Walter Mutze.
Issue price: Unknown.

22-69-1.32
1941 *Strassburg Cathedral.*
Artist: Walter Mutze.
Issue price: Unknown.

22-69-1.33
1942 *Marianburg Castle.*
Artist: Walter Mutze.
Issue price: Unknown.

22-69-1.34
1943 *Winter Idyll.*
Artist: Amadeus Dier.
Issue price: Unknown.

22-69-1.35
1944 *Wood Scape.*
Artist: Willi Hein.
Issue price: Unknown.

22-69-1.36
1945 *Christmas Peace.*
Artist: Alfred Mundel.
Issue price: Unknown.

22-69-1.37
1946 *Christmas in an Alpine Valley.*
Artist: Willi Hein.
Issue price: Unknown.

22-69-1.38
1947 *The Dillingen Madonna.*
Artist: Louis Hagen.
Issue price: Unknown.

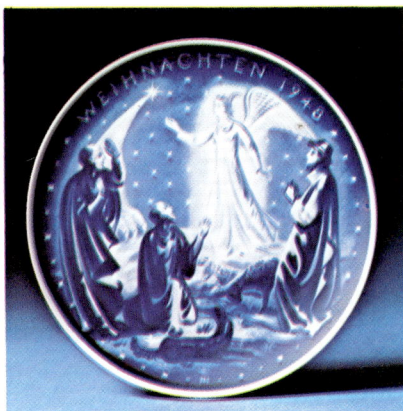

22-69-1.39
1948 *Message to the Shepherds.*
Artist: Richard Hoffman.
Issue price: Unknown.

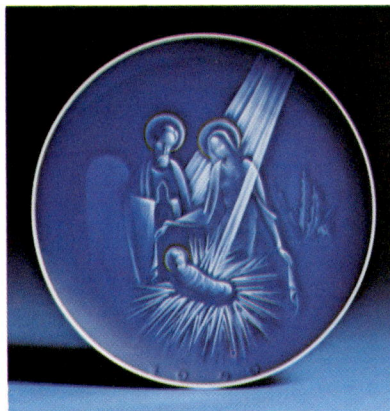

22-69-1.40
1949 *The Holy Family.*
Artist: Prof. Karl.
Issue price: Unknown.

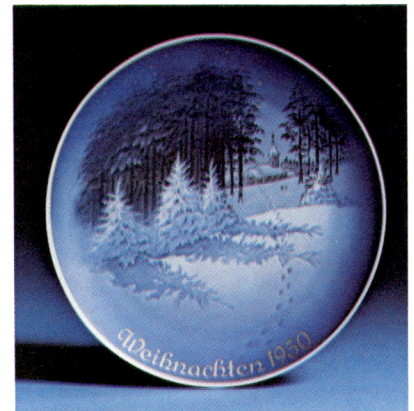

22-69-1.41
1950 *Christmas in the Forest.*
Artist: Willi Hein.
Issue price: Unknown.

22-69-1.42
1951 *Star of Bethlehem.*
Artist: Anne V. Groote.
Issue price: Unknown.

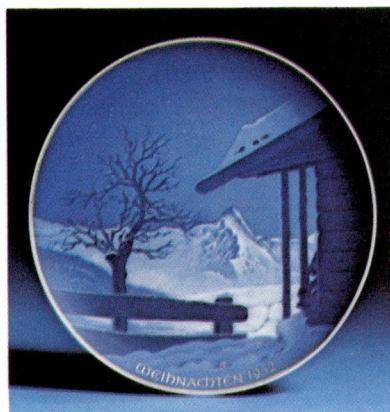

22-69-1.43
1952 *Christmas in the Alps.*
Artist: Willi Hein.
Issue price: Unknown.

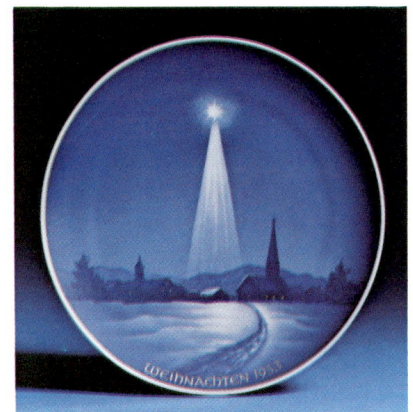

22-69-1.44
1953 *The Holy Light.*
Artist: Willi Hein.
Issue price: Unknown.

22-69-1.45
1954 *Christmas Eve.*
Artist: Willi Hein.
Issue price: Unknown.

22-69-1.46
1955 *Christmas in a Village.*
Artist: Willi Hein.
Issue price: Unknown.

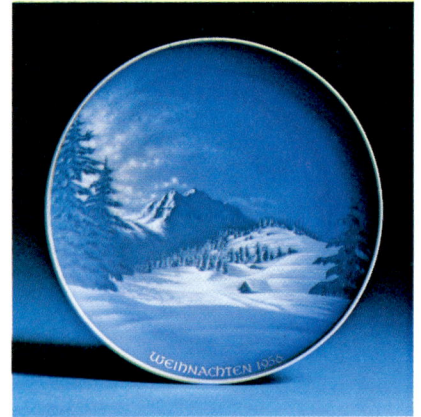

22-69-1.47
1956 *Christmas in the Alps.*
Artist: Willi Hein.
Issue price: Unknown.

22-69-1.48
1957 *Christmas by the Sea.*
Artist: Willi Hein.
Issue price: Unknown.

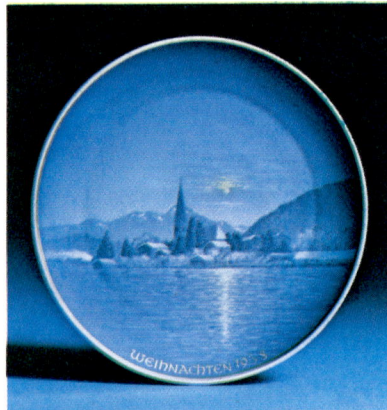

22-69-1.49
1958 *Christmas Eve.*
Artist: Willi Hein.
Issue price: Unknown.

22-69-1.50
1959 *Midnight Mass.*
Artist: Willi Hein.
Issue price: Unknown.

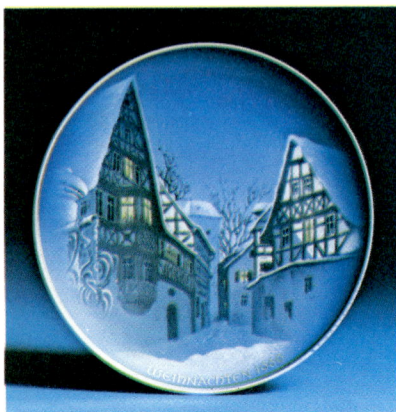

22-69-1.51
1960 *Christmas in a Small Village.*
Artist: Willi Hein.
Issue price: Unknown.

22-69-1.52
1961 *Solitary Christmas.*
Artist: Willi Hein.
Issue price: Unknown.

22-69-1.53
1962 *Christmas Eve.*
Artist: Willi Hein.
Issue price: Unknown.

(Selb, Rothbühl, Selb-Plössberg, München, Kronach, Amberg,
Bad Soden, Neusorg)

22-69-1.54
1963 *Silent Night.*
Artist: Willi Hein.
Issue price: Unknown.

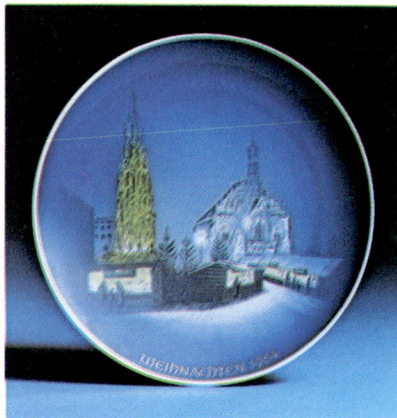

22-69-1.55
1964 *Christmas Market in Nurnberg.*
Artist: Georg Kuspert.
Issue price: Unknown.

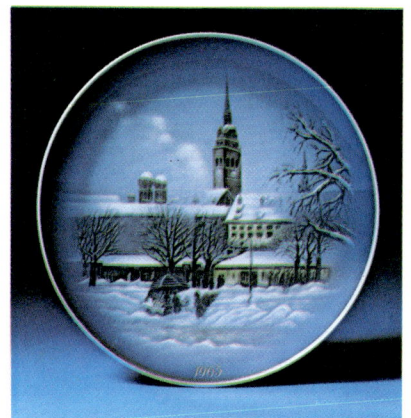

22-69-1.56
1965 *Christmas in Munich.*
Artist: Georg Kuspert.
Issue price: Unknown.

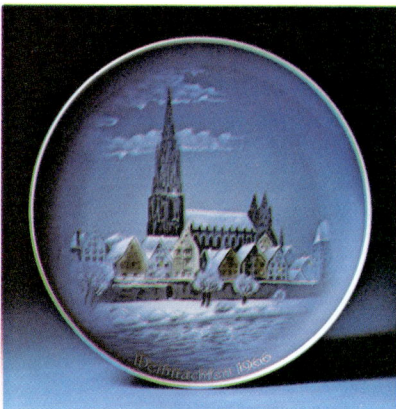

22-69-1.57
1966 *Christmas in Ulm.*
Artist: Georg Kuspert.
Issue price: Unknown.

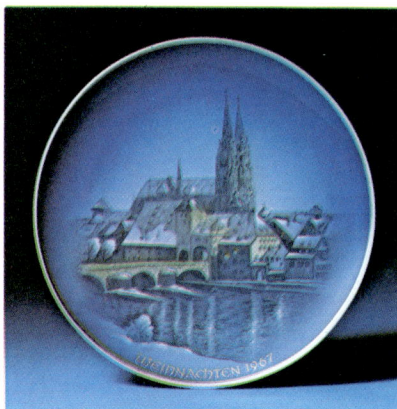

22-69-1.58
1967 *Christmas in Regensburg.*
Artist: Georg Kuspert.
Issue price: Unknown.

22-69-1.59
1968 *Christmas in Bremen.*
Artist: Georg Kuspert.
Issue price: Unknown.

22-69-1.60
1969 *Christmas in Rothenburg.*
Artist: Georg Kuspert.
Issue price: Unknown.

22-69-1.61
1970 *Christmas in Cologne.*
Artist: Georg Kuspert.
Issue price: Unknown.

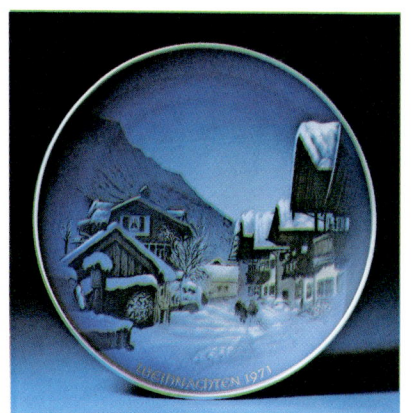

22-69-1.62
1971 *Christmas in Garmisch.*
Artist: Georg Kuspert.
Issue price: $66.00.

22-69-1.63
1972 *Christmas Celebration in Franconia.*
Artist: Georg Kuspert.
Issue price: $66.00.

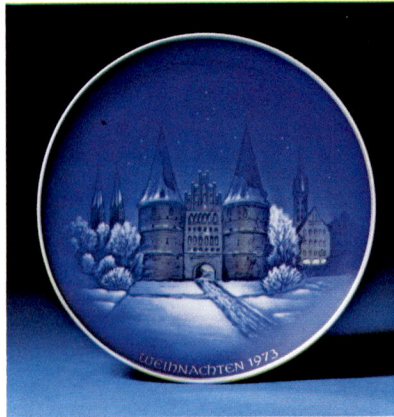

22-69-1.64
1973 *Christmas in Lübeck-Holstein.*
Artist: Georg Kuspert.
Issue price: $84.00.

22-69-1.65
1974 *Christmas in Wurzburg.*
Artist: Georg Kuspert.
Issue price: $85.00.

22-69-1.66
1975 *Freiburg Cathedral.*
Artist: Helmut Drexler.
Issue price: $75.00.

22-69-1.67
1976 *The Castle of Cochem.*
Artist: Helmut Drexler.
Issue price: $95.00.

22-69-1.68
1977 *Hannover Town Hall.*
Artist: Helmut Drexler.
Issue price: $125.00.

22-69-1.69
1978 *Cathedral at Aachen.*
Artist: Helmut Drexler.
Issue price: $150.00.

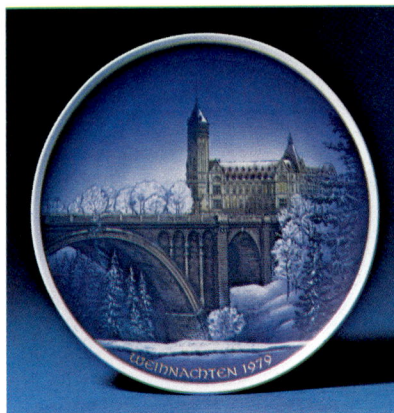

22-69-1.70
1979 *Cathedral in Luxenburg.*
Artist: Helmut Drexler.
Issue price: $165.00.

(Selb, Rothbühl, Selb-Plössberg, München, Kronach, Amberg, Bad Soden, Neusorg)

Wiinblad Christmas Series

Artist: Bjørn Wiinblad. Artist's signature appears on front

Overglaze porcelain partially hand painted in 18 colors with 18k gold rim

Diameter: 29 centimeters (11½ inches)

Attached back hanger

Edition size: Undisclosed

Not numbered; without certificate

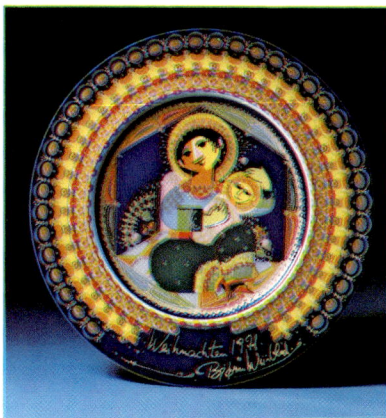

22-69-2.1
1971 *Maria and Child.*
Artist: Bjørn Wiinblad.
Issue price: $100.00.

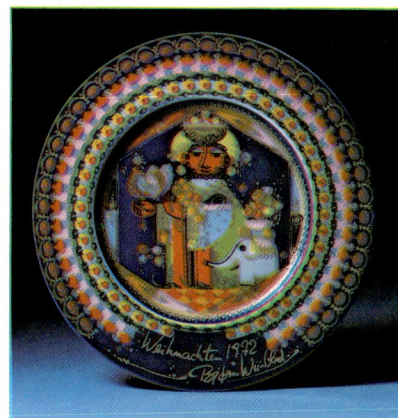

22-69-2.2
1972 *Caspar.*
Artist: Bjørn Wiinblad.
Issue price: $100.00.

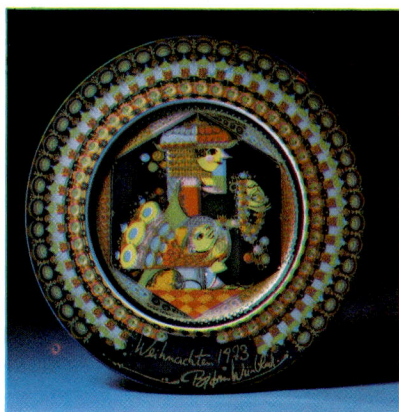

22-69-2.3
1973 *Melchior.*
Artist: Bjørn Wiinblad.
Issue price: $125.00.

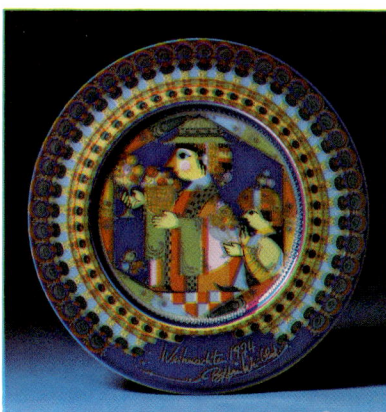

22-69-2.4
1974 *Balthazar.*
Artist: Bjørn Wiinblad.
Issue price: $125.00.

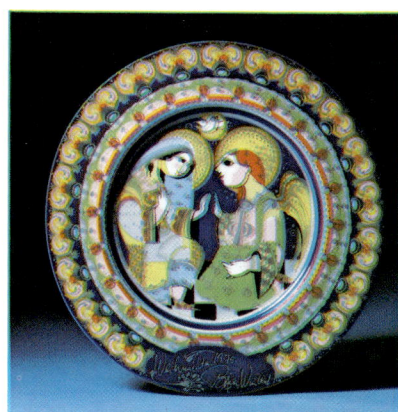

22-69-2.5
1975 *The Annunciation.*
Artist: Bjørn Wiinblad.
Issue price: $195.00.

22-69-2.6
1976 *Angel with Trumpet.*
Artist: Bjørn Wiinblad.
Issue price: $195.00.

22-69-2.7
1977 *Adoration of the Shepherds.*
Artist: Bjørn Wiinblad.
Issue price: $225.00.

22-69-2.8
1978 *Angel with Harp.*
Artist: Bjørn Wiinblad.
Issue price: $275.00.

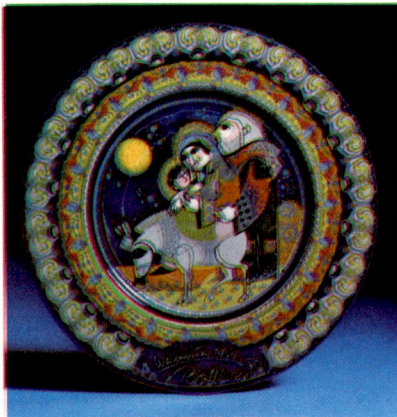

22-69-2.9
1979 *Exodus from Egypt.*
Artist: Bjørn Wiinblad.
Issue price: $310.00.

Fantasies and Fables Series

Artist: Bjørn Wiinblad. Artist's
  signature appears on front
Overglaze porcelain
Diameter: 16.5 centimeters
  (6½ inches)
Attached back hanger
Edition size: Undisclosed
Not numbered, without certificate

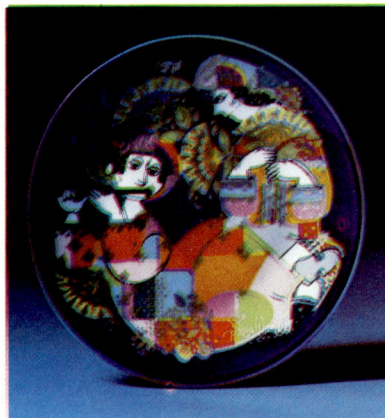

22-69-4.1
1976 *Oriental Night Music.*
Artist: Bjørn Wiinblad.
Issue price: $50.00.

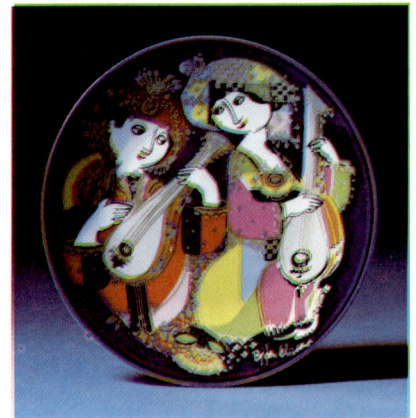

22-69-4.2
1977 *The Mandolin Players.*
Artist: Bjørn Wiinblad.
Issue price: $55.00.

The Nobility of Children Series

Artist: Edna Hibel. Artist's
  signature appears on front
Overglaze porcelain
Diameter: 25.5 centimeters
  (10 inches)
Attached back hanger
Edition size limited to 12,750
Numbered with certificate

22-69-6.1
1976 *La Contessa Isabella.*
Artist: Edna Hibel.
Issue price: $120.00.

22-69-6.2
1977 *Le Marquis Maurice-Pierre.*
Artist: Edna Hibel.
Issue price: $120.00.

(Selb, Rothbühl, Selb-Plössberg, München, Kronach, Amberg, Bad Soden, Neusorg)

22-69-6.3
1979 *Baronesse Johanna-Maryke Van Vollendam Tot Marken.*
Artist: Edna Hibel.
Issue price: $130.00.

Oriental Gold Series

Artist: Edna Hibel. Artist's signature appears on front
Overglaze porcelain
Diameter: 25.5 centimeters (10 inches)
Attached back hanger
Edition size limited to 2,000
Numbered with certificate

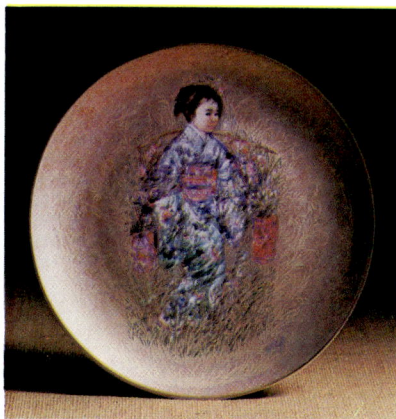

22-69-8.1
1976 *Yasuko.*
Artist: Edna Hibel.
Issue price: $275.00.

22-69-8.2
1977 *Mr. Obata.*
Artist: Edna Hibel.
Issue price: $275.00.

22-69-8.3
1978 *Sakura.*
Artist: Edna Hibel.
Issue price: $295.00.

22-69-8.4
1979 *Michio.*
Artist: Edna Hibel.
Issue price: $325.00.

The pottery now known as Royal Bayreuth began in 1794 in the mountain village of Tettau as the Königlich Privilegierter. Porzellanfabrik Tettau, the first porcelain manufacturer in Bavaria. Now a subsidiary of Royal Tettau, Royal Bayreuth began its first limited-edition *Christmas Series* in 1972. The series which depicts Bavarian winter scenes, was followed in 1973 by a *Mother's Day Series* with art by contemporary artists. The *Antique American Art Series* began in 1976.

Christmas Series

Artist: As indicated
Overglaze porcelain
Diameter: 20.5 centimeters
 (8 inches)
Attached back hanger
Edition size: As indicated
Numbered without certificate

22-73-1.1
1972 *Carriage in the Village.*
Artist: Unknown.
Issue price: $15.00.
Edition size limited to 4,000.

22-73-1.2
1973 *Snow Scene.*
Artist: Unknown.
Issue price: $16.50.
Edition size limited to 5,000.

22-73-1.3
1974 *The Old Mill.*
Artist: Unknown.
Issue price: $24.00.
Edition size limited to 4,000.

22-73-1.4
1975 *Forest Chalet 'Serenity'.*
Artist: Georg Rotger.
Issue price: $27.50.
Edition size limited to 4,000.

22-73-1.5
1976 *Christmas in the Country.*
Artist: Ken Zylla.
Issue price: $40.00.
Edition size limited to 5,000.

22-73-1.6
1977 *Peace on Earth.*
Artist: Frank Kecskes, Jr.
Issue price: $40.00.
Edition size limited to 5,000.

22-73-1.7
1978 *Peaceful Interlude.*
Artist: Ron Stewart.
Issue price: $45.00.
Edition size limited to 5,000.

Mother's Day Series

Artist: As indicated. Artist's signature appears on back until 1975, on front thereafter

Overglaze porcelain

Diameter: 19.5 centimeters (7¾ inches)

Attached back hanger

Edition size: As indicated

Numbered without certificate

22-73-2.1
1973 *Consolation.*
Artist: Ozz Franka.
Issue price: $16.50.
Edition size limited to 4,000.

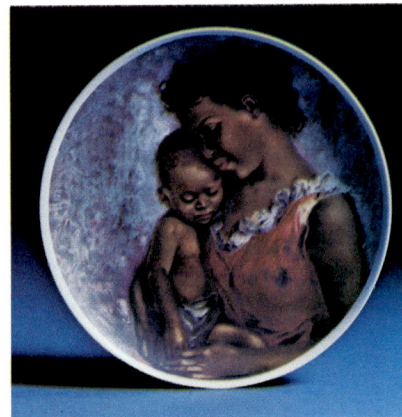

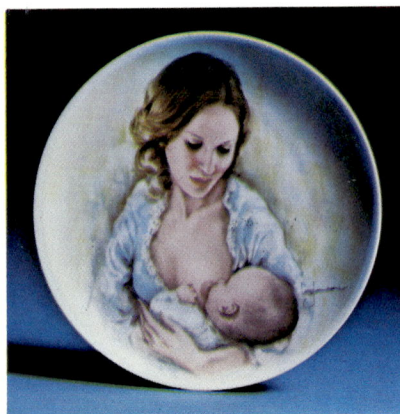

22-73-2.2
1974 *Young Americans.*
Artist: Leo Jansen.
Issue price: $25.00.
Edition size limited to 4,000.

22-73-2.3
1975 *Young Americans II.*
Artist: Leo Jansen.
Issue price: $25.00.
Edition size limited to 5,000.

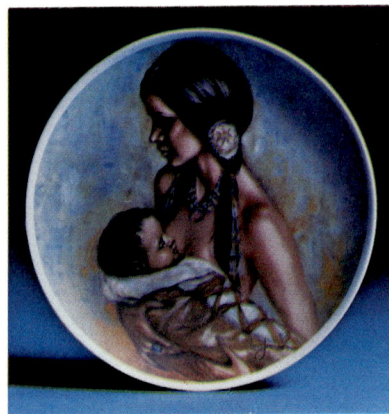

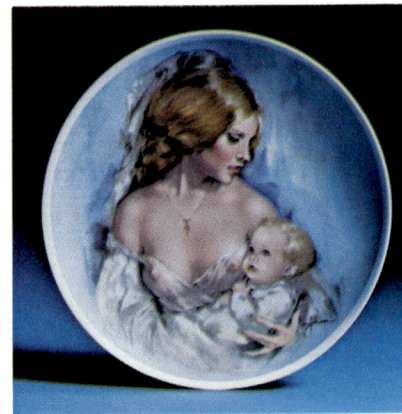

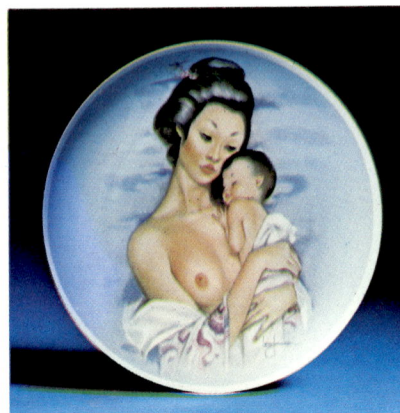

22-73-2.4
1976 *Young Americans III.*
Artist: Leo Jansen.
Issue price: $30.00.
Edition size limited to 5,000.

22-73-2.5
1977 *Young Americans IV.*
Artist: Leo Jansen.
Issue price: $40.00.
Edition size limited to 5,000.

22-73-2.6
1978 *Young Americans V.*
Artist: Leo Jansen.
Issue price: $45.00.
Edition size limited to 5,000.

22-73-2.7
1979 *Young Americans VI.*
Artist: Leo Jansen.
Issue price: $60.00.
Edition size limited to 5,000

ROYAL BAYREUTH

(Tettau)

Antique American Art Series

Artist: As indicated. Artist's
   signature appears on front

Overglaze porcelain

Diameter: 25 centimeters
   (9⅞ inches)

Attached back hanger

Edition size limited to 3,000

Numbered without certificate

22-73-5.1
1976 *Farmyard Tranquility.*
Artist: Henry C. Bryant.
Issue price: $50.00.

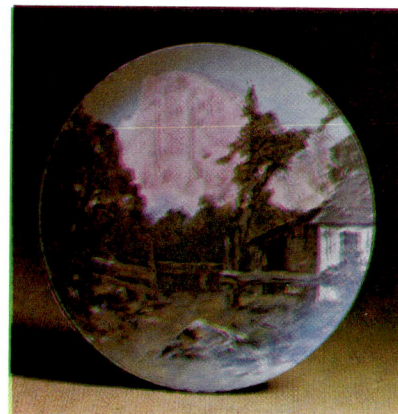

22-73-5.2
1977 *Half Dome.*
Artist: Thomas Hill.
Issue price: $55.00.

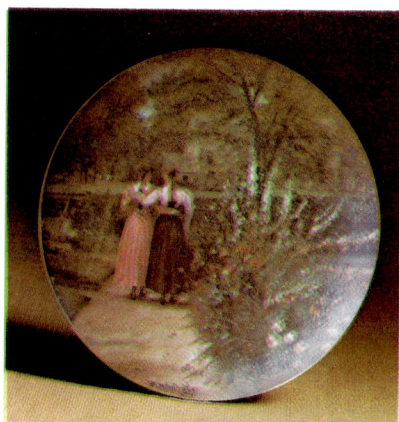

22-73-5.3
1978 *Down Memory Lane.*
Artist: Thomas Worthington
Whittredge.
Issue price: $65.00.

Plates currently issued by Royale are produced by the Staatliche Porzellanmanufaktur, Berlin. This renowned porcelain factory was established in 1763. Prior to 1972 Royale plates were produced by the Kaiser factory (see Germany, KAISER). Royale issues plaques and ornaments, as well as plates and lead crystal items. Royale's *Christmas Series* began in 1969 and ended in 1977.

Christmas Series
Artist: Jack Polusynski
Underglaze porcelain decorated in
cobalt blue; bas-relief since 1971
Diameter: 19 centimeters
(7½ inches)
Pierced foot rim
Edition size: As indicated
Not numbered;without certificate

22-77-1.1
1969 *Christmas Fair in Ebeltoft.*
Artist: Jack Polusynski.
Issue price: $12.00. Edition size limited
to announced quantity of 6,000.

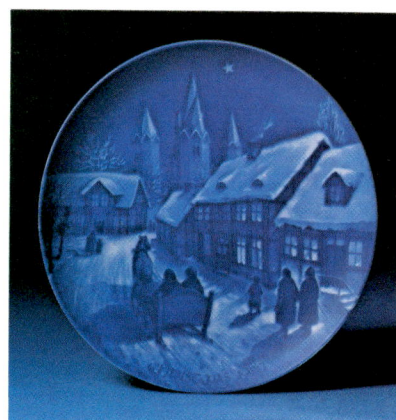

22-77-1.2
1970 *Midnight Mass at Kalundborg
Church.* Artist: Jack Polusynski.
Issue price: $13.00. Edition size limited
to announced quantity of 10,000.

22-77-1.3
1971 *Christmas Night in a Village.*
Artist: Jack Polusynski.
Issue price: $16.00. Edition size limited
to announced quantity of 8,000.

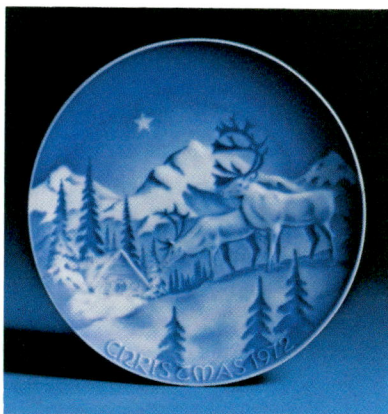

22-77-1.4
1972 *Elks.*
Artist: Jack Polusynski.
Issue price: $16.00. Edition size limited
to announced quantity of 8,000.

22-77-1.5
1973 *Christmas Dawn.*
Artist: Jack Polusynski.
Issue price: $20.00. Edition size limited
to announced quantity of 6,000.

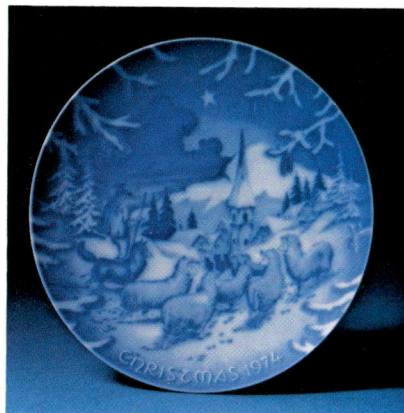

22-77-1.6
1974 *Village at Christmas.*
Artist: Jack Polusynski.
Issue price: $22.00. Edition size limited
to announced quantity of 5,000.

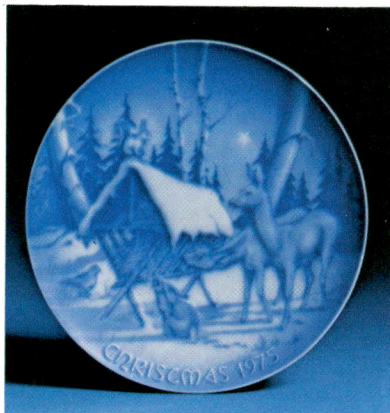

22-77-1.7
1975 *Feeding Time.*
Artist: Jack Polusynski.
Issue price: $26.00. Edition size limited
to announced quantity of 5,000.

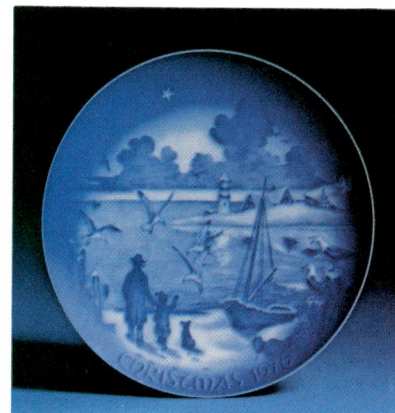

22-77-1.8
1976 *Christmas at the Seaport.*
Artist: Jack Polusynski.
Issue price: $27.50. Edition size limited
to announced quantity of 5,000.

22-77-1.9
1977 *Sledding.*
Artist: Jack Polusynski.
Issue price: $30.00. Edition size limited
to announced quantity of 5,000.

22-85-0.0

Schmid was established in Boston in the 1930s. Since then the firm has been a specialized importer of porcelain bells and mugs as well as plates. Schmid limited-edition plates are produced by the Hutschenreuther factory in Germany, a noted manufacturer of porcelain figurines and tableware.

Both the *Christmas Series*, which began in 1971, and the *Mother's Day Series*, which started the following year, feature art created by the late Berta Hummel before she entered the Franciscan convent at Siessen in 1934. (See Germany, GOEBEL). The Hummel plates bear her signature depending on whether Berta Hummel had signed the original artwork.

The *Ferrandiz Mother and Child Series* opened in 1977.

GERMANY
SCHMID
(Selb)

Christmas Series

Artist: Berta Hummel. Artist's signature or initials appear on front except 1975

Overglaze porcelain

Diameter: 19.5 centimeters (7¾ inches)

Attached back hanger

Edition size undisclosed, limited by year of issue

Not numbered; without certificate

22-85-1.1
1971 *Angel in a Christmas Setting.*
Artist: Berta Hummel.
Issue price: $15.00.

22-85-1.2
1972 *Angel with Flute.*
Artist: Berta Hummel.
Issue price: $15.00.

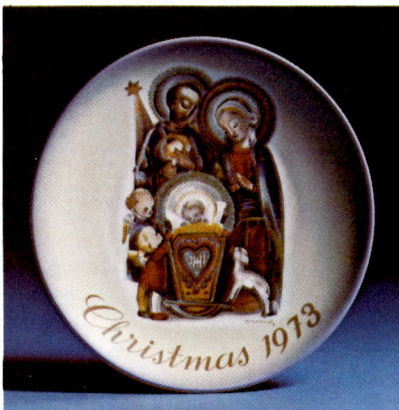

22-85-1.3
1973 *The Nativity.*
Artist: Berta Hummel.
Issue price: $15.00.

22-85-1.4
1974 *The Guardian Angel.*
Artist: Berta Hummel.
Issue price: $18.50.

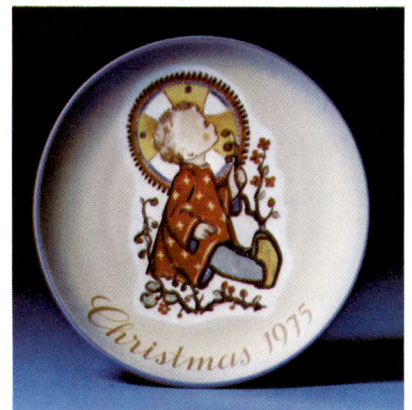

22-85-1.5
1975 *Christmas Child.*
Artist: Berta Hummel.
Issue price: $25.00.

22-85-1.6
1976 *Sacred Journey.*
Artist: Berta Hummel.
Issue price: $27.50.

22-85-1.7
1977 *Herald Angel.*
Artist: Berta Hummel.
Issue price: $27.50.

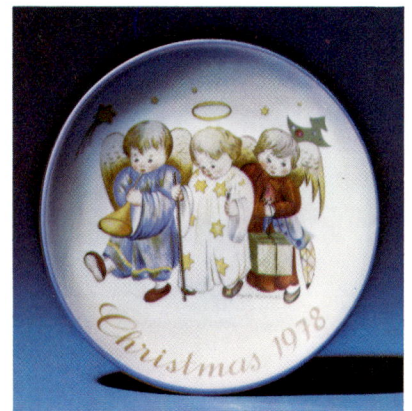

22-85-1.8
1978 *Heavenly Trio.*
Artist: Berta Hummel.
Issue price: $32.50.

22-85-1.9
1979 *Starlight Angel*.
Artist: Berta Hummel.
Issue price: $38.00.

Mother's Day Series

Artist: Berta Hummel. Artist's
signature or initials appears on
front except 1976
Overglaze porcelain
Diameter: 19.5 centimeters
(7¾ inches)
Attached back hanger
Edition size undisclosed, limited
by year of issue
Not numbered; without certificate

22-85-2.1
1972 *Playing Hooky*.
Artist: Berta Hummel.
Issue price: $15.00.

22-85-2.2
1973 *The Little Fisherman*.
Artist: Berta Hummel.
Issue price: $15.00.

22-85-2.3
1974 *The Bumblebee*.
Artist: Berta Hummel.
Issue price: $18.50.

22-85-2.4
1975 *Message of Love*.
Artist: Berta Hummel.
Issue price: $25.00.

22-85-2.5
1976 *Devotion for Mother*.
Artist: Berta Hummel.
Issue price: $27.50.

SCHMID
(Selb)

22-85-2.6
1977 *Moonlight Return.*
Artist: Berta Hummel.
Issue price: $27.50.

22-85-2.7
1978 *Afternoon Stroll.*
Artist: Berta Hummel.
Issue price: $32.50.

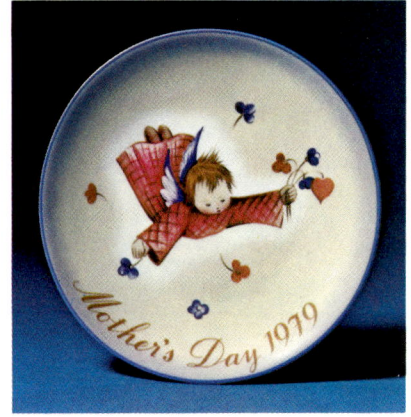

22-85-2.8
1979 *Cherub's Gift.*
Artist: Berta Hummel.
Issue price: $38.00.

Ferrandiz Mother and Child Series

Artist: Juan Ferrandiz
Overglaze porcelain
Diameter: 25.5 centimeters
　(10 inches)
Pierced foot rim
Edition size limited to 10,000
Numbered without certificate

22-85-3.1
1977 *Orchard Mother and Child.*
Artist: Juan Ferrandiz.
Issue price: $65.00.

22-85-3.2
1978 *Pastoral Mother and Child.*
Artist: Juan Ferrandiz.
Issue price: $75.00.

22-85-3.3
1979 *Floral Mother.*
Artist: Juan Ferrandiz.
Issue price: $95.00.

Belleek Pottery Ltd., maker of thin, translucent parian china, was established in 1857 by David McBirney and Robert W. Armstrong on the banks of the River Erne near the small village of Belleek in County Fermanagh, Ireland. The site is near deposits of clay discovered when the owner of Castle Caldwell in Fermanagh became interested in the brilliant whitewash used on local cottages and found that his entire estate lay on a bed of feldspar clay.

When combined with metallic washes, this clay produces the unique iridescent effect for which Belleek is known—a mother-of-pearl luster that has been used on tea sets, figurines, and tableware. Queen Victoria and her son, the Prince of Wales, were among those who commissioned elaborate table services from the firm.

During the 1880s and 1890s some workers from Belleek were brought to the United States to produce an American Belleek, but the resulting porcelain was heavier and less translucent than the Irish product. Belleek ware is still made today much as it was a century ago.

Belleek's *Christmas Series*, based on Irish subjects, began in 1970 and ended in 1977. The *Irish Wild Life Christmas Series* began in 1978.

BELLEEK

(Belleek, County Fermanagh)

Christmas Series
Artist: Undisclosed
Parian china
Diameter: 19 centimeters
 (7½ inches)
No hanger
Edition size limited to announced
 quantity of 7,500
Not numbered;without certificate

26-8-1.1
1970 *Castle Caldwell.*
Artist: Undisclosed.
Issue price: $25.00.

26-8-1.2
1971 *Celtic Cross.*
Artist: Undisclosed.
Issue price: $25.00.

26-8-1.3
1972 *Flight of the Earls.*
Artist: Undisclosed.
Issue price: $30.00.

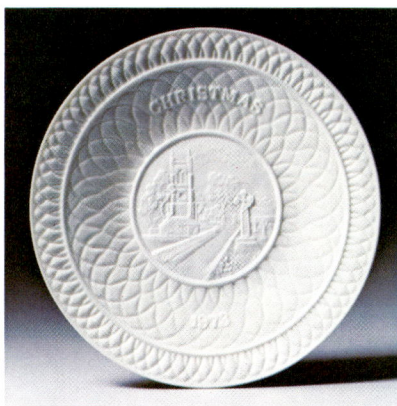

26-8-1.4
1973 *Tribute to W. B. Yeats.*
Artist: Undisclosed.
Issue price: $38.50.

26-8-1.5
1974 *Devenish Island.*
Artist: Undisclosed.
Issue price: $45.00.

26-8-1.6
1975 *The Celtic Cross.*
Artist: Undisclosed.
Issue price: $48.00.

26-8-1.7
1976 *Dove of Peace.*
Artist: Undisclosed.
Issue price: $55.00.

26-8-1.8
1977 *Wren.*
Artist: Undisclosed.
Issue price: $55.00.

*Irish Wild Life
Christmas Series*
Artist: Undisclosed
Parian china
Diameter: 23 centimeters
(9 inches)
No hanger
Edition size undisclosed
Not numbered; without certificate

26-8-2.1
1978 *A Leaping Salmon.*
Artist: Undisclosed.
Issue price: $55.00.

GREAT BRITAIN
ROYAL DOULTON
(Burslem, Stoke-on-Trent, Staffordshire)

One of the oldest surviving English china manufacturers, Doulton & Company traces its origin in 1815 to the small stoneware pottery of John Doulton and John Watts near Vauxhall Gardens, London. Within a few years the pottery was moved to Lambeth, where it remained until it was relocated to its present site at Burslem in 1877. There Doulton took over an established pottery and began producing fine earthenware and china.

In 1887 the honor of knighthood was bestowed upon Henry Doulton by Queen Victoria and in 1901 the company received the Royal warrant giving it authority to use *Royal* with its name.

The Royal Doulton *Christmas Series*, which began in 1972, depicts Christmas scenes in countries around the world. It ended in 1978.

The Collector's International collection began with the *Mother and Child Series* in 1973. These plates show mothers and children of various countries. Other series in the Collector's International group are by contemporary artists and include the *Commedia Dell' Arte Series* begun in 1974 and ended in 1978; the *Flower Garden Series* and *Ports of Call Series*, both started in 1975; and *The Log of the "Dashing Wave"* and *Reflections on China Series* which began in 1976. The *Valentine's Day Series* also began in 1976 with artwork from Victorian period prints.

Beswick Christmas Series

Artist: As indicated

Earthenware in hand-cast bas-relief hand painted in 15 colors

Diameter: 20.5 centimeters (8 inches square)

Pierced foot rim

Edition size limited to 15,000

Numbered without certificate

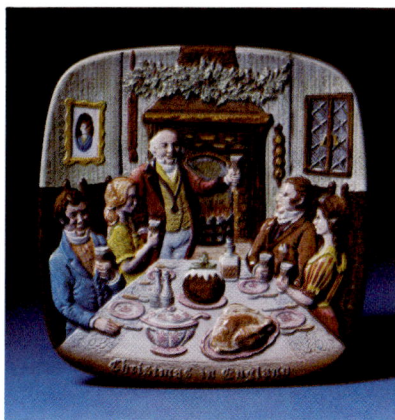

26-69-1.1
1972 *Christmas in England.*
Artist: Harry Sales.
Issue price: $35.00.

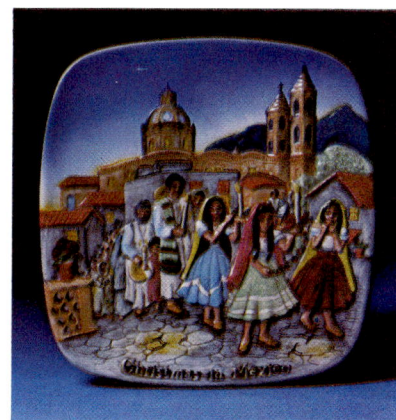

26-69-1.2
1973 *Christmas in Mexico.*
Artist: Chavela Castrejon.
Issue price: $37.50.

26-69-1.3
1974 *Christmas in Bulgaria.*
Artist: Dimitri Yordanov.
Issue price: $37.50.

26-69-1.4
1975 *Christmas in Norway.*
Artist: Alton Toby.
Issue price: $45.00.

26-69-1.5
1976 *Christmas in Holland.*
Artist: Alton Toby.
Issue price: $50.00.

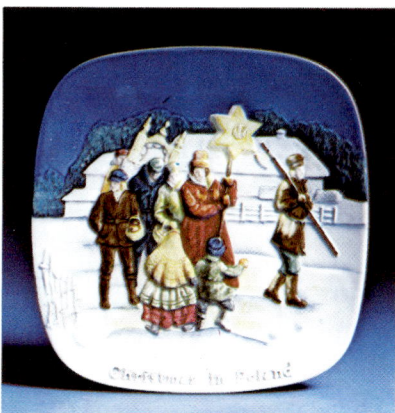

26-69-1.6
1977 *Christmas in Poland.*
Artist: Alton Toby.
Issue price: $50.00.

26-69-1.7
1978 *Christmas in America.*
Artist: Alton Toby.
Issue price: $55.00.

Mother and Child Series
Artist: Edna Hibel. Artist's
    signature appears on front
Bone china
Diameter: 21 centimeters
    (8¼ inches)
No hanger
Edition size limited to 15,000
Numbered since 1974, without
    certificate

26-69-2.1
1973 *Colette and Child.*
Artist: Edna Hibel.
Issue price: $40.00.
Edition size limited to announced
quantity of 15,000.

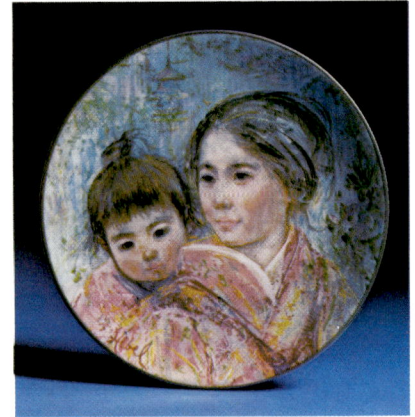

26-69-2.2
1974 *Sayuri and Child.*
Artist: Edna Hibel.
Issue price: $40.00.

26-69-2.3
1975 *Kristina and Child.*
Artist: Edna Hibel.
Issue price: $50.00.

26-69-2.4
1976 *Marilyn and Child.*
Artist: Edna Hibel.
Issue price: $55.00.

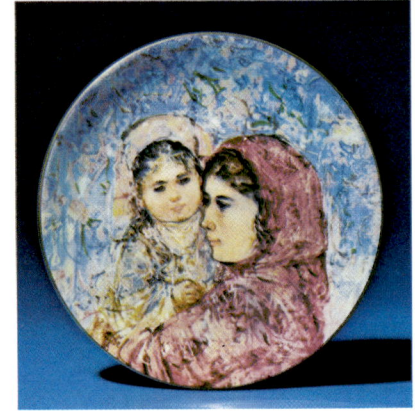

26-69-2.5
1977 *Lucia and Child.*
Artist: Edna Hibel.
Issue price: $60.00.

Maker had
no photo at
press time

26-69-2.6
1978 *Kathleen and Child.*
Artist: Edna Hibel.
Issue price: $65.00.

GREAT BRITAIN
ROYAL DOULTON
(Burslem, Stoke-on-Trent, Staffordshire)

Commedia Dell' Arte Series
Artist: LeRoy Neiman. Artist's
  signature appears on front
Bone china
Diameter: 25.5 centimeters
  (10 inches)
No hanger
Edition size limited to 15,000
Numbered without certificate

26-69-3.1
1974 *Harlequin.*
Artist: LeRoy Neiman.
Issue price: $50.00.

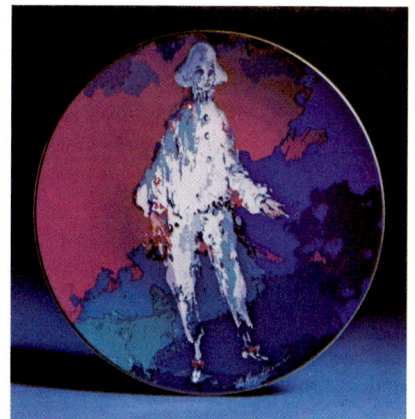

26-69-3.2
1976 *Pierrot.*
Artist: LeRoy Neiman.
Issue price: $60.00.

26-69-3.3
1977 *Columbine.*
Artist: LeRoy Neiman.
Issue price: $70.00.

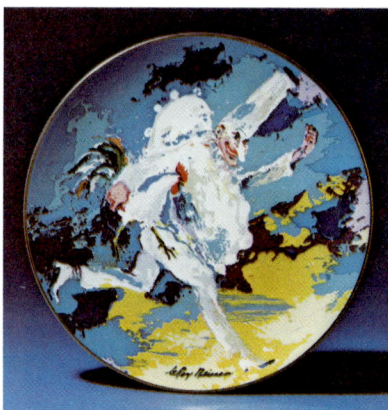

26-69-3.4
1978 *Punchinello.*
Artist: LeRoy Neiman.
Issue price: $70.00.

Flower Garden Series
Artist: Hahn Vidal. Artist's
  signature appears on front
Bone china
Diameter: 26.5 centimeters
  (10½ inches)
No hanger
Edition size limited to 15,000
Numbered without certificate

26-69-4.1
1975 *Spring Harmony.*
Artist: Hahn Vidal.
Issue price: $60.00.

26-69-4.2
1976 *Dreaming Lotus.*
Artist: Hahn Vidal.
Issue price: $65.00.

26-69-4.3
1977 *From a Poet's Garden.*
Artist: Hahn Vidal.
Issue price: $70.00.

26-69-4.4
1978 *Country Bouquet.*
Artist: Hahn Vidal.
Issue price: $70.00.

Ports of Call Series

Artist: Dong Kingman. Artist's
  signature appears on front
Bone china
Diameter: 26.5 centimeters
  (10½ inches)
No hanger
Edition size limited to 15,000
Numbered without certificate

26-69-5.1
1975 *Fisherman's Wharf (San Francisco).*
Artist: Dong Kingman.
Issue price: $60.00.

26-69-5.2
1976 *Royal Street (New Orleans).*
Artist: Dong Kingman.
Issue price: $65.00.

26-69-5.3
1977 *Grand Canal (Venice).*
Artist: Dong Kingman.
Issue price: $70.00.

26-69-5.4
1978 *Montmartre (Paris).*
Artist: Dong Kingman.
Issue price: $70.00.

The Log of the "Dashing Wave" Series

Artist: John Stobart. Artist's signature appears on front

Bone china

Diameter: 26.5 centimeters (10½ inches)

No hanger

Edition size limited to 15,000

Numbered without certificate

26-69-6.1
1976 *Sailing with the Tide.*
Artist: John Stobart.
Issue price: $65.00.

26-69-6.2
1977 *Running Free.*
Artist: John Stobart.
Issue price: $70.00.

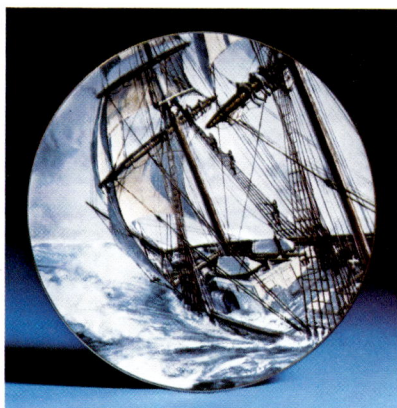

26-69-6.3
1978 *Rounding the Horn.*
Artist: John Stobart.
Issue price: $70.00.

26-69-6.4
1979 *Hong Kong.*
Artist: John Stobart.
Issue price: $75.00.

Valentine's Day Series

Artist: Unknown. Reproduced from nineteenth-century Victorian prints

Bone china

Diameter: 21 centimeters (8¼ inches)

No hanger

Edition size undisclosed, limited by period of issue

Not numbered; without certificate

26-69-7.1
1976 *Victorian Boy and Girl.*
Artist: Unknown.
Issue price: $25.00.

26-69-7.2
1977 *My Sweetest Friend.*
Artist: Unknown.
Issue price: $25.00.

26-69-7.3
1978 *If I Loved You.*
Artist: Unknown.
Issue price: $25.00.

26-69-7.4
1979 *My Valentine.*
Artist: Unknown.
Issue price: $29.95.

Reflections on China Series
Artist: Chen Chi. Artist's signature
   appears on front
Bone china
Diameter: 26.5 centimeters
   (10½ inches)
No hanger
Edition size limited to 15,000
Numbered without certificate

26-69-8.1
1976 *Garden of Tranquility.*
Artist: Chen Chi.
Issue price: $70.00.

26-69-8.2
1977 *Imperial Palace.*
Artist: Chen Chi.
Issue price: $70.00.

26-69-8.3
1978 *Temple of Heaven.*
Artist: Chen Chi.
Issue price: $75.00.

The Worcester Porcelain Company, the oldest porcelain manufactory in England today, was established at Worcester, England, in 1751. Two of its original stockholders—Dr. John Wall, a physician and amateur artist, and William Davis, an apothecary—are credited with perfecting a formula for making soft-paste porcelain from soapstone (steatite). Their formula was used until the introduction of bone china in the nineteenth century.

In 1788, King George III gave the company permission to call itself "Manufacturers to their Majesties." After undergoing a number of changes in ownership, the firm was reorganized in 1862 as the Royal Worcester Porcelain Company in recognition of its long history of royal patronage. More recently in 1976, Royal Worcester merged with Spode; however, each company has retained its own trademark.

Royal Worcester makes two types of collector's plates: bone china, made at Worcester, England; and pewter, made in the United States (see United States, ROYAL WORCESTER).

In 1972, Royal Worcester introduced a series of twelve annual plates, the *Doughty Bird Series*, based on the porcelain sculptures of American birds by Dorothy Doughty.

Doughty Bird Series
Artist: Dorothy Doughty. Artist's signature appears on back

Bone china with hand-painted bas-relief

Diameter: 20.5 centimeters (8 inches)

No hanger

Edition size: As indicated

Not numbered;without certificate

26-78-1.1
1972 *Redstarts and Beech.*
Artist: Dorothy Doughty.
Issue price: $125.00. Edition size
limited to announced quantity of 2,750.

26-78-1.2
1973 *Myrtle Warbler and Cherry.*
Artist: Dorothy Doughty.
Issue price: $175.00. Edition size
limited to announced quantity of 3,000.

26-78-1.3
1974 *Blue-Grey Gnatcatchers.*
Artist: Dorothy Doughty.
Issue price: $195.00. Edition size
limited to announced quantity of 3,000.

26-78-1.4
1975 *Blackburnian Warbler.*
Artist: Dorothy Doughty.
Issue price: $195.00. Edition size
limited to announced quantity of 3,000.

26-78-1.5
1976 *Blue-Winged Sivas and Bamboo.*
Artist: Dorothy Doughty.
Issue price: $195.00. Edition size
limited to announced quantity of 3,000.

26-78-1.6
1977 *Paradise Wydah.*
Artist: Dorothy Doughty.
Issue price: $195.00. Edition size
limited to announced quantity of 3,000.

26-78-1.7
1978 *Bluetits and Witch Hazel.*
Artist: Dorothy Doughty.
Issue price: $200.00. Edition size
limited to announced quantity of 3,000.

Maker had
no photo at
press time

26-78-1.8
1979 *Mountain Bluebird and Pine.*
Artist: Dorothy Doughty.
Issue price: $195.00.

Spode

Josiah Spode I established the Spode Works at Stoke-on-Trent, England, in 1776 after spending nearly thirty years learning every facet of the pottery business. From the beginning the Spode name was highly respected, and the firm has been awarded the Royal warrant by each English monarch since George III.

Josiah Spode perfected the process by which animal bone ash is added to china clay to produce bone china, which is pearly white and more translucent than hard-paste porcelain. His formula came to be known as English bone china and remains the standard to this day.

Upon Spode's death in 1797 his son, Josiah Spode II, continued the trade, with William Copeland in charge of sales. Josiah Spode III in turn headed the business, but upon his death Copeland became sole owner and from 1847 his descendants operated the firm, calling it W. T. Copeland & Sons, Ltd. Between 1967 and 1976 the firm was owned by Carborundum Company, but in 1976 Spode merged with Royal Worcester of England. The Spode trademark has been retained and the present factory is located on the site of the original pottery.

Spode's bone china *Christmas Series* began in 1970 and draws its theme from old English carols. The plate itself reproduces an original eighteenth-century Spode model. Decorations of the 1970 and 1971 plates are in gold; thereafter, decorations are gold with a second color which is changed every two years.

Christmas Series
Artist: Gillian West
Bone china
Diameter: 20.5 centimeters
  (8 inches)
No hanger
Edition size undisclosed, limited
  by year of issue
Not numbered;without certificate

26-86-1.1
1970 *Partridge in a Pear Tree.*
Artist: Gillian West.
Issue price: $35.00.

26-86-1.2
1971 *In Heaven the Angels Singing.*
Artist: Gillian West.
Issue price: $35.00.

26-86-1.3
1972 *We Saw Three Ships A-Sailing.*
Artist: Gillian West.
Issue price: $35.00.

26-86-1.4
1973 *We Three Kings of Orient Are.*
Artist: Gillian West.
Issue price: $35.00.

26-86-1.5
1974 *Deck the Halls.*
Artist: Gillian West.
Issue price: $35.00.

26-86-1.6
1975 *Christbaum.*
Artist: Gillian West.
Issue price: $45.00.

26-86-1.7
1976 *Good King Wenceslas.*
Artist: Gillian West.
Issue price: $45.00.

26-86-1.8
1977 *The Holly and the Ivy.*
Artist: Gillian West.
Issue price: $45.00.

26-86-1.9
1978 *While Shepherds Watched.*
Artist: Gillian West.
Issue price: $45.00.

26-86-1.10
1979 *Away in a Manger.*
Artist: Gillian West.
Issue price: $50.00.

Josiah Wedgwood I, Fellow of the Royal Society, was known as the "father of English potters." He founded the firm that bears his name in 1759 and built a new factory which he called "Etruria" ten years later.

Wedgwood himself developed many of the processes and materials used by the firm to this day. He is perhaps best known for his "Jasper ware" which he perfected in 1774. A vitreous, unglazed stoneware, Jasper is pure white in its original form but can be stained to produce a wide variety of colored backgrounds—green, lilac, yellow, maroon, black, and most popular of all, classic "Wedgwood blue"—onto which white bas-relief decorations are applied by hand.

Although potters in England and abroad tried to duplicate Jasper ware, none were successful and the Wedgwood name is so firmly linked with Jasper to this day that many people mistakenly think it is the only ware Wedgwood produces, and that it is made only in blue.

In 1940, having outgrown the pottery at Etruria, the firm moved to what has been described as the most up-to-date pottery in the world near the village of Barlaston, Stoke-on-Trent, England.

There, in 1969, the firm celebrated the two-hundredth anniversary of the Etruria pottery by introducing a Christmas series of classic Wedgwood blue and white Jasper collector's plates commemorating famous English monuments.

In 1972 Wedgwood began a series of *Mothers* plates, issued annually, made in Jasper ware, and bearing designs created for Wedgwood in the late eighteenth century.

The *Bicentennial of American Independence Series*, also in blue and white Jasper, is a six-plate series which began in 1972 and closed in 1976. It commemorates events which led to American independence.

The *Blossoming of Suzanne Series*, started in 1977, was the first series to bear the name of Wedgwood on bone china. A second series with artwork by Mary Vickers began in 1979. Made in Queen's Ware, it is entitled the *Mary Vicker's My Memories Series*.

Christmas Series
Modeler: Tom Harper
Jasper stoneware
Diameter: 20.5 centimeters
  (8 inches)
No hanger
Edition size undisclosed, limited
  by year of issue
Not numbered; without certificate

26-90-1.1
1969 *Windsor Castle.*
Modeler: Tom Harper.
Issue price: $25.00.

26-90-1.2
1970 *Christmas in Trafalgar Square.*
Modeler: Tom Harper.
Issue price: $30.00.

26-90-1.3
1971 *Picadilly Circus, London.*
Modeler: Tom Harper.
Issue price: $30.00.

26-90-1.4
1972 *St. Paul's Cathedral.*
Modeler: Tom Harper.
Issue price: $35.00.

26-90-1.5
1973 *The Tower of London.*
Modeler: Tom Harper.
Issue price: $40.00.

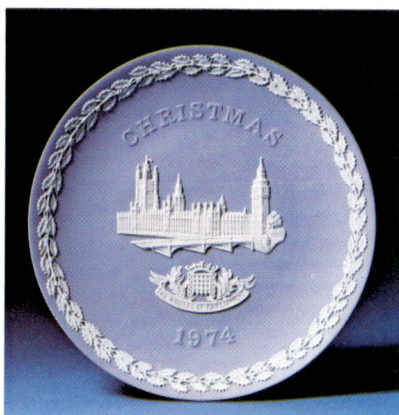

26-90-1.6
1974 *The Houses of Parliament.*
Modeler: Tom Brarper.
Issue price: $40.00.

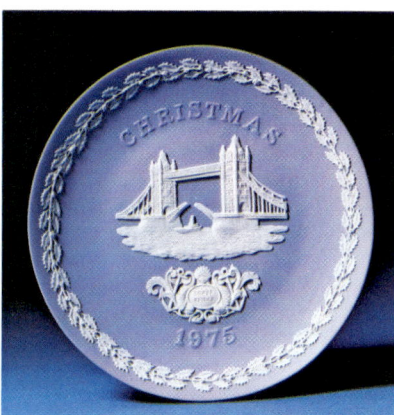

26-90-1.7
1975 *Tower Bridge.*
Modeler: Tom Harper.
Issue price: $45.00.

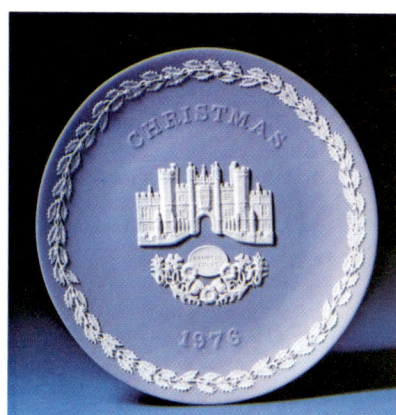

26-90-1.8
1976 *Hampton Court.*
Modeler: Tom Harper.
Issue price: $55.00.

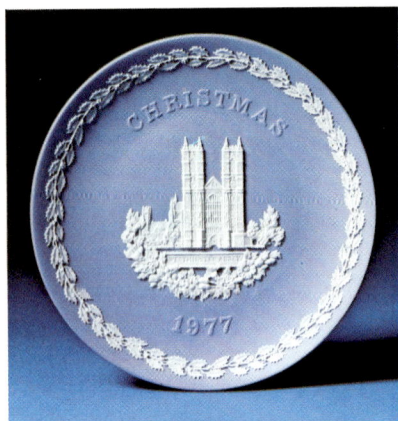

26-90-1.9
1977 *Westminster Abbey.*
Modeler: Tom Harper.
Issue price: $55.00.

26-90-1.10
1978 *The Horse Guards.*
Modeler: Tom Harper.
Issue price: $60.00.

26-90-1.1
1979 *Buckingham Palace.*
Artist: Wedgwood Design Studio.
Issue price: $65.00.

Mothers Series

Artist: As indicated

Jasper stoneware

Diameter: 16.5 centimeters
(6½ inches)

No hanger

Edition size undisclosed, limited
by year of issue

Not numbered; without certificate

26-90-2.1
1971 *Sportive Love.*
Artist: Lady Elizabeth Templetown.
Issue price: $20.00.

26-90-2.2
1972 *The Sewing Lesson.*
Artist: Emma Crewe.
Issue price: $20.00.

26-90-2.3
1973 *The Baptism of Achilles.*
Artist: Lady Elizabeth Templetown.
Issue price: $25.00.

26-90-2.4
1974 *Domestic Employment.*
Artist: Lady Elizabeth Templetown.
Issue price: $30.00.

26-90-2.5
1975 *Mother and Child.*
Artist: Lady Elizabeth Templetown.
Issue price: $35.00.

26-90-2.6
1976 *The Spinner.*
Artist: William Hackwood.
Issue price: $35.00.

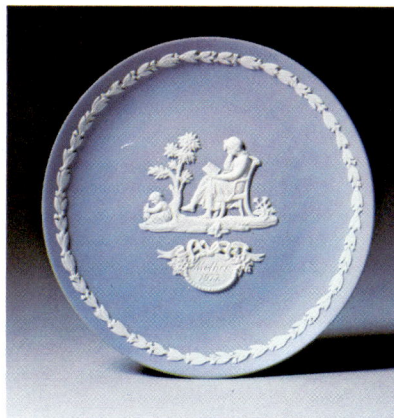

26-90-2.7
1977 *Leisure Time.*
Artist: William Hackwood.
Issue price: $35.00.

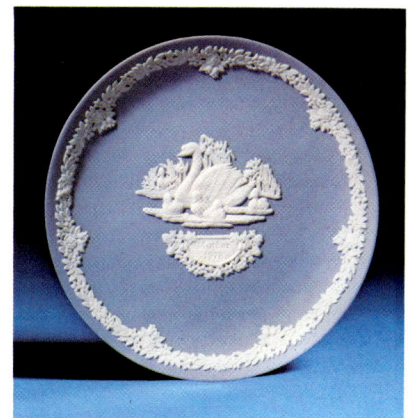

26-90-2.8
1978 *Swan and Cygnets.*
Artist: Wedgwood Design Studio,
Barlaston.
Issue price: $40.00.

26-90-2.9
1979 *Deer and Fawn.*
Artist: Wedgwood Design Studio.
Issue price: $45.00.

Bicentennial of American Independence Series

Modeler: Undisclosed
Jasper Stoneware
Diameter: 20.5 centimeters
  (8 inches)
No hanger
Edition size undisclosed, limited
  by year of issue
Not numbered without certificate

26-90-3.1
1972 *Boston Tea Party.*
Modeler: Undisclosed.
Issue price: $30.00.

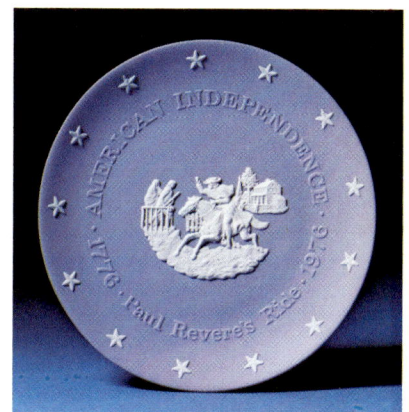

26-90-3.2
1973 *Paul Revere's Ride.*
Modeler: Undisclosed.
Issue price: $35.00.

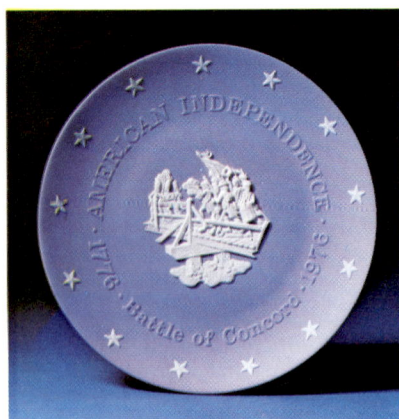

26-90-3.3
1974 *Battle of Concord.*
Modeler: Undisclosed.
Issue price: $40.00.

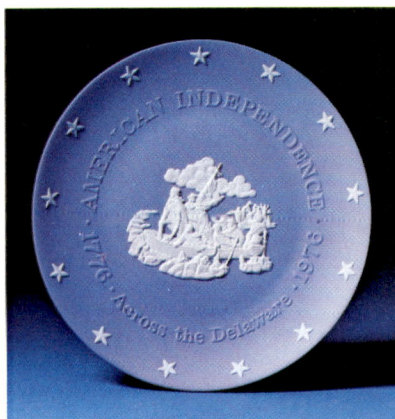

26-90-3.4
1975 *Across the Delaware.*
Modeler: Undisclosed.
Issue price: $45.00.

26-90-3.5
1975 *Victory at Yorktown.*
Modeler: Undisclosed.
Issue price: $45.00.

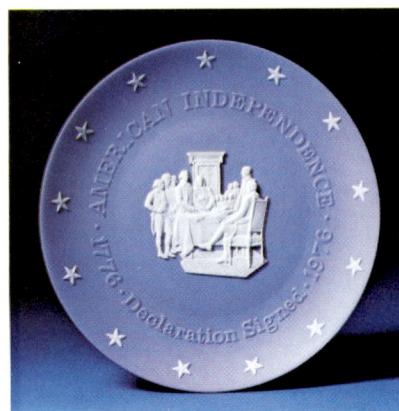

26-90-3.6
1976 *Declaration Signed.*
Modeler: Undisclosed.
Issue price: $45.00.

Blossoming of Suzanne Series

Artist: Mary Vickers
Bone china
Diameter: 23.5 centimeters
(9¼ inches)
No hanger
Edition size limited to 24,000
Numbered with certificate

26-90-4.1
1977 *Innocence.*
Artist: Mary Vickers.
Issue price: $60.00.

26-90-4.2
1978 *Cherish.*
Artist: Mary Vickers.
Issue price: $60.00.

26-90-4.3
1979 *Wistful.*
Artist: Mary Vickers.
Issue price: $60.00.

Mary Vicker's My Memories Series

Artist: Mary Vickers

Queen's ware

Diameter: 20.5 centimeters
  (8 inches)

No hanger

Edition size undisclosed, limited
  by period of issue

Numbered with certificate

26-90-5.1
1979 *Be My Friend.*
Artist: Mary Vickers.
Issue price: $37.50.

The House of Anri, which claims to be the world's largest wood-carving manufactory, is a family firm established in 1916 by Anton Riffeser Sr. and is headed by his son, Anton Jr. The factory is located in the Tyrolean Alps, an area with a long tradition of wood carving.

Anri's *Christmas Series* began in 1971. Using a process known as "toriart," the plates are molded and carved in wood material and hand painted to produce a three-dimensional effect. Each plate is mounted in a circular European maple frame.

Christmas Series

Artist: Joseph Malfertheiner
Hand-painted molded wood material
Diameter: 30.5 centimeters (12 inches)
Attached back hanger
Edition size: As indicated
Numbered since 1972, without certificate

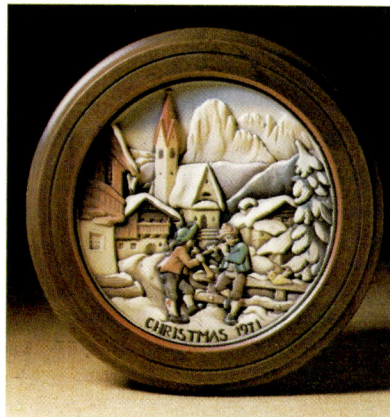

38-4-1.1
1971 *St. Jakob in Groden.*
Artist: Joseph Malfertheiner.
Issue price: $37.50. Edition size limited to announced quantity of 10,000.

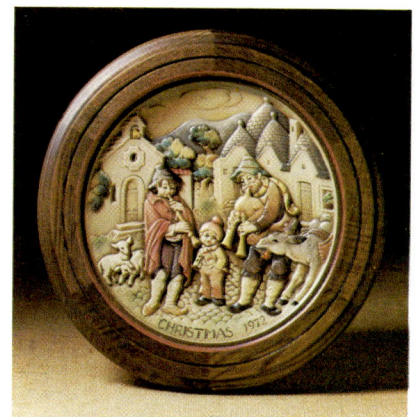

38-4-1.2
1972 *Pipers at Alberobello.*
Artist: Joseph Malfertheiner.
Issue price: $45.00.
Edition size limited to 10,000.

38-4-1.3
1973 *Alpine Horn.*
Artist: Joseph Malfertheiner.
Issue price: $45.00.
Edition size limited to 10,000.

38-4-1.4
1974 *Young Man and Girl.*
Artist: Joseph Malfertheiner.
Issue price: $50.00.
Edition size limited to 10,000.

38-4-1.5
1975 *Christmas in Ireland.*
Artist: Joseph Malfertheiner.
Issue price: $60.00.
Edition size limited to 10,000.

38-4-1.6
1976 *Alpine Christmas.*
Artist: Joseph Malfertheiner.
Issue price: $65.00.
Edition size limited to 10,000.

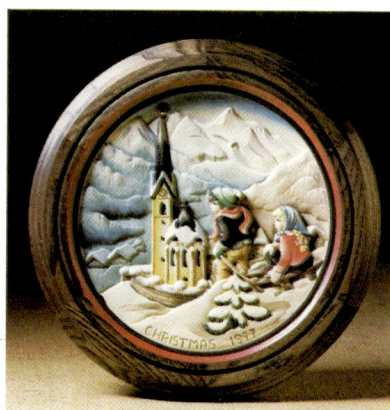

38-4-1.7
1977 *Legend of Heiligenblut.*
Artist: Joseph Malfertheiner.
Issue price: $65.00.
Edition size limited to 6,000.

38-4-1.8
1978 *The Klöckler Singers.*
Artist: Joseph Malfertheiner.
Issue price: $80.00.
Edition size limited to 6,000.

38-4-1.9
1979 *The Moss Gatherers of Villnoess.*
Artist: Undisclosed.
Issue price: $135.00.
Edition size limited to 6,000
sequentially numbered.

King's Porcelain was established in the original Giuseppe Cappe factory in the 1960s. The factory had been known for its Cappe figurines of which King's has retained the original molds.

King's *Flowers of America Series* began in 1973 and ended in 1977.

Flowers of America Series

Artist: Aldo Falchi.
Artist's signature appears
  on back since 1975

High relief porcelain, hand
  painted with a gold border
Diameter: 22.5 centimeters
  (8¾ inches)
Attached back hanger
Edition size limited to 1,000
Numbered without certificate

38-43-2.1
1973 *Pink Carnation.*
Artist: Aldo Falchi.
Issue price: $85.00.

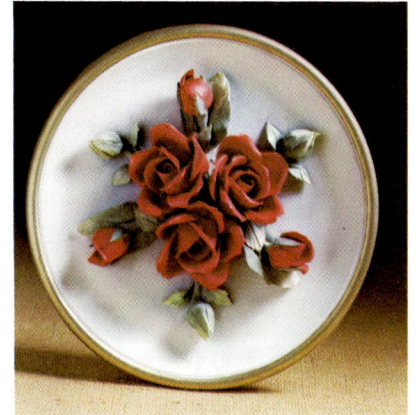

38-43-2.2
1974 *Red Roses.*
Artist: Aldo Falchi.
Issue price: $100.00.

38-43-2.3
1975 *Yellow Dahlia.*
Artist: Aldo Falchi.
Issue price: $110.00.

38-43-2.4
1976 *Bluebells.*
Artist: Aldo Falchi.
Issue price: $130.00.

38-43-2.5
1977 *Anemones.*
Artist: Aldo Falchi.
Issue price: $130.00.

CREATIVE
WORLD
CW

The Veneto Flair factory was established in 1946 by a consortium of potters and painters. Creative World of White Plains, New York, acts as importer and distributor of the Veneto Flair collector's plates.

A centuries-old technique is used to create the Veneto Flair plates. The resulting decorated and glazed earthenware is known as majolica or faience pottery. In this ancient process, terra cotta is hand thrown on a potter's wheel and the design is incised with a scalpel on the baked clay. Colors are then hand applied and the plates undergo a series of paintings and firings before a final firing at extreme temperatures, producing Veneto Flair's characteristic mosaic-effect finish.

In 1971, Veneto Flair entered the limited-edition plate market with a single issue, the Bellini "Madonna" plate. That same year the firm inaugurated a *Christmas Series* which ended in 1974. The *Last Supper Series*, based on da Vinci's painting, and a *Dog Series* both began in 1972 and ended in 1976. Veneto Flair's *Mosaic Series* began in 1973, closed after the '74 issue, but reopened in 1977. The annual *Christmas Card Series* started in 1975 and ended in 1978. The *Valentine's Day Series* began in 1977.

Bellini Plate

Artist: Vincente Tiziano
    (after Bellini's *Madonna*)
Terra cotta
Diameter: 21.5 centimeters
    (8½ inches)
Pierced foot rim
Edition size limited to 500
Numbered with certificate

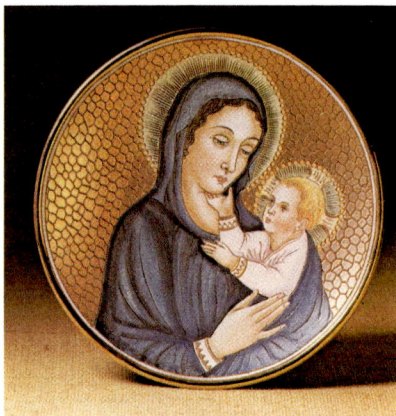

38-84-1.1
1971 *Madonna*.
Artist: Vincente Tiziano.
Issue price: $45.00.

Christmas Series

Artist: Vincente Tiziano
Terra Cotta
Diameter: 21.5 centimeters
    (8½ inches)
Pierced foot rim
Edition size: As indicated
Numbered with certificate

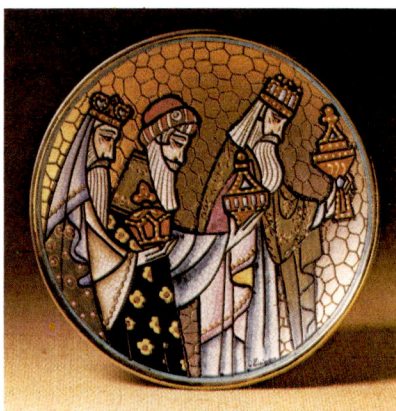

38-84-2.1
1971 *Three Kings*.
Artist: Vincente Tiziano.
Issue price: $45.00.
Edition size limited to 1,500.

38-84-2.2
1972 *Shepherds*.
Artist: Vincente Tiziano.
Issue price: $45.00.
Edition size limited to 2,000.

38-84-2.3
1973 *Christ Child*.
Artist: Vincente Tiziano.
Issue price: $55.00.
Edition size limited to 2,000.

38-84-2.4
1974 *Angel*.
Artist: Vincente Tiziano.
Issue price: $55.00.
Edition size limited to 2,000.

Dog Series

Artist: Vincente Tiziano
Terra cotta
Diameter: 21.5 centimeters
  (8½ inches)
Pierced foot rim
Edition size limited to 2,000
Numbered with certificate

38-84-5.1
1972 German Shepherd.
Artist: Vincente Tiziano.
Issue price: $37.50.

38-84-5.2
1973 Poodle.
Artist: Vincente Tiziano.
Issue price: $37.50.

38-84-5.3
1974 Doberman.
Artist: Vincente Tiziano.
Issue price: $37.50.

38-84-5.4
1975 Collie.
Artist: Vincente Tiziano.
Issue price: $40.00.

38-84-5.5
1976 Dachshund.
Artist: Vincente Tiziano.
Issue price: $45.00.

Last Supper Series

Artist: Vincente Tiziano (after
  Leonardo da Vinci's *Last Supper*)
Terra cotta
Diameter: 21.5 centimeters
  (8½ inches)
Pierced foot rim
Edition size limited to 2,000
Numbered with certificate

38-84-6.1
*1972 Apostles Matthew, Thaddaeus and
Simon.*
Artist: Vincente Tiziano.
Issue price: $100.00.

38-84-6.2
*1973 Apostles Bartholomew, James and
Andrew.*
Artist: Vincente Tiziano.
Issue price: $70.00.

VENETO FLAIR

(Treviso)

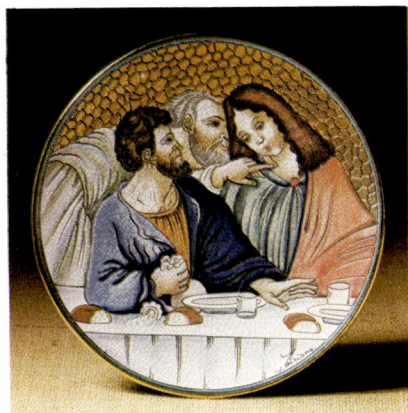

38-84-6.3
1974 *Apostles Thomas, James and Philip.*
Artist: Vincente Tiziano.
Issue price: $70.00.

38-84-6.4
1975 *Apostles Judas, Peter and John.*
Artist: Vincente Tiziano.
Issue price: $70.00.

38-84-6.5
1976 *Jesus Christ.*
Artist: Vincente Tiziano.
Issue price: $70.00.

Mosaic Series

Artist: Vincente Tiziano
Terra cotta
Diameter: 16.5 centimeters
  (6½ inches)
Pierced foot rim
Edition size: As indicated
Numbered with certificate

38-84-9.1
1973 *Justinian.*
Artist: Vincente Tiziano.
Issue price: $50.00.
Edition size limited to 500.

38-84-9.2
1974 *Pelican.*
Artist: Vincente Tiziano.
Issue price: $50.00.
Edition size limited to 1,000.

38-84-9.3
1977 *Theodora.*
Artist: Vincente Tiziano.
Issue price: $50.00.
Edition size limited to 500.

Christmas Card Series

Artist: Vincente Tiziano
Terra cotta
Diameter: 18.5 centimeters
(7¼ inches)
Pierced foot rim
Edition size limited to 5,000
Numbered with certificate

38-84-11.1
1975 *Christmas Eve.*
Artist: Vincente Tiziano.
Issue price: $45.00.

38-84-11.2
1976 *The Old North Church.*
Artist: Vincente Tiziano.
Issue price: $50.00.

38-84-11.3
1977 *Log Cabin Christmas.*
Artist: Vincente Tiziano.
Issue price: $50.00.

38-84-11.4
1978 *Dutch Christmas.*
Artist: Vincente Tiziano.
Issue price: $50.00.

Valentine's Day Series

Artist: Vincente Tiziano
Terra cotta
Diameter: 18.5 centimeters
(7¼ inches)
Pierced foot rim
Edition size limited to 3,000
Numbered with certificate

38-84-12.1
1977 *Valentine Boy.*
Artist: Vincente Tiziano.
Issue price: $45.00.

38-84-12.2
1978 *Valentine Girl.*
Artist: Vincente Tiziano.
Issue price: $45.00.

VENETO FLAIR

(Treviso)

38-84-12.3
1979 *Hansel.*
Artist: Vincente Tiziano.
Issue price: $60.00.

ITALY
STUDIO DANTE DI VOLTERADICI
(Volterra)

Located near Tuscany, world center for the mining and carving of alabaster, the Studio Dante di Volteradici continues the Italian tradition of alabaster sculpturing.

Di Volteradici's *Grand Opera Series*, commissioned by the Museo Teatrale alla Scala to commemorate the two-hundredth anniversary of La Scala Opera House, began in 1976. *Madonne Viventi, Living Madonnas Series*, its first proprietary series, started in 1978.

Grand Opera Series
Artist: Gino Ruggeri. Artist's
  signature appears on front
Ivory alabaster
Diameter: 21.5 centimeters
  (8½ inches)
Attached back hanger
Edition size undisclosed, limited
  by period of issue
Numbered with certificate

38-90-1.1
1976 *Rigoletto.*
Artist: Gino Ruggeri.
Issue price: $35.00.

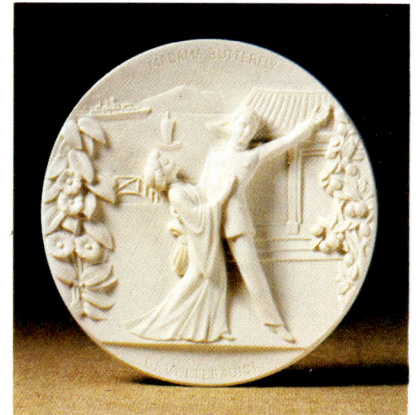

38-90-1.2
1977 *Madama Butterfly.*
Artist: Gino Ruggeri.
Issue price: $35.00.

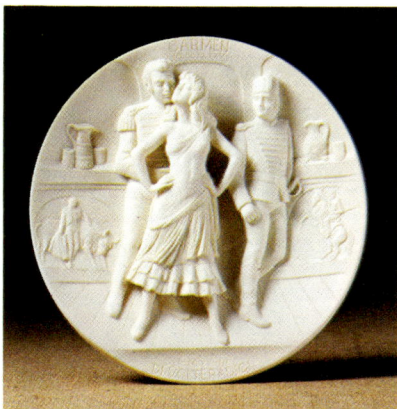

38-90-1.3
1978 *Carmen.*
Artist: Gino Ruggeri.
Issue price: $40.00.

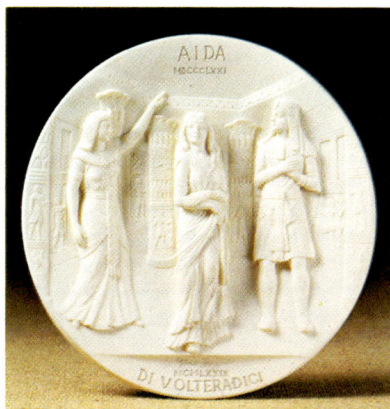

38-90-1.4
1979 *Aida.*
Artist: Gino Ruggeri.
Issue price: $40.00.

Madonne Viventi Series
(Living Madonnas Series)
Artist: as indicated; artist's
  signature appears on front
Ivory alabaster
Diameter: 21.5 centimeters
  (8½ inches)
Attached back hanger
Edition size undisclosed, limited
  by period of issue
Numbered with certificate

38-90-2.1
1978 *Madonna Pensosa.*
(Pensive Madonna)
Artist: Ado Santini.
Issue price: $45.00.

38-90-2.2
1979 *Madonna Serena.*
(Serene Madonna)
Artist: Alberto Santangela.
Issue price: $45.00.

Although the present Fukagawa Porcelain factory was organized in the 1880s in Arita by the Fukagawa family, the heritage of its Izumistone porcelain goes back some three centuries to the discovery of kaolin deposits on the island of Kyushu, Japan.

It was there, on the slopes of Mount Izumi, that the Korean master potter Ri Sampei ended his twenty-year search for a pure white clay base to be used in the manufacture of fine porcelain. As the direct result of his discovery, a number of small porcelain workshops—the first in all Japan—sprang up in the nearby town of Arita, and delicate plates and saucers were being shipped to the West from the harbor city of Imari decades before porcelain manufacture began in Europe.

The establishment of Fukagawa Porcelain was actually a merger of a number of small workshops whose standards and techniques dated to the time of Ri Sampei. In 1913, Fukagawa was granted the title "Purveyor to the Imperial Household," which indicates patronage from the royal family of Japan. In recognition of this honor, all Fukagawa ceramics bear the imprint "Imperial."

The factory, which is still in the hands of the Fukagawa family, continues to employ the original Izumiyama clay from Mount Izumi to give its porcelain a uniquely white body.

In 1977, Fukagawa issued its first series of collector's plates—the *Warabe No Haiku* (*Haiku* about Children) *Series.*

Warabe No Haiku Series
(*Haiku* about children)

Artist: Suetomi. Artist's signature
and seal appear on front

Overglaze porcelain

Diameter: 26 centimeters
(10¼ inches)

No hanger

Edition size undisclosed, limited
by period of issue

Numbered with certificate

Original Haiku poem appears on
front

42-23-1.1
1977 *Under the Plum Branch.*
Artist: Suetomi.
Issue price: $38.00.

42-23-1.2
1978 *Child of Straw.*
Artist: Suetomi.
Issue price: $42.00.

Maker had
no photo at
press time

42-23-1.3
1979 *Dragon Dance.*
Artist: Suetomi.
Issue price: $42.00.

Schmid
THE CREATIVE HAND

A Japanese subsidiary of Schmid (see Germany, SCHMID) produces several series of plates based on contemporary cartoon characters. The *Peanuts Christmas Series* and the *Peanuts Mother's Day Series* began in 1972. The *Peanuts Valentine's Day Series* began in 1977. Artwork for all plates is designed or approved by Charles Schultz.

The *Disney Christmas Series* began in 1973 and the *Disney Mother's Day Series* in 1974. Artwork for these series is by Walt Disney Productions.

The *Raggedy Ann Christmas Series* began in 1975, the *Raggedy Ann Mother's Day Series* in 1976 and the *Raggedy Ann Valentine's Day Series* began in 1978. Artwork is by the Bobbs-Merrill Company.

JAPAN
SCHMID
(Seito City)

Peanuts Christmas Series

Artist: Charles Schultz. Artist's signature appears on front with the exception of the 1975 issue

Overglaze porcelain

Diameter: 19 centimeters (7½ inches)

Attached back hanger

Edition size undisclosed, limited by year of issue, as indicated

Not numbered except as indicated; without certificate

42-85-1.1
1972 *Snoopy Guides the Sleigh.*
Artist: Charles Schultz.
Issue price: $10.00.

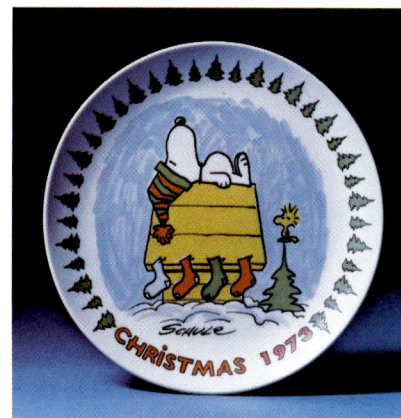

42-85-1.2
1973 *Christmas Eve at the Doghouse.*
Artist: Charles Schultz.
Issue price: $10.00.

42-85-1.3
1974 *Christmas Eve at the Fireplace.*
Artist: Charles Schultz.
Issue price: $10.00.

42-85-1.4
1975 *Woodstock, Santa Claus.*
Artist: Charles Schultz.
Issue price: $12.50.

42-85-1.5
1976 *Woodstock's Christmas.*
Artist: Charles Schultz.
Issue price: $13.00.

42-85-1.6
1977 *Deck the Doghouse.*
Artist: Charles Schultz.
Issue price: $13.00.

42-85-1.7
1978 *Filling the Stocking.*
Artist: Charles Schultz.
Issue price: $15.00.

42-85-1.8
1979 *Christmas at Hand.*
Artist: Charles Schultz.
Issue price: $17.50.
Edition size limited to 15,000 sequentially numbered.

42-85-2.1

Peanuts Mother's Day Series

Artist: Charles Schultz. Artist's signature appears on front except 1975

Overglaze porcelain

Diameter: 19 centimeters (7½ inches)

Attached back hanger

Edition size undisclosed, limited by year of issue, as indicated

Not numbered except as indicated; without certificate

42-85-2.1
1972 *Linus.*
Artist: Charles Schultz.
Issue price: $10.00.

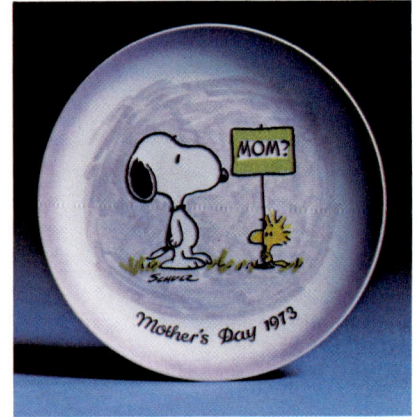

42-85-2.2
1973 *Mom?*
Artist: Charles Schultz.
Issue price: $10.00.

42-85-2.3
1974 *Snoopy and Woodstock on Parade.*
Artist: Charles Schultz.
Issue price: $10.00.

42-85-2.4
1975 *A Kiss for Lucy.*
Artist: Charles Schultz.
Issue price: $12.50.

42-85-2.5
1976 *Linus and Snoopy.*
Artist: Charles Schultz.
Issue price: $13.00.

42-85-2.6
1977 *Dear Mom.*
Artist: Charles Schultz.
Issue price: $13.00.

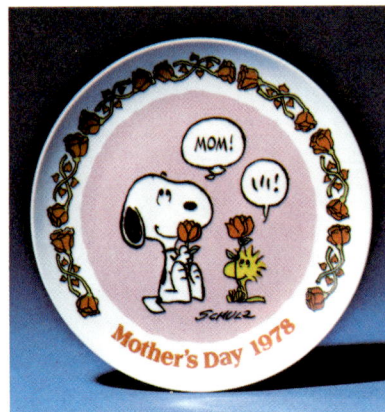

42-85-2.7
1978 *Thoughts that Count.*
Artist: Charles Schultz.
Issue price: $15.00.

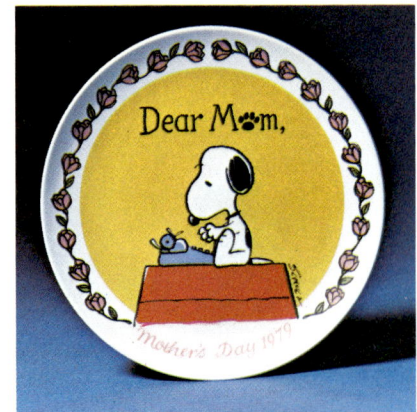

42-85-2.8
1979 *A Special Letter.*
Artist: Charles Schultz.
Issue price: $17.50.
Edition size limited to 10,000 sequentially numbered.

Disney Christmas Series

Artist: Walt Disney Productions
Overglaze porcelain
Diameter: 19 centimeters
   (7½ inches)
Attached back hanger
Edition size undisclosed, limited
  by year of issue, as indicated
Not numbered except as indicated;
  without certificate

42-85-3.1
1973 *Sleigh Ride*.
Artist: Walt Disney Productions.
Issue price: $10.00.

42-85-3.2
1974 *Decorating the Tree*.
Artist: Walt Disney Productions.
Issue price: $10.00.

42-85-3.3
1975 *Caroling*.
Artist: Walt Disney Productions.
Issue price: $12.50.

42-85-3.4
1976 *Building a Snowman*.
Artist: Walt Disney Productions.
Issue price: $13.00.

42-85-3.5
1977 *Down the Chimney*.
Artist: Walt Disney Productions.
Issue price: $13.00.

42-85-3.6
1978 *Night Before Christmas*.
Artist: Walt Disney Productions.
Issue price: $15.00.

42-85-3.7
1979 *Santa's Surprise*.
Artist: Walt Disney Productions.
Issue price: $17.50.
Edition size limited to 15,000
sequentially numbered.

Disney Mother's Day Series
Artist: Walt Disney Productions
Overglaze porcelain
Diameter: 19 centimeters
    (7½ inches)
Attached back hanger
Edition size undisclosed, limited
    by year of issue, as indicated
Not numbered except as indicated;
    without certificate

42-85-4.1
1974 *Flowers for Mother.*
Artist: Walt Disney Productions.
Issue price: $10.00.

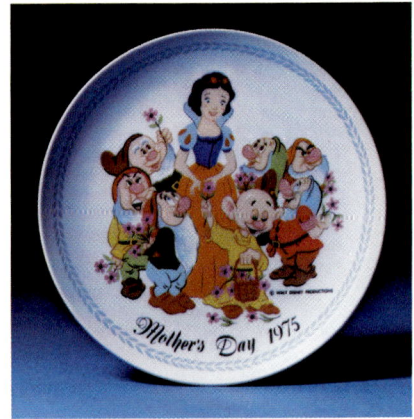

42-85-4.2
1975 *Snow White and the Seven Dwarfs.*
Artist: Walt Disney Productions.
Issue price: $12.50.

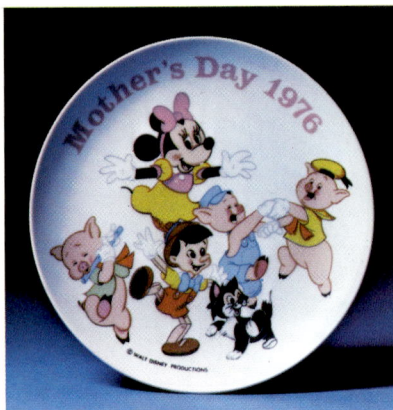

42-85-4.3
1976 *Minnie Mouse and Friends.*
Artist: Walt Disney Productions.
Issue price: $13.00.

42-85-4.4
1977 *Pluto's Pals.*
Artist: Walt Disney Productions.
Issue price: $13.00.

42-85-4.5
1978 *Flowers for Bambi.*
Artist: Walt Disney Productions.
Issue price: $15.00.

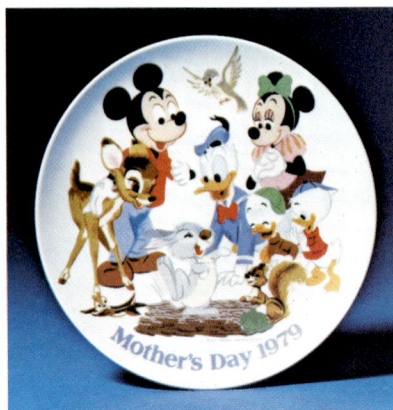

42-85-4.6
1979 *Happy Feet.*
Artist: Walt Disney Productions.
Issue price: $17.50.
Edition size limited to 10,000
sequentially numbered.

Raggedy Ann Christmas Series

Artist: The Bobbs-Merrill Company, Inc.
Overglaze porcelain
Diameter: 19 centimeters (7½ inches)
Attached back hanger
Edition size undisclosed, limited by year of issue, as indicated
Not numbered except as indicated; without certificate

42-85-5.1
1975 *Gifts of Love.*
Artist: The Bobbs-Merrill Company, Inc.
Issue price: $12.50.

42-85-5.2
1976 *Raggedy Ann Skates.*
Artist: The Bobbs-Merrill Company, Inc.
Issue price: $13.00.

42-85-5.3
1977 *Decorating Tree.*
Artist: The Bobbs-Merrill Company, Inc.
Issue price: $13.00.

42-85-5.4
1978 *Checking the List.*
Artist: The Bobbs-Merrill Company, Inc.
Issue price: $15.00.

42-85-5.5
1979 *Little Helper.*
Artist: The Bobbs-Merrill Company, Inc. Issue price: $17.50.
Edition size limited to 15,000 sequentially numbered.

Raggedy Ann Mother's Day Series

Artist: The Bobbs-Merrill Company, Inc.
Overglaze porcelain
Diameter: 19 centimeters (7½ inches)
Attached back hanger
Edition size undisclosed, limited by year of issue
Not numbered; without certificate

42-85-6.1
1976 *Motherhood.*
Artist: The Bobbs-Merrill Company, Inc.
Issue price: $13.00.

42-85-6.2
1977 *Bouquet of Love.*
Artist: The Bobbs-Merrill Company, Inc.
Issue price: $13.00.

42-85-6.3
1978 *Hello Mom*.
Artist: The Bobbs-Merrill
Company, Inc.
Issue price: $15.00.

42-85-6.4
1979 *High Spirits*.
Artist: The Bobbs-Merrill Company,
Inc. Issue price: $17.50.
Edition size limited to 10,000
sequentially numbered.

Peanuts Valentine's Day Series

Artist: Charles Schultz. Artist's
  signature appears on front
Overglaze porcelain
Diameter: 19 centimeters
  (7½ inches)
Attached back hanger
Edition size undisclosed, limited
  by year of issue
Not numbered; without certificate

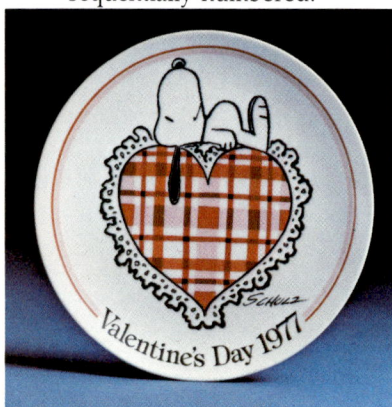

42-85-7.1
1977 *Home Is Where the Heart Is*.
Artist: Charles Schultz.
Issue price: $13.00.

42-85-7.2
1978 *Heavenly Bliss*.
Artist: Charles Schultz.
Issue price: $13.00.

42-85-7.3
1979 *Love Match*.
Artist: Charles Schultz.
Issue price: $17.50.

SCHMID

(Seito City)

Raggedy Ann Valentine's Day Series
Artist: The Bobbs-Merrill Co., Inc.
Overglaze porcelain
Diameter: 19 centimeters
 (7½ inches)
Attached back hanger
Not numbered; without certificate

42-85-8.1
1978 *As Time Goes By*.
Artist: The Bobbs-Merrill Company, Inc.
Issue price: $13.00.

42-85-8.2
1979 *Daisies Do Tell*.
Artist: The Bobbs-Merrill Company, Inc.
Issue price: $17.50.

Johan Jeremiason established Porsgrund, Norway's only porcelain factory, in 1885. Jeremiason began his business by importing English clay which was modeled by ceramist Carl Bauer. Porcelain tableware and decorative wares have been produced since then.

In 1909 Porsgrund produced a small edition of a Christmas plate entitled "Christmas Flowers." A *Christmas Series* based on religious themes was introduced in 1968 and ended with the 1977 issue. In 1978 Porsgrund began a nostalgic Christmas series entitled the *Traditional Norwegian Christmas Series*. The *Mother's Day Series* began in 1970 and the *Father's Day Series* in 1971. The *Easter Series* began in 1972 and closed in 1977.

Christmas Series
Artist: Gunnar Bratlie
Underglaze porcelain decorated in
cobalt blue
Diameter: 18 centimeters
(7 inches)
Pierced foot rim
Edition size undisclosed, limited
by year of issue
Not numbered; without certificate

54-61-1.1
1968 *Church Scene.*
Artist: Gunnar Bratlie.
Issue price: $12.00.

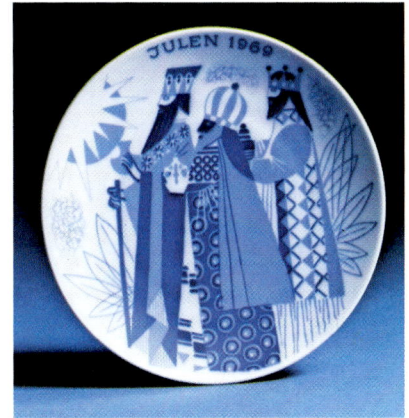

54-61-1.2
1969 *Three Kings.*
Artist: Gunnar Bratlie.
Issue price: $12.00.

54-61-1.3
1970 *Road to Bethlehem.*
Artist: Gunnar Bratlie.
Issue price: $12.00.

54-61-1.4
1971 *A Child Is Born in Bethlehem.*
Artist: Gunnar Bratlie.
Issue price: $12.00.

54-61-1.5
1972 *Hark, the Herald Angels Sing.*
Artist: Gunnar Bratlie.
Issue price: $12.00.

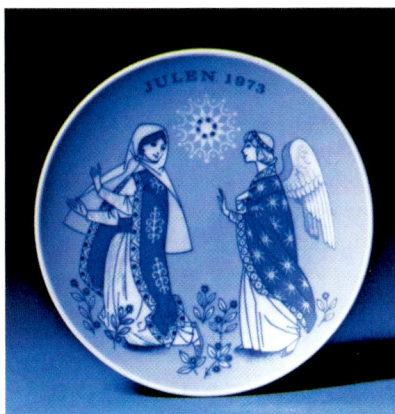

54-61-1.6
1973 *Promise of the Savior.*
Artist: Gunnar Bratlie.
Issue price: $15.00.

54-61-1.7
1974 *The Shepherds.*
Artist: Gunnar Bratlie.
Issue price: $15.00.

54-61-1.8
1975 *Jesus on the Road to the Temple.*
Artist: Gunnar Bratlie.
Issue price: $19.50.

54-61-1.9
1976 *Jesus and the Elders.*
Artist: Gunnar Bratlie.
Issue price: $22.00.

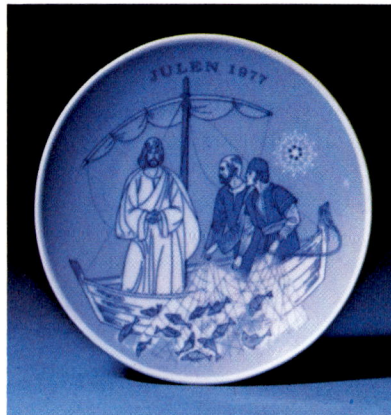

54-61-1.10
1977 *The Draught of Fish.*
Artist: Gunnar Bratlie.
Issue price: $24.00.

Mother's Day Series
Artist: Gunnar Bratlie
Underglaze porcelain decorated in
  cobalt blue
Diameter: 12.5 centimeters
  (5 inches)
Pierced foot rim
Edition size undisclosed, limited
  by year of issue
Not numbered; without certificate

54-61-2.1
1970 *Mare and Foal.*
Artist: Gunnar Bratlie.
Issue price: $7.50.

54-61-2.2
1971 *Boy and Geese.*
Artist: Gunnar Bratlie.
Issue price: $7.50.

54-61-2.3
1972 *Doe and Fawn.*
Artist: Gunnar Bratlie.
Issue price: $10.00.

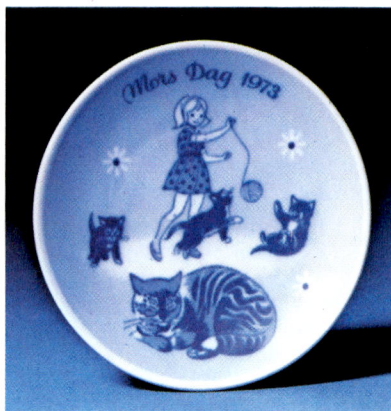

54-61-2.4
1973 *Cat and Kittens.*
Artist: Gunnar Bratlie.
Issue price: $10.00.

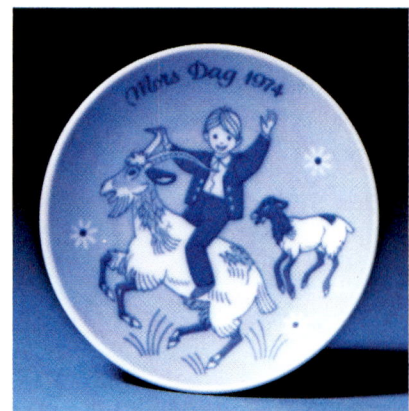

54-61-2.5
1974 *Boy and Goats.*
Artist: Gunnar Bratlie.
Issue price: $10.00.

54-61-2.6
1975 *Dog and Puppies.*
Artist: Gunnar Bratlie.
Issue price: $12.50.

54-61-2.7
1976 *Girl and Calf.*
Artist: Gunnar Bratlie.
Issue price: $15.00.

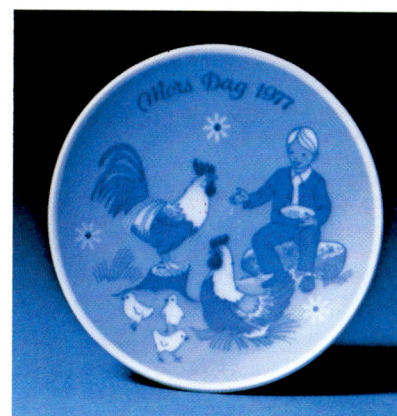

54-61-2.8
1977 *Boy and Chickens.*
Artist: Gunnar Bratlie.
Issue price: $16.50.

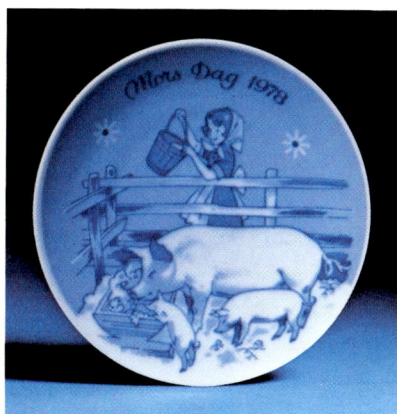

54-61-2.9
1978 *Girl and Pigs.*
Artist: Gunnar Bratlie.
Issue price: $17.50.

54-61-2.10
1979 *Boy and Reindeer.*
Artist: Gunnar Bratlie.
Issue price: $19.50.

Father's Day Series
Artist: Gunnar Bratlie
Underglaze porcelain decorated in cobalt blue
Diameter: 12.5 centimeters (5 inches)
Pierced foot rim
Edition size undisclosed, limited by year of issue
Not numbered; without certificate

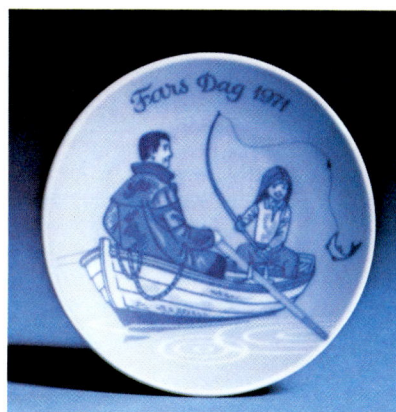

54-61-3.1
1971 *Fishing.*
Artist: Gunnar Bratlie.
Issue price: $10.00.

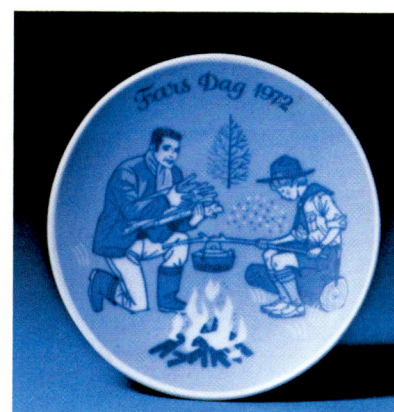

54-61-3.2
1972 *Cookout.*
Artist: Gunnar Bratlie.
Issue price: $10.00.

54-61-3.3
1973 *Sledding.*
Artist: Gunnar Bratlie.
Issue price: $10.00.

54-61-3.4
1974 *Father and Son.*
Artist: Gunnar Bratlie.
Issue price: $10.00.

54-61-3.5
1975 *Skating.*
Artist: Gunnar Bratlie.
Issue price: $12.50.

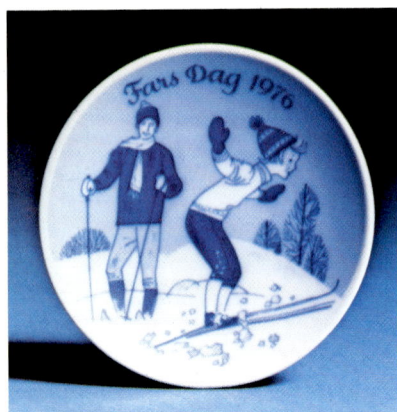

54-61-3.6
1976 *Skiing.*
Artist: Gunnar Bratlie.
Issue price: $15.00.

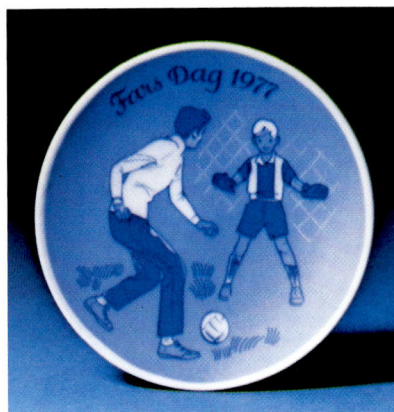

54-61-3.7
1977 *Soccer.*
Artist: Gunnar Bratlie.
Issue price: $16.50.

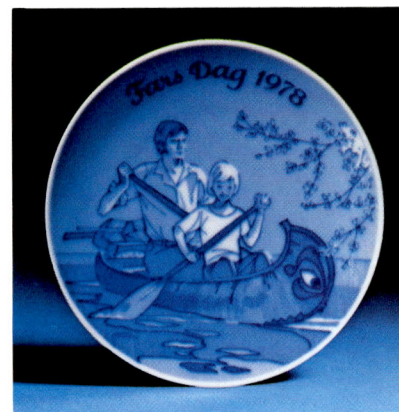

54-61-3.8
1978 *Canoeing.*
Artist: Gunnar Bratlie.
Issue price: $17.50.

54-61-3.9
1979 *Father and Daughter.*
Artist: Gunnar Bratlie.
Issue price: $19.50.

PORSGRUND

(Porsgrunn, Telemark County)

Easter Series

Artist: Grete Roenning

Underglaze porcelain decorated in
cobalt blue

Diameter: 18 centimeters
(7 inches)

Pierced foot rim

Edition size undisclosed, limited
by year of issue

Not numbered; without certificate

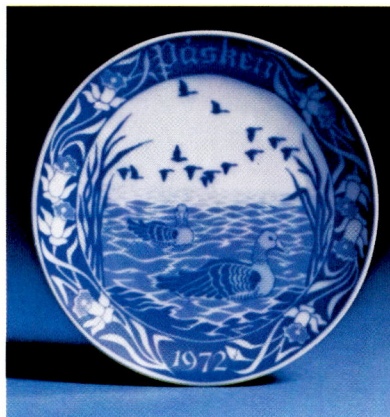

54-61-4.1
1972 *Ducks*.
Artist: Grete Roenning.
Issue price: $12.00.

54-61-4.2
1973 *Birds*.
Artist: Grete Roenning.
Issue price: $12.00.

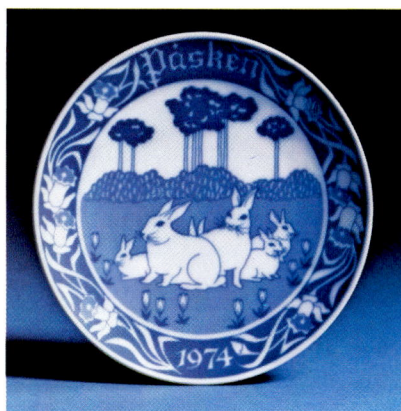

54-61-4.3
1974 *Bunnies*.
Artist: Grete Roenning.
Issue price: $15.00.

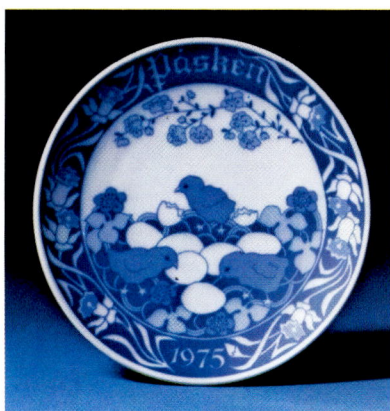

54-61-4.4
1975 *Chicks*.
Artist: Grete Roenning.
Issue price: $19.50.

54-61-4.5
1976 *Sheep in the Field*.
Artist: Grete Roenning.
Issue price: $22.00.

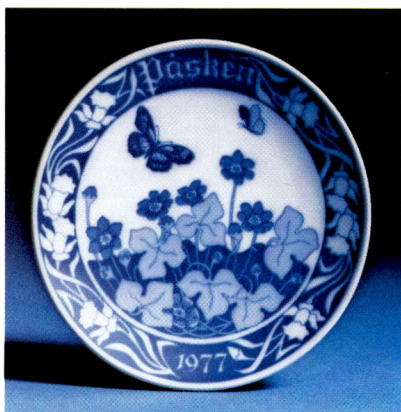

54-61-4.6
1977 *Butterflies*.
Artist: Grete Roenning.
Issue price: $24.00.

Traditional Norwegian Christmas Series

Artist: Gunnar Bratlie. Artist's initials appear on back

Underglaze porcelain decorated in cobalt blue

Diameter: 18 centimeters (7 inches)

Pierced foot rim

Edition size undisclosed, limited by year of issue

Not numbered; without certificate

54-61-5.1
1978 *Guests Are Coming for Christmas Eve.*
Artist: Gunnar Bratlie.
Issue price: $27.00.

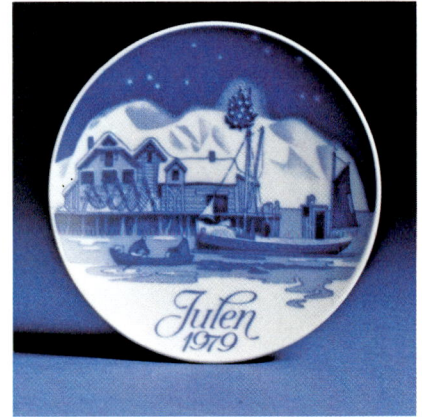

54-61-5.2
1979 *Home for Christmas.*
Artist: Gunnar Bratlie.
Issue price: $30.00.

LLADRÓ

The Lladró Porcelain factory was established in the 1950s by three Lladró brothers—Juan, Jose, and Vincente, sons of a peasant. At night, they studied porcelain designing, modeling, and firing and built their first kiln while in their teens. By 1970 their factory was one of the best equipped in Europe and had become known for its vases and figurines. Lladró initiated both its limited-edition *Christmas Series* and *Mother's Day Series* in 1971.

SPAIN
LLADRÓ
(Tabernes Blanques, Valencia)

Christmas Series
Artist: Undisclosed
White bisque center in bas-relief
  with underglaze porcelain
  border and 14k gold trim
Diameter: 20.5 centimeters
  (8 inches)
No hanger
Edition size undisclosed, limited
  by year of issue
Not numbered;without certificate

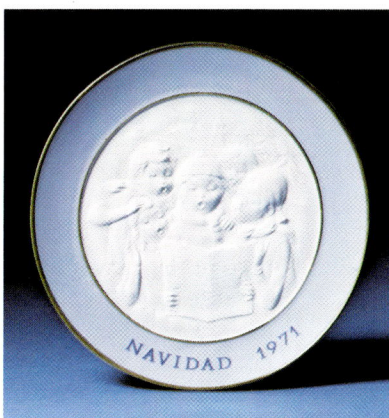

72-46-1.1
1971 *Caroling*.
Artist: Undisclosed.
Issue price: $27.50.

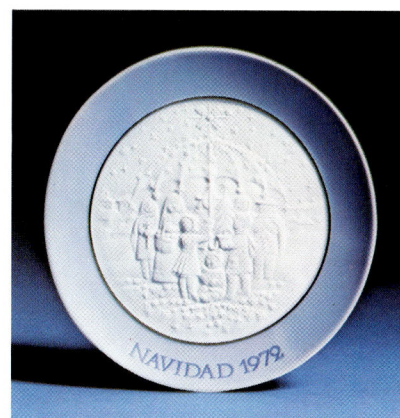

72-46-1.2
1972 *Carolers*.
Artist: Undisclosed.
Issue price: $35.00.

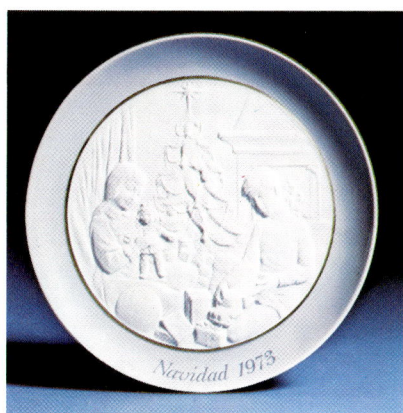

72-46-1.3
1973 *Boy and Girl*.
Artist: Undisclosed.
Issue price: $45.00.

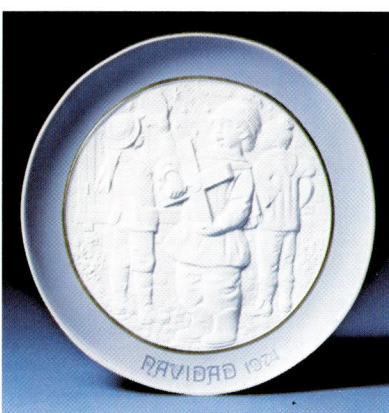

72-46-1.4
1974 *Carolers*.
Artist: Undisclosed.
Issue price: $55.00.

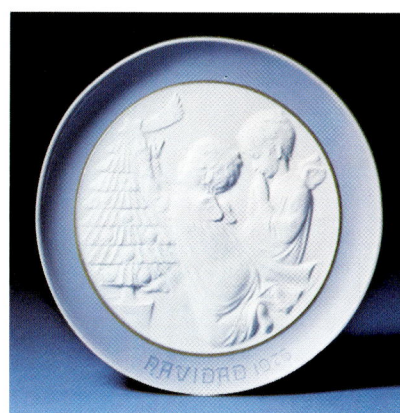

72-46-1.5
1975 *Cherubs*.
Artist: Undisclosed.
Issue price: $60.00.

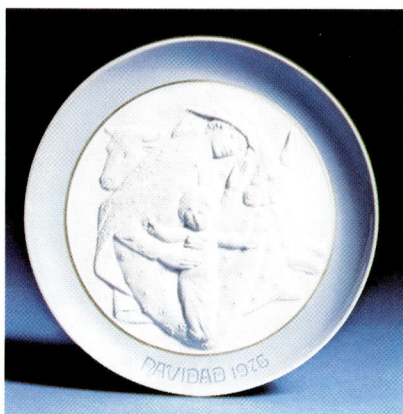

72-46-1.6
1976 *Christ Child*.
Artist: Undisclosed.
Issue price: $60.00.

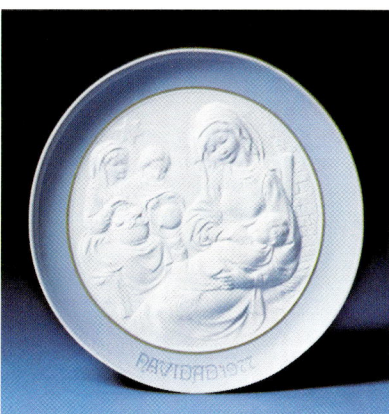

72-46-1.7
1977 *Nativity Scene*.
Artist: Undisclosed.
Issue price: $80.00.

Mother's Day Series

Artist: Undisclosed

White bisque center in bas-relief with underglaze porcelain border and 14k gold trim

Diameter: 20.5 centimeters (8 inches)

No hanger

Edition size undisclosed, limited by year of issue

Not numbered; without certificate

72-46-2.1
1971 *Kiss of the Child.*
Artist: Undisclosed.
Issue price: $27.50.

72-46-2.2
1972 *Bird and Chicks.*
Artist: Undisclosed.
Issue price: $27.50.

72-46-2.3
1973 *Mother and Children.*
Artist: Undisclosed.
Issue price: $35.00.

72-46-2.4
1974 *Mother Nursing.*
Artist: Undisclosed.
Issue price: $45.00.

72-46-2.5
1975 *Mother and Child.*
Artist: Undisclosed.
Issue price: $60.00.

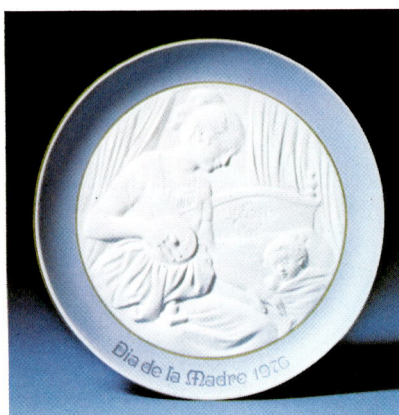

72-46-2.6
1976 *Tender Vigil.*
Artist: Undisclosed.
Issue price: $60.00.

72-46-2.7
1977 *Mother and Daughter.*
Artist: Undisclosed.
Issue price: $67.50.

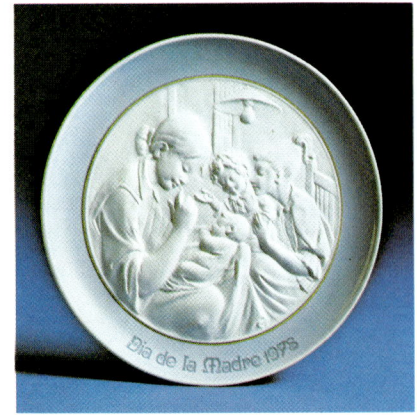

72-46-2.8
1978 *The New Arrival.*
Artist: Undisclosed.
Issue price: $80.00.

SANTA CLARA
PORCELANA

Santa Clara porcelain is made in the
Alvarez porcelain factory in Spain. The
Santa Clara *Christmas Series* began in 1970.

Christmas Series

Artist: Undisclosed
Underglaze porcelain with 24k
  gold decoration
Diameter: 20.5 centimeters
  (8 inches)
Pierced foot rim
Edition size: As indicated
Numbered since 1971,
  without certificate

72-72-1.1
1970 *Christmas Message.*
Artist: Undisclosed.
Issue price: $18.00. Edition size limited
to announced quantity of 10,000.

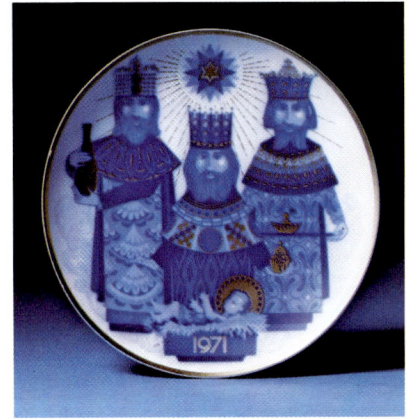

72-72-1.2
1971 *Three Wise Men.*
Artist: Undisclosed.
Issue price: $18.00.
Edition size limited to 10,000.

72-72-1.3
1972 *Children in the Woods.*
Artist: Undisclosed.
Issue price: $20.00.
Edition size limited to 10,000.

72-72-1.4
1973 *Archangel.*
Artist: Undisclosed.
Issue price: $25.00.
Edition size limited to 5,000.

72-72-1.5
1974 *Spirit of Christmas.*
Artist: Undisclosed.
Issue price: $25.00.
Edition size limited to 10,000.

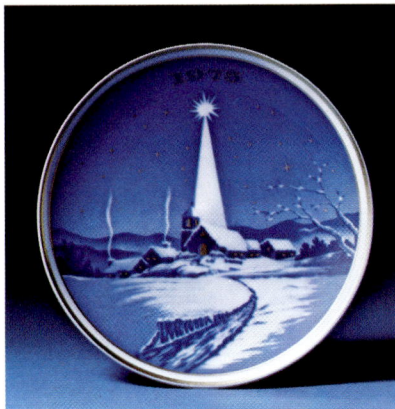

72-72-1.6
1975 *Christmas Eve in the Country.*
Artist: Undisclosed.
Issue price: $27.50.
Edition size limited to 10,000.

72-72-1.7
1976 *Madonna and Child.*
Artist: Undisclosed.
Issue price: $25.00.
Edition size limited to 5,000.

72-72-1.8
1977 *Mother and Child.*
Artist: Undisclosed.
Issue price: $27.50.
Edition size limited to 10,000.

72-72-1.9
1978 *Angel With Flowers.*
Artist: Undisclosed.
Issue price: $32.00.

Orrefors was originally established in 1726 as an ironworks. In 1898 they began manufacturing glass ink bottles and window glass. Although the ironworks was no longer profitable, Johan Ekman purchased the property in 1913. He was interested in improving the facilities for glassmaking and recognized the importance of the valuable forest land of the area as fuel for glass furnaces. He eventually built an entire community around the glassworks.

Orrefors crystal is made from a mixture of seashore sand and potash, plus a heavy lead content. The ornamentation is created by master blowers who apply liquid molten glass in desired shapes.

In 1970 Orrefors began its *Annual Cathedral Series*, made in clear crystal, depicting famous places of worship. This series ended in 1978. The *Mother's Day Series*, made in cobalt crystal, started in 1971. These plates are handmade with the designs engraved in the crystal and filled with 24k gold, a technique developed by the artist, John Selbing.

Annual Cathedral Series
Artist: John Selbing
Leaded crystal with engraved
    designs inlaid in 24k gold
Diameter: 25.5 centimeters
    (10 inches)
No hanger
Edition size: As indicated
Numbered since 1975, without
    certificate

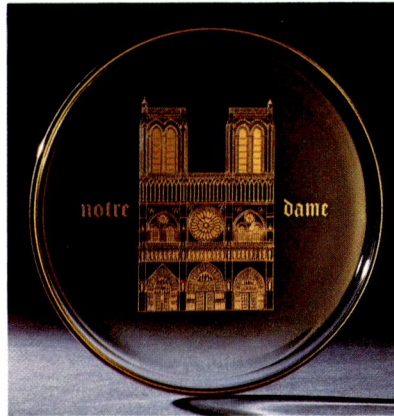

76-57-1.1
1970 *Notre Dame Cathedral.*
Artist: John Selbing.
Issue price: $50.00. Edition size limited
to announced quantity of 5,000.

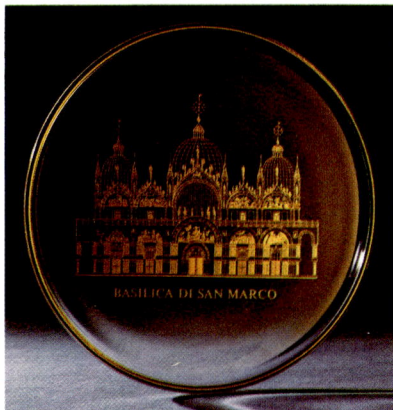

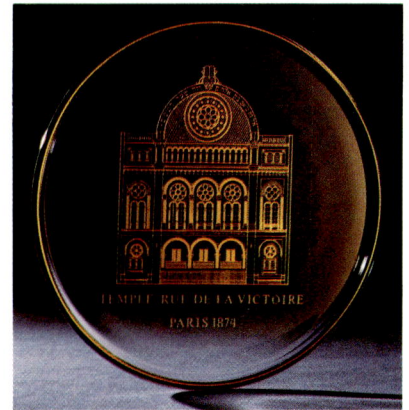

76-57-1.2
1971 *Westminster Abbey.*
Artist: John Selbing.
Issue price: $50.00. Edition size limited
to announced quantity of 5,000.

76-57-1.3
1972 *Basilica di San Marco.*
Artist: John Selbing.
Issue price: $50.00. Edition size limited
to announced quantity of 5,000.

76-57-1.4
1973 *Cologne Cathedral.*
Artist: John Selbing.
Issue price: $50.00. Edition size limited
to announced quantity of 5,000.

76-57-1.5
1974 *Temple Rue de la Victoire, Paris.*
Artist: John Selbing.
Issue price: $60.00. Edition size limited
to announced quantity of 5,000.

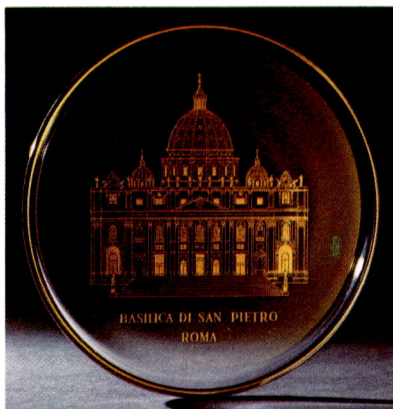

76-57-1.6
1975 *Basilica di San Pietro, Rome.*
Artist: John Selbing.
Issue price: $85.00.
Edition size limited to 5,000.

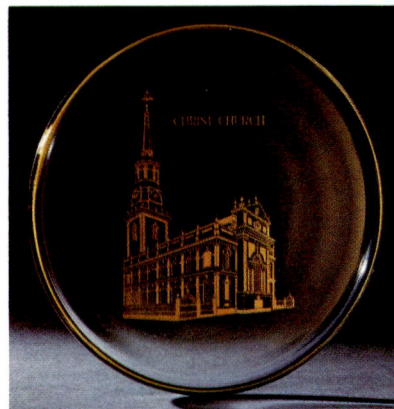

76-57-1.7
1976 *Christ Church, Philadelphia.*
Artist: John Selbing.
Issue price: $85.00.
Edition size limited to 3,000.

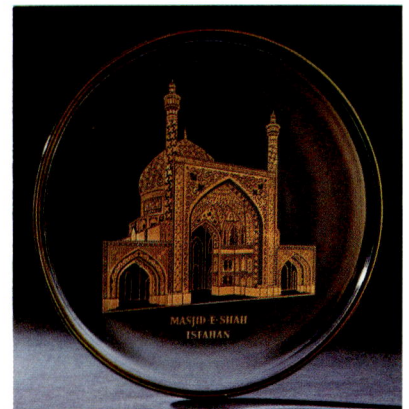

76-57-1.8
1977 *Masjid-E-Shah.*
Artist: John Selbing.
Issue price: $90.00.
Edition size limited to 3,000.

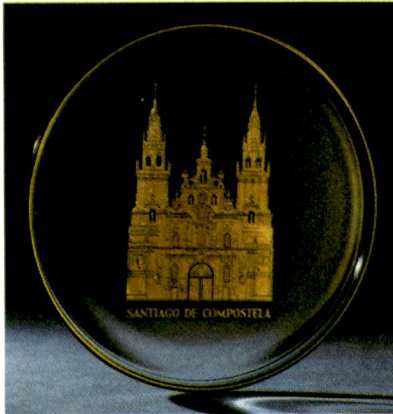

76-57-1.9
1978 *Santiago de Compostelá.*
Artist: John Selbing.
Issue price: $95.00.
Edition size limited to 3,000.

Mother's Day Series

Artist: John Selbing
Leaded cobalt crystal with
    engraved designs inlaid in 24k
    gold
Diameter: 20.5 centimeters
    (8 inches)
Attached back hanger since 1973
Edition size: As indicated
Numbered since 1975, without
    certificate

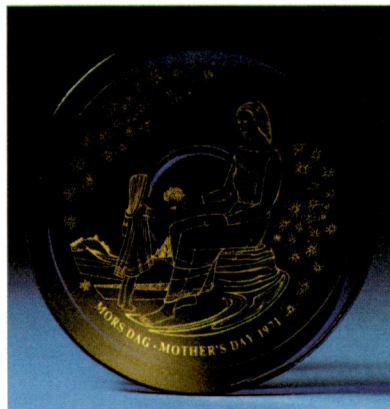

76-57-2.1
1971 *Flowers for Mother.*
Artist: John Selbing.
Issue price: $45.00. Edition size limited
to announced quantity of 2,500.

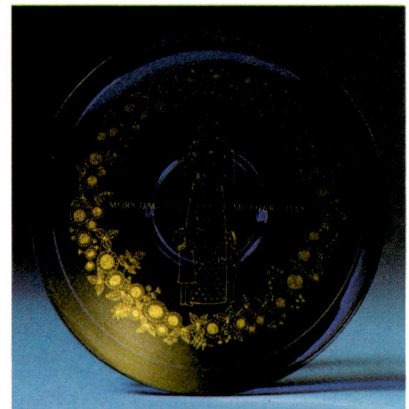

76-57-2.2
1972 *Mother and Children.*
Artist: John Selbing.
Issue price: $45.00. Edition size limited
to announced quantity of 2,500.

76-57-2.3
1973 *Mother and Child.*
Artist: John Selbing.
Issue price: $50.00. Edition size limited
to announced quantity of 2,500.

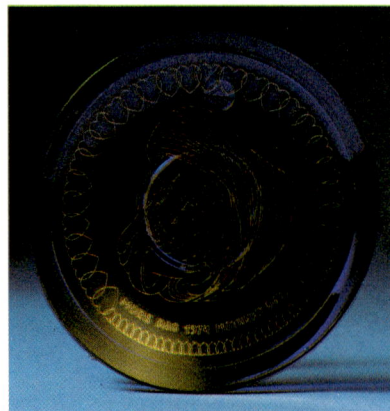

76-57-2.4
1974 *Mother and Child.*
Artist: John Selbing.
Issue price: $50.00. Edition size limited
to announced quantity of 5,000.

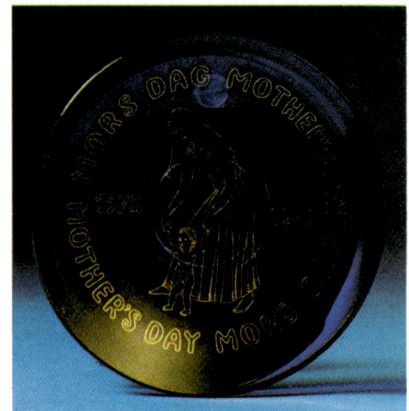

76-57-2.5
1975 *Mother and Child.*
Artist: John Selbing.
Issue price: $60.00.
Edition size limited to 2,500.

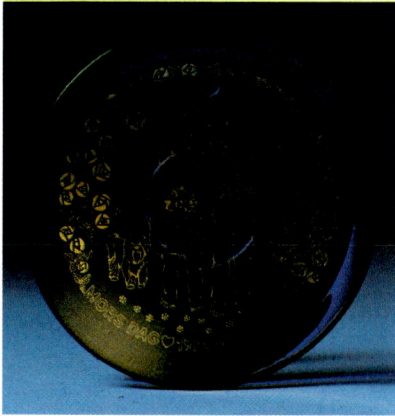

76-57-2.6
1976 *Children and Puppy.*
Artist: John Selbing.
Issue price: $75.00.
Edition size limited to 2,500.

76-57-2.7
1977 *Child and Dove.*
Artist: John Selbing.
Issue price: $85.00.
Edition size limited to 1,500.

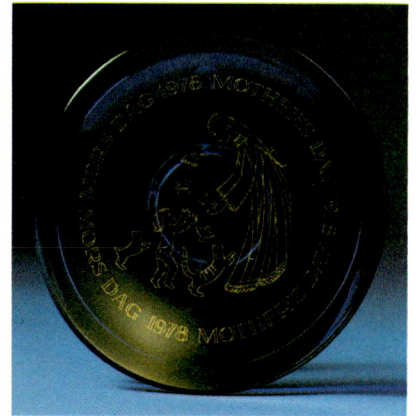

76-57-2.8
1978 *Mother and Child.*
Artist: John Selbing.
Issue price: $90.00.
Edition size limited to 1,500.

The Rörstrand Porcelain factory is
Sweden's oldest pottery and the second
oldest in Europe. Originally founded in
Stockholm in 1726 under government
patronage, the plant was later moved
inland to Lidkoping for safety during World
War II.

In addition to ceramics made of stoneware
and high-fired earthenware, Rörstrand
produces dinnerware, kitchenware, wall
plaques, and other decorative art, including
collector's plates. In 1968 Rörstrand began
its series of square Christmas plates with
designs derived from Swedish folk tales
and traditions.

Christmas Series

Artist: Gunnar Nylund

Underglaze porcelain decorated in Scandia blue

Diameter: 19 centimeters
(7½ inches square)

Pierced foot rim

Edition size undisclosed, limited by year of issue

Not numbered; without certificate

76-69-1.1
1968 *Bringing Home the Tree.*
Artist: Gunnar Nylund.
Issue price: $12.00.

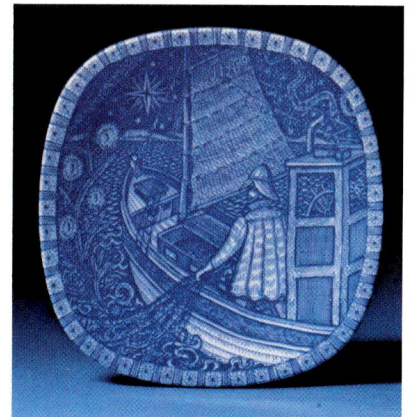

76-69-1.2
1969 *Fisherman Sailing Home.*
Artist: Gunnar Nylund.
Issue price: $13.50.

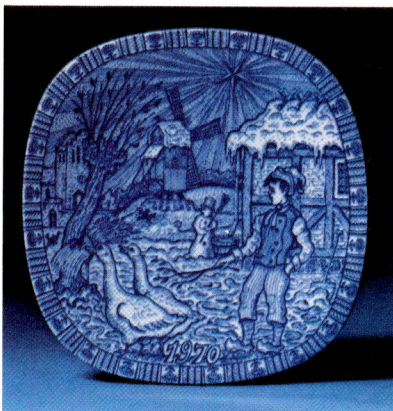

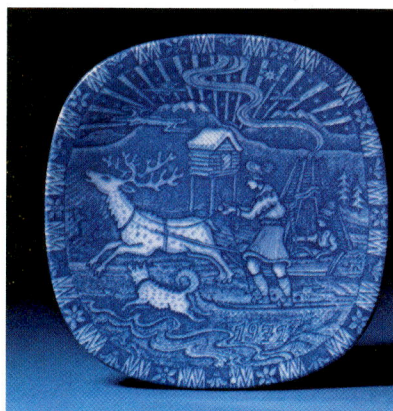

76-69-1.3
1970 *Nils with His Geese.*
Artist: Gunnar Nylund.
Issue price: $13.50.

76-69-1.4
1971 *Nils in Lapland.*
Artist: Gunnar Nylund.
Issue price: $15.00.

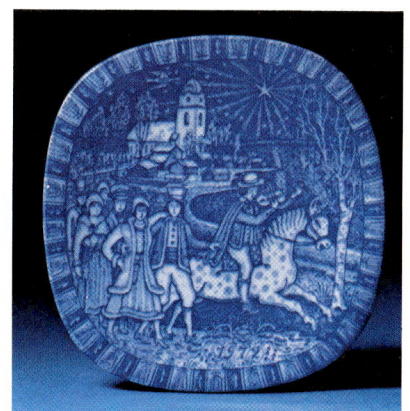

76-69-1.5
1972 *Dalecarlian Fiddler.*
Artist: Gunnar Nylund.
Issue price: $15.00.

76-69-1.6
1973 *Farm in Smaland.*
Artist: Gunnar Nylund.
Issue price: $16.00.

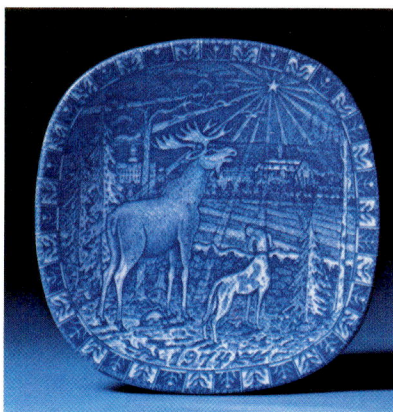

76-69-1.7
1974 *Vadstena.*
Artist: Gunnar Nylund.
Issue price: $19.00.

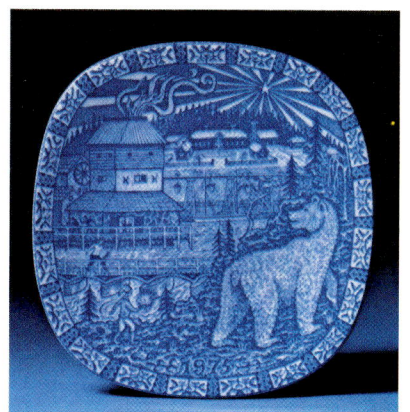

76-69-1.8
1975 *Nils in Vastmanland.*
Artist: Gunnar Nylund.
Issue price: $20.00.

76-69-1.9
1976 *Nils in Uppland.*
Artist: Gunnar Nylund.
Issue price: $20.00.

76-69-1.10
1977 *Nils in Värmland.*
Artist: Gunnar Nylund.
Issue price: $29.50.

76-69-1.11
1978 *Nils in Fjallbacka.*
Artist: Gunnar Nylund.
Issue price: $32.50.

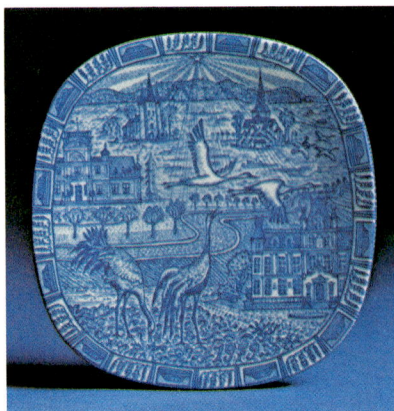

76-69-1.12
1979 *Nils in Vaestergoetland.*
Artist: Gunnar Nylund.
Issue price: $38.50.

Artists of the World

Initially organized as DeGrazia of Scottsdale, the company was founded by James LaFond and represented only Arizona artist Ted DeGrazia. The present name, Artists of the World, was adopted in 1977 when the company's scope was enlarged to include additional artists.

Children of Aberdeen, a proprietary issue with artwork by Kee Fung Ng, began in 1979 and depicts the children who live on boats anchored at the fishing village of Aberdeen near Hong Kong.

Children of Aberdeen Series
Artist: Kee Fung Ng
China
Diameter: 26 centimeters
  (10 inches)
No hanger
Edition size unannounced
Numbered with certificate

84-3-1.1
1979 *Girl with Little Brother.*
Artist: Kee Fung Ng.
Issue price: $50.00.

Fairmont

FINE CHINA

ARTISTS OF THE WORLD

Fairmont China entered the collector's plate market with three series: the *Holiday Series* with artwork by Ted DeGrazia, the *Famous Clowns Series* with artwork by comedian Red Skelton, and the *Ruffin Annual Series* with artwork by Don Ruffin. In 1977, they issued the third plate in the *Irene Spencer Annual Series* and in 1978 the third plate in the *DeGrazia Children Series*, both originally started by Gorham. (See United States, GORHAM). The *Irene Spencer's Special Requests Series* was started by Fairmont in 1978.

UNITED STATES
FAIRMONT
(Pasadena, California)

Holiday Series
Artist: Ted DeGrazia. Artist's
  signature appears on front; first
  500 autographed on back
China trimmed in gold
Diameter: 26 centimeters
  (10¼ inches)
No hanger
Edition size: As indicated
Numbered since 1977,
  without certificate

84-14-1.1
1976 *The Festival of Lights.*
Artist: Ted DeGrazia.
Issue price: $45.00; autographed:
$100.00. Edition size limited to
announced quantity of 10,000.

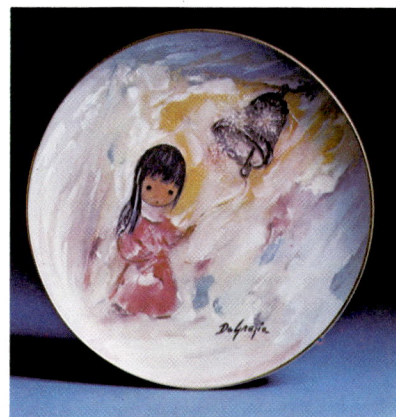

84-14-1.2
1977 *The Bell of Hope.*
Artist: Ted DeGrazia.
Issue price: $45.00;
autographed: $100.00.
Edition size limited to 10,000.

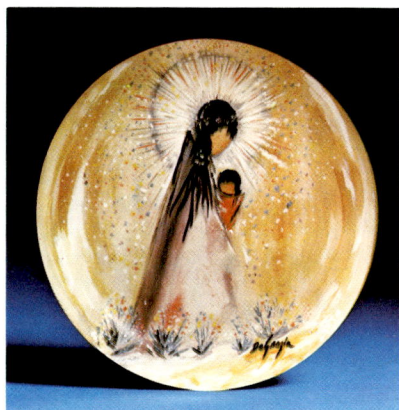

84-14-1.3
1978 *Little Madonna.*
Artist: Ted DeGrazia.
Issue price: $45.00;
autographed: $100.00.
Edition size limited to 10,000.

84-14-1.4
1979 *The Nativity.*
Artist: Ted DeGrazia.
Issue price: $50.00;
autographed $100.00.
Edition size limited to 10,000.

Famous Clowns Series
Artist: Red Skelton. Artist's
  signature appears on front
China trimmed in gold
Diameter: 21.5 centimeters
  (8½ inches)
No hanger
Edition size limited to 10,000
Numbered without certificate

84-14-2.1
1976 *Freddie the Freeloader.*
Artist: Red Skelton.
Issue price: $55.00.

84-14-2.2
1977 *W. C. Fields.*
Artist: Red Skelton.
Issue price: $55.00.

84-14-2.3
1978 *Happy*.
Artist: Red Skelton.
Issue price: $55.00.

84-14-2.4
1979 *The Pledge*.
Artist: Red Skelton.
Issue price: $55.00.

Irene Spencer Annual Series

Artist: Irene Spencer. Artist's signature appears on front and back

China trimmed in gold

Diameter: 21.5 centimeters (8½ inches)

No hanger

Edition size limited to 10,000

Numbered without certificate

84-14-3.1
1977 *Patient Ones*.
Artist: Irene Spencer.
Issue price: $42.50.

84-14-3.2
1978 *Yesterday, Today and Tomorrow*.
Artist: Irene Spencer.
Issue price: $47.50.

DeGrazia Children Series

Artist: Ted DeGrazia. Artist's signature appears on front; first 500 autographed on back

China trimmed in gold

Diameter: 26 centimeters (10¼ inches)

No hanger

Edition size limited to 10,000

Numbered without certificate

84-14-4.1
1978 *Flower Girl*.
Artist: Ted DeGrazia.
Issue price: $45.00;
autographed: $100.00.

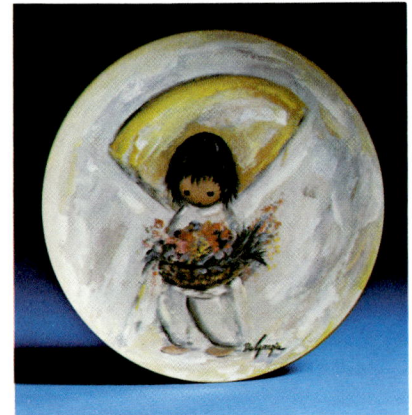

84-14-4.2
1979 *Flower Boy*.
Artist: Ted DeGrazia.
Issue price: $45.00;
autographed: $100.00.

Irene Spencer's Special Requests

Artist: Irene Spencer. Artist's signature appears on front

China trimmed in gold

Diameter: 26 centimeters (10¼ inches)

No hanger

Edition size limited to 10,000

Numbered without certificate

84-14-7.1
1978 *Hug Me.*
Artist: Irene Spencer.
Issue price: $55.00.

84-14-7.2
1979 *Sleep Little Baby.*
Artist: Irene Spencer.
Issue price: $65.00.

Classical American Beauties

Artist: Vincent

China banded in gold

Diameter: 26 centimeters (10¼ inches)

No hanger

Edition size limited to 7,500

Numbered without certificate

84-14-8.1
1979 *Colleen.*
Artist: Vincent.
Issue price: $60.00.

Ruffin Annual Series

Artist: Don Ruffin

China banded in gold

Diameter: 26 centimeters (10¼ inches)

No hanger

Edition size as indicated

Numbered without certificate

84-14-9.1
1976 *Navajo Lullaby.*
Artist: Don Ruffin.
Issue price: $40.00.
Edition size limited to 10,000.

84-14-9.2
1977 *Through the Years.*
Artist: Don Ruffin
Issue price: $45.00.
Edition size limited to 5,000.

84-14-9.3
1978 *Child of the Pueblo.*
Artist: Don Ruffin.
Issue price: $50.00.
Edition size limited to 5,000.

84-14-9.4
1979 *Colima Madonna.*
Artist: Don Ruffin.
Issue price: $50.00.
Edition size limited to 5,000.

The Franklin Mint, considered the world's largest private mint, was established in Philadelphia in 1965 by Joseph Segal. The firm specializes in medallic art forms, minting coins for foreign governments, and has several international subsidiaries and branches.

The Franklin Mint entered the limited-edition plate field in 1970 with the six-plate *Rockwell Christmas Series*, made in sterling silver. This series ended in 1975. The Franklin Mint *Mother's Day Series* began in 1972 and ended in 1976.

Rockwell Christmas Series
Artist: Norman Rockwell. Artist's signature appears on front
Etched sterling silver
Diameter: 20.5 centimeters (8 inches)
No hanger
Edition size: As indicated
Numbered; with certificate since 1972

84-19-1.1
1970 *Bringing Home the Tree.*
Artist: Norman Rockwell.
Issue price: $100.00.
Edition size limited to 18,321.

84-19-1.2
1971 *Under the Mistletoe.*
Artist: Norman Rockwell.
Issue price: $100.00.
Edition size limited to 24,792.

84-19-1.3
1972 *The Carolers.*
Artist: Norman Rockwell.
Issue price: $125.00.
Edition size limited to 29,074.

84-19-1.4
1973 *Trimming the Tree.*
Artist: Norman Rockwell.
Issue price: $125.00.
Edition size limited to 18,010.

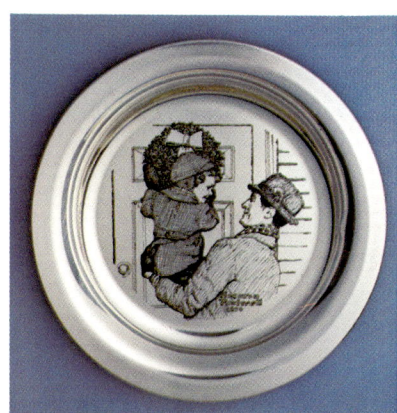

84-19-1.5
1974 *Hanging the Wreath.*
Artist: Norman Rockwell.
Issue price: $175.00.
Edition size limited to 12,822.

84-19-1.6
1975 *Home for Christmas.*
Artist: Norman Rockwell.
Issue price: $180.00.
Edition size limited to 11,059.

Mother's Day Series

Artist: Irene Spencer. Artist's
  signature appears on front
Etched sterling silver
Diameter: 20.5 centimeters
  (8 inches)
No hanger
Edition size: As indicated
Numbered without certificate

84-19-2.1
1972 *Mother and Child.*
Artist: Irene Spencer.
Issue price: $125.00.
Edition size limited to 21,987.

84-19-2.2
1973 *Mother and Child.*
Artist: Irene Spencer.
Issue price: $125.00.
Edition size limited to 6,154.

84-19-2.3
1974 *Mother and Child.*
Artist: Irene Spencer.
Issue price: $150.00.
Edition size limited to 5,116.

84-19-2.4
1975 *Mother and Child.*
Artist: Irene Spencer.
Issue price: $175.00.
Edition size limited to 2,704.

84-19-2.5
1976 *Mother and Child.*
Artist: Irene Spencer.
Issue price: $180.00.
Edition size limited to 1,858.

GORHAM
EST. 1831

In 1831 Jabez Gorham, a silversmith, established the Gorham Corporation — a division of Textron and one of the world's largest producers of sterling silver. The firm manufactures silverware and holloware, figurines and ornaments.

Gorham Corporation acquired crystal and china manufacturing companies in 1970, enabling it to produce limited-edition plates in china as well as silver.

Gorham's *Rockwell Four Seasons Series*, which began in 1971, creates four plates (spring, summer, fall and winter) each year. A *Christmas Series*, also with artwork by Norman Rockwell, was started in 1974. In 1975 the *Irene Spencer Annual Series* began. The *DeGrazia Children Series* and the *Sugar and Spice Series* began in 1976. The *Prince Tatters Series* was started in 1977.

Since 1977, Fairmont China has made the *Irene Spencer Annual* plates and in 1978 they also began making the *DeGrazia Children* plates. (See United States, FAIRMONT).

GORHAM

(Providence, Rhode Island)

*Rockwell Four
Seasons Series*

Artist: Norman Rockwell. Artist's
signature appears on front

China trimmed in 24k gold

Diameter: 26.5 centimeters
(10½ inches)

No hanger

Edition size undisclosed, limited
by year of issue

Not numbered; without certificate

Issued in sets of four

84-24-1.1-1
1971 *A Boy and His Dog;
A Boy Meets His Dog.*
Artist: Norman Rockwell.
Issue price: $50.00 the set.

84-24-1.1-2
1971 *Adventurers Between Adventures.*

84-24-1.1-3
1971 *A Mysterious Malady.*

84-24-1.1-4
1971 *Price of Parenthood.*

84-24-1.2-1
1972 *Young Love; Flying Colors.*
Artist: Norman Rockwell.
Issue price: $60.00 the set.

84-24-1.2-2
1972 *Beguiling Buttercup.*

84-24-1.2-3
1972 *A Scholarly Pace.*

84-24-1.2-4
1972 *Downhill Daring.*

84-24-1.3-1
1973 *The Ages of Love;*
Sweet Song So Young.
Artist: Norman Rockwell.
Issue price: $60.00 the set.

84-24-1.3-2
1973 *Flowers in Tender Bloom.*

84-24-1.3-3
1973 *Fondly Do We Remember.*

84-24-1.3-4
1973 *Gaily Sharing Vintage.*

84-24-1.4-1
1974 *Grandpa and Me; Day Dreamers.*
Artist: Norman Rockwell.
Issue price: $60.00 the set.

84-24-1.4-2
1974 *Goin' Fishin'.*

84-24-1.4-3
1974 *Pensive Pals.*

84-24-1.4-4
1974 *Gay Blades.*

84-24-1.5-1
1975 *Me and My Pal; Young Man's*
Fancy.
Artist: Norman Rockwell.
Issue price: $70.00 the set.

84-24-1.5-2
1975 *Fisherman's Paradise.*

84-24-1.5-3
1975 *Disastrous Daring.*

84-24-1.5-4
1975 *A Lickin' Good Bath.*

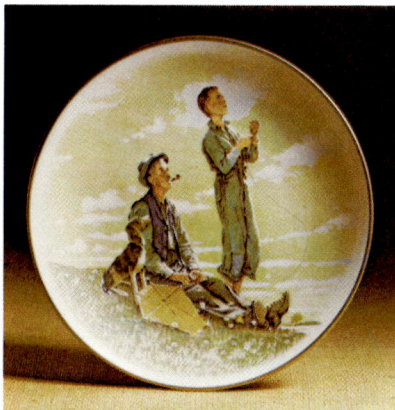

84-24-1.6-1
1976 *Grand Pals; Soaring Spirits.*
Artist: Norman Rockwell.
Issue price: $70.00 the set.

84-24-1.6-2
1976 *Fish Finders.*

84-24-1.6-3
1976 *Ghostly Gourds.*

84-24-1.6-4
1976 *Snow Sculpture.*

84-24-1.7-1
1977 *Going on Sixteen; Sweet Serenade.*
Artist: Norman Rockwell.
Issue price: $75.00 the set.

84-24-1.7-2
1977 *Sheer Agony.*

84-24-1.7-3
1977 *Pilgrimage.*

84-24-1.7-4
1977 *Chilling Chore.*

84-24-1.8-1
1978 *The Tender Years; Spring Tonic.*
Artist: Norman Rockwell.
Issue price: $100.00 the set.

84-24-1.8-2
1978 *Cool Aid.*

84-24-1.8-3
1978 *Chilly Reception.*

84-24-1.8-4
1978 *New Year Look.*

84-24-1.9-1
1979 *A Helping Hand;*
Closed for Business.
Artist: Norman Rockwell.
Issue price: $100.00 the set.

84-24-1.9-2
1979 *Swatters Rights.*

84-24-1.9-3
1979 *The Coal Season's Coming.*

(Providence, Rhode Island)

84-24-1.9-4
1979 Year End Count.

Rockwell Christmas Series

Artist: Norman Rockwell. Artist's
  signature appears on front
China trimmed in 24k gold
Diameter: 21.5 centimeters
  (8½ inches)
No hanger
Edition size undisclosed, limited
  by year of issue
Not numbered; without certificate

84-24-3.1
1974 Tiny Tim.
Artist: Norman Rockwell.
Issue price: $12.50.

84-24-3.2
1975 Good Deeds.
Artist: Norman Rockwell.
Issue price: $17.50.

84-24-3.3
1976 Christmas Trio.
Artist: Norman Rockwell.
Issue price: $19.50.

84-24-3.4
1977 Yuletide Reckoning.
Artist: Norman Rockwell.
Issue price: $19.50.

84-24-3.5
1978 Planning Christmas Visits.
Artist: Norman Rockwell.
Issue price: $24.50.

84-24-3.6
1979 *Santa's Helpers*.
Artist: Norman Rockwell.
Issue price: $24.50.

Irene Spencer Annual

Artist: Irene Spencer. Artist's
signature appears on front
China trimmed in 24k gold
Diameter: 21.5 centimeters
(8½ inches)
No hanger
Edition size limited to announced
quantity of 10,000
Not numbered; without certificate

84-24-4.1
1975 *Dear Child*.
Artist: Irene Spencer.
Issue price: $37.50.

84-24-4.2
1976 *Promises to Keep*.
Artist: Irene Spencer.
Issue price: $40.00.

DeGrazia Children Series

Artist: Ted DeGrazia. Artist's
signature appears on front
China trimmed in 24k gold
Diameter: 26.5 centimeters
(10½ inches)
No hanger
Edition size: As indicated
Not numbered; without certificate

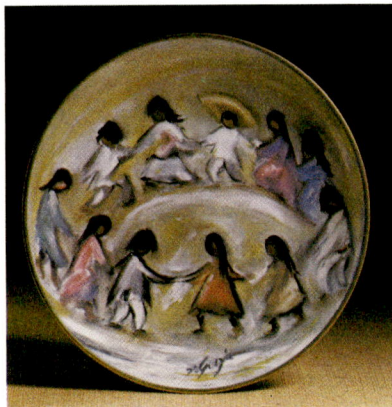

84-24-5.1
1976 *Los Niños*.
Issue price: $35.00.
Edition size limited to announced
quantity of 5,000.

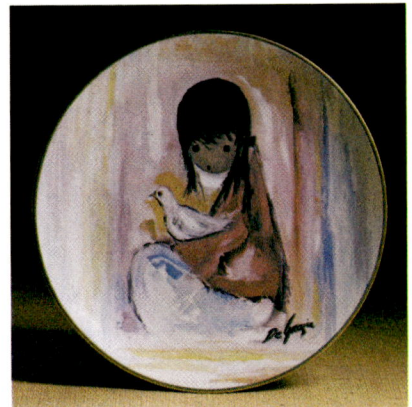

84-24-5.2
1977 *The White Dove*.
Issue price: $40.00.
Edition size limited to announced
quantity of 10,000.

GORHAM

(Providence, Rhode Island)

Sugar and Spice Series
Artist: Leo Jansen. Artist's
  signature appears on front
China trimmed in 24k gold
Diameter: 21.5 centimeters
  (8½ inches)
No hanger
Edition size limited to 7,500
Numbered without certificate

84-24-6.1
1976 *Dana and Debbie.*
Artist: Leo Jansen.
Issue price: $40.00.

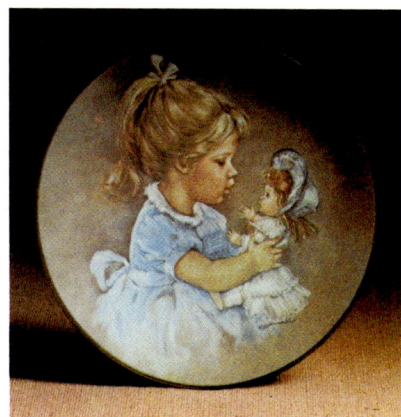

84-24-6.2
1977 *Becky and Baby.*
Artist: Leo Jansen.
Issue price: $42.50.

84-24-6.3
1978 *Jeanette and Julie.*
Artist: Leo Jansen.
Issue price: $47.50.

Prince Tatters Series

Artist: Leo Jansen. Artist's
   signature appears on front

China trimmed in 24k gold

Diameter: 21.5 centimeters
   (8½ inches)

No hanger

Edition size limited to 7,500

Numbered without certificate

84-24-8.1
1977 *Johnny and Duke.*
Artist: Leo Jansen.
Issue price: $40.00.

84-24-8.2
1978 *Randy and Rex.*
Artist: Leo Jansen.
Issue price: $42.50.

84-24-8.3
1979 *Furry Friends.*
Artist: Leo Jansen.
Issue price: $47.50.

84-31-0.0

UNITED STATES
INCOLAY

(San Fernando, California)

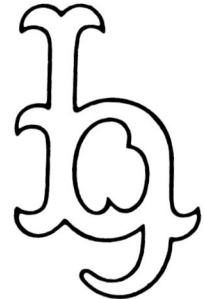

**Incolay Studios
of California**

Incolay Studios has been creating cameo objets d'art in Incolay stone since 1969. Incolay stone is a combination of minerals including two ingredients necessary for true cameos: semi-precious carnelian and crystal quartz.

Incolay Studios began its first series of collector's plates, *The Romantic Poets Collection*, in 1977. The series is inspired by the poetry of early nineteenth-century poets.

Romantic Poets Collection

Artist: Gayle Bright Appleby.
  Artist's signature appears on
  front

Incolay stone with high relief
  cameos

Diameter: 26 centimeters
  (10¼ inches)

Attached back hanger

Edition size undisclosed, limited
  by announced period of issue

Numbered with certificate

84-31-1.1
1977 She Walks in Beauty.
Artist: Gayle Bright Appleby.
Issue price: $60.00.

84-31-1.2
1978 A Thing of Beauty Is a Joy Forever.
Artist: Gayle Bright Appleby.
Issue price: $60.00.

84-31-1.3
1979 To A Skylark.
Artist: Gayle Bright Appleby.
Issue price: $60.00.

84-34-0.0

International Silver Company, one of the world's largest manufacturers of silver and silver-plated ware, traces its origin to a pewter shop established by Ashbil Griswold in Meriden in 1808. Rogers Brothers, developers of a silver electroplating process, became affiliated with the firm in 1862, and International Silver was incorporated in 1898.

The firm introduced limited-edition pewter plates in 1972 with its six-plate United States Bicentennial *We Are One Series*. The *Christmas Series* began in 1974.

We Are One
Bicentennial Series

Artist: Manuel de Oliviero (after) works by Carl Sundberg); artist's signature appears on back

Pewter with sculpted designs in high relief

Diameter: 22 centimeters (8¾ inches)

Attached back hanger

Edition size limited to 7,500

Numbered with certificate

84-34-1.1
1972 *Declaration of Independence.*
Artist: Manuel de Oliveiro.
Issue price: $40.00.

84-34-1.2
1973 *The Midnight Ride of Paul Revere.*
Artist: Manuel de Oliveiro.
Issue price: $40.00.

84-34-1.3
1973 *Stand at Concord Bridge.*
Artist: Manuel de Oliveiro.
Issue price: $40.00.

84-34-1.4
1974 *Crossing the Delaware.*
Artist: Manuel de Oliveiro.
Issue price: $50.00.

84-34-1.5
1974 *Battle of Valley Forge.*
Artist: Manuel de Oliveiro.
Issue price: $50.00.

84-34-1.6
1975 *Surrender at Yorktown.*
Artist: Manuel de Oliveiro.
Issue price: $50.00.

Christmas Series

Artist: As indicated. Artist's
  signature appears on back
Pewter with sculpted designs in
  high relief
Diameter: 24 centimeters
  (9⅜ inches)
Attached back hanger
Edition size limited to 7,500
Numbered with certificate

84-34-2.1
1974 *Tiny Tim.*
Artist: Carl Sundberg.
Issue price: $75.00.

84-34-2.2
1975 *Caught.*
Artist: Beverly Chase (after a work by
Thomas Nast).
Issue price: $75.00.

84-34-2.3
1976 *Bringing Home the Tree.*
Artist: Albert Petitto (after a work by
Emilie Mary Osborn).
Issue price: $75.00.

84-34-2.4
1977 *Fezziwig's Christmas Ball.*
Artist: Albert Petitto (after a work by
John Leech).
Issue price: $75.00.

84-34-2.5
1978 *Allelulia.*
Artist: Albert Petitto (after a work by
Uldis Klavina).
Issue price: $75.00.

84-34-2.6
1979 *Rejoice.*
Artist: Albert Pettito (after an Old
World engraving c. 1800).
Issue price: $100.00.

The story of Kern Collectibles began in 1969 when Oscar L. Kern founded Commemorative Imports, a distributor of limited-edition collectibles. Mr. Kern expanded his business one step further in 1972 with the establishment of Kern Collectibles. Since its first year, Kern Collectibles has issued limited-edition plates produced especially for the company by several of the world's fine china manufacturers.

The *Cowboy Artists Series*, produced for Kern Collectibles by Pickard, began in 1976. (See United States, PICKARD). The *Runci Mother's Day Series* started in 1977.

UNITED STATES
KERN COLLECTIBLES
(Stillwater, Minnesota)

Cowboy Artists Series
Artist: As indicated
China with 24k gold rim
Diameter: 29.5 centimeters
    (11⅝ inches)
Attached back hanger
Edition size: As indicated
Numbered; without certificate
Issued in pairs

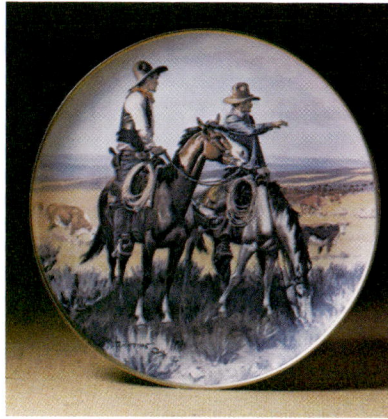

84-38-5.1
1976 *Out There.*
Artist: John Hampton.
Issue price: $130.00 (pair).
Edition size limited to 3,000.

84-38-5.1
1976 *Cutting Out a Stray.*
Artist: Charlie Dye.

84-38-5.2
1977 *The Broken Cinch.*
Artist: George Phippen.
Issue price: $130.00 (pair).
Edition size limited to 1,000.

84-38-5.2
1977 *No Place to Cross.*
Artist: Joe Beeler.

Runci Mother's Day Series
Artist: Edward Runci
Overglaze porcelain
Diameter: 19 centimeters
    (7½ inches)
Attached back hanger
Edition size limited to 5,000
Numbered without certificate

84-38-6.1
1977 *Darcy.*
Artist: Edward Runci.
Issue price: $50.00.

84-38-6.2
1978 *A Moment to Reflect.*
Artist: Edward Runci.
Issue price: $55.00.

84-38-6.3
1979 *Fulfillment*.
Artist: Edward Runci.
Issue price: $45.00.

The Knowles heritage of fine china can be traced to the early nineteenth century when Isaac Knowles, father of Edwin, established the family firm — Knowles, Taylor and Knowles — in East Liverpool, Ohio. The site was chosen for its proximity to deposits of high-quality kaolin clay. The firm became well known for its production of Lotus Ware.

After apprenticing with Knowles, Taylor and Knowles, Edwin established his own company in Newell, West Virginia. By the late 1880s, Edwin M. Knowles had become a preeminent force in American china. He was honored by election to the presidency of the United States Potters Association.

After his death, the company ceased operations for a period of time until entering into an affiliation with the Bradford Exchange in order to preserve its time-honored name.

Since 1975 the Edwin M. Knowles name has appeared on issues certified by the Rockwell Society of America (see United States, ROCKWELL SOCIETY). The *Wizard of Oz*, first proprietary series to bear the name of Knowles, began in 1977. The *Americana Holidays Series* and the *Gone With The Wind Series*, which is endorsed by Metro-Goldwyn-Mayer, began in 1978.

UNITED STATES
EDWIN M. KNOWLES
(Newell, West Virginia)

Wizard of Oz Series

Artist: James Auckland. Artist's
  signature appears on front
China
Diameter: 21.5 centimeters
  (8½ inches)
No hanger
Edition size undisclosed, limited
  by announced period of issue
Numbered with certificate

84-41-1.1
1977 *Over the Rainbow.*
Artist: James Auckland.
Issue price: $19.00.

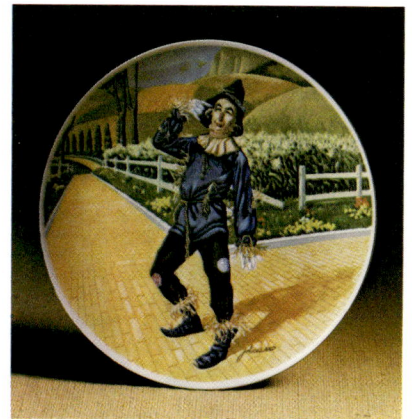

84-41-1.2
1978 *If I Only Had a Brain.*
Artist: James Auckland.
Issue price: $19.00.

84-41-1.3
1978 *If I Only Had a Heart.*
Artist: James Auckland.
Issue price: $19.00.

84-41-1.4
1978 *If I Were King of the Forest.*
Artist: James Auckland.
Issue price: $19.00.

84-41-1.5
1979 *The Wicked Witch of the West.*
Artist: James Auckland.
Issue price: $19.00.

84-41-1.6
1979 *Follow the Yellow Brick Road.*
Artist: James Auckland.
Issue price: $19.00.

Americana Holidays Series
Artist: Don Spaulding
China
Diameter: 21.5 centimeters
(8½ inches)
No hanger
Edition size undisclosed, limited
by period of issue
Numbered with certificate

Maker had
no photo at
press time

84-41-2.1
1978 *Fourth of July*.
Artist: Don Spaulding.
Issue price: $26.00.

84-41-2.2
1979 *Thanksgiving*.
Artist: Don Spaulding.
Issue price: $26.00.

EDWIN M. KNOWLES

(Newell, West Virginia)

Gone With the Wind Series

Artist: Raymond Kursár
China
Diameter: 21.5 centimeters
(8½ inches)
No hanger
Edition size undisclosed, limited
by period of issue
Numbered with certificate

84-41-3.1
1978 *Scarlett.*
Artist: Raymond Kursár.
Issue price: $21.50.

LENOX

Walter Scott Lenox and his partner, Jonathan Coxon, Sr., established the Ceramic Art Company in Trenton, New Jersey, in 1889. In 1895 Lenox bought out Coxon and operated the business alone until it was reorganized in 1906 as Lenox, Inc. The plant later moved to Pomona. The firm's early products were bowls, vases, figurines, and later, tableware. All were made in "American Belleek," named for the town in Ireland where this creamy, ivory-tinted ware was first produced.

During World War I, Lenox was commissioned to supply President Wilson with a complete 1,700 piece dinner service, the first wholly American china ever used in the White House. Later both Presidents Franklin Roosevelt and Harry Truman commissioned Lenox to make sets of dinnerware. The etched gold and green Truman service is still in use at the White House.

In 1970 Lenox introduced its *American Bird Series* using paintings by renowned wildlife artist, Edward Marshall Boehm. The *Boehm Woodland Wildlife Series* began in 1973 with artwork adapted from original Boehm sculptures.

American Bird Series

Artist: Edward Marshall Boehm.
  Artist's name appears on back
China with 24k gold decoration
Diameter: 26.5 centimeters
  (10½ inches)
No hanger
Edition size undisclosed
Not numbered;without certificate

84-47-1.1
1970 *Wood Thrush.*
Artist: Edward Marshall Boehm.
Issue price: $35.00.

84-47-1.2
1971 *Goldfinch.*
Artist: Edward Marshall Boehm.
Issue price: $35.00.

84-47-1.3
1972 *Mountain Bluebird.*
Artist: Edward Marshall Boehm.
Issue price: $37.50.

84-47-1.4
1973 *Meadowlark.*
Artist: Edward Marshall Boehm.
Issue price: $41.00.

84-47-1.5
1974 *Rufous Hummingbird.*
Artist: Edward Marshall Boehm.
Issue price: $45.00.

84-47-1.6
1975 *American Redstart.*
Artist: Edward Marshall Boehm.
Issue price: $50.00.

84-47-1.7
1976 *Cardinal.*
Artist: Edward Marshall Boehm.
Issue price: $53.00.

84-47-1.8
1977 *Robins.*
Artist: Edward Marshall Boehm.
Issue price: $55.00.

84-47-1.9
1978 Mockingbirds.
Artist: Edward Marshall Boehm.
Issue price: $58.00.

Boehm Woodland Wildlife Series

Artist: Edward Marshall Boehm.
  Artist's name appears on back
China with 24k gold decoration
Diameter: 26.5 centimeters
  (10½ inches)
No hanger
Edition size undisclosed
Not numbered; without certificate

84-47-3.1
1973 Raccoons.
Artist: Edward Marshall Boehm.
Issue price: $50.00.

84-47-3.2
1974 Red Fox.
Artist: Edward Marshall Boehm.
Issue price: $52.50.

84-47-3.3
1975 Rabbits.
Artist: Edward Marshall Boehm.
Issue price: $58.50.

84-47-3.4
1976 Eastern Chipmunks.
Artist: Edward Marshall Boehm.
Issue price: $62.50.

84-47-3.5
1977 Beaver.
Artist: Edward Marshall Boehm.
Issue price: $67.50.

UNITED STATES
LENOX
(Pomona, New Jersey)

84-47-3.6
1978 *White Tail Deer.*
Artist: Edward Marshall Boehm.
Issue price: $70.00.

84-47-3.7
1979 *Squirrels.*
Artist: Edward Marshall Boehm.
Issue price: $76.00.

Pickard

Pickard was established in Edgerton, Wisconsin, in 1894 by Wilder Austin Pickard, then moved to Chicago in 1897. For some forty years the Pickard China Studio, as the firm was then known, was a decorating company employing artists to hand paint white blanks of bowls, pitchers and other items obtained from factories in Europe.

In 1920 Pickard was incorporated and in 1938 moved to Antioch, Illinois, the site of the present pottery. Here the firm began making its own fine china. Today Pickard, Inc. is headed by Henry Pickard, a third generation descendant of the founder, making it the only American china company in the hands of the founding family.

In 1970 Pickard introduced its *Wildlife Series*. These plates were issued in pairs during the first four years of the series, but from 1974 individual plates were issued. The *Christmas Series* began in 1976, and in 1978 Pickard began the *Children of Renoir Series* in which two plates are issued each year.

PICKARD

(Antioch, Illinois)

Lockhart Wildlife Series
Artist: James Lockhart. Artist's
  signature appears on front
China with 23k gold design on the
  border
Diameter: As indicated
No hanger
Edition size: As indicated
Numbered with certificate

84-50-1.1
1970 *Woodcock.*
Artist: James Lockhart.
Diameter: 10½ inches.
Issue price: $150.00 (pair).
Edition size limited to 2,000.

84-50-1.1
1970 *Ruffed Grouse.*

84-50-1.2
1971 *Green-Winged Teal.*
Artist: James Lockhart.
Diameter: 10½ inches.
Issue price: $150.00 (pair).
Edition size limited to 2,000.

84-50-1.2
1971 *Mallard.*

84-50-1.3
1972 *Mockingbird.*
Artist: James Lockhart.
Diameter: 10½ inches.
Issue price: $162.50 (pair).
Edition size limited to 2,000.

84-50-1.3
1972 *Cardinal.*

84-50-1.4
1973 *Wild Turkey.*
Artist: James Lockhart.
Diameter: 10½ inches.
Issue price: $162.50 (pair).
Edition size limited to 2,000.

84-50-1.4
1973 *Ring-Necked Pheasant.*

84-50-1.5
1974 *American Bald Eagle.*
Artist: James Lockhart.
Diameter: 13 inches.
Issue price: $150.00.
Edition size limited to 2,000.

84-50-1.6
1975 *White-Tailed Deer.*
Artist: James Lockhart.
Diameter: 11 inches.
Issue price: $100.00.
Edition size limited to 2,500.

84-50-1.7
1976 *The American Buffalo.*
Artist: James Lockhart.
Diameter: 13 inches.
Issue price: $165.00.
Edition size limited to 2,500.

84-50-1.8
1977 *Great Horned Owl.*
Artist: James Lockhart.
Diameter: 11 inches.
Issue price: $100.00.
Edition size limited to 2,500.

84-50-1.9
1978 *American Panther.*
Artist: James Lockhart.
Diameter: 13 inches.
Issue price: $175.00.
Edition size limited to 2,000.

84-50-1.10
1979 *The Red Foxes.*
Artist: James Lockhart.
Issue price: $120.00.
Edition size limited to 2,500.

Christmas Series

Artist: As indicated
China with 23k gold design on the
    border
Diameter: 21.5 centimeters
    (8⅜ inches)
No hanger
Edition size: As indicated
Numbered without certificate

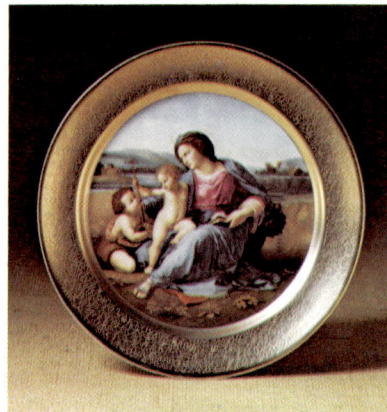

84-50-2.1
1976 *The Alba Madonna.*
Artist: Raphael.
Issue price: $60.00.
Edition size limited to 7,500.

84-50-2.2
1977 *The Nativity.*
Artist: Lorenzo Lotto.
Issue price: $65.00.
Edition size limited to 7,500.

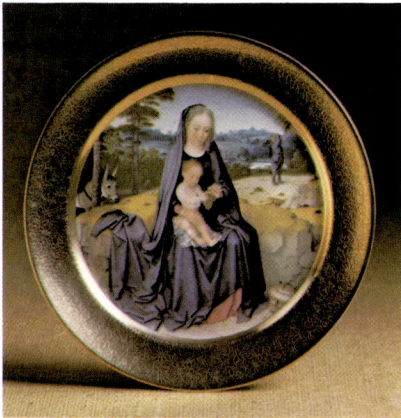

84-50-2.3
1978 *The Rest on the Flight into Egypt.*
Artist: Gerard David.
Issue price: $65.00.
Edition size limited to 10,000.

The Children of Renoir Series

Artist: Auguste Renoir. Artist's
name appears on back
China with 23k gold rim
Diameter: 21 centimeters
(8¼ inches)
No hanger
Edition size limited to 5,000
Numbered without certificate

84-50-4.1
1978 *A Girl with a Watering Can.*
Artist: Auguste Renoir.
Issue price: $50.00.

84-50-4.2
1978 *Child in White.*
Artist: Auguste Renoir.
Issue price: $50.00.

84-50-4.3
1979 *Girl With Hoop.*
Artist: Auguste Renoir.
Issue price: $55.00.

84-60-0.0

Reco

Reco International was founded in 1967 by Heio W. Reich who continues as its president. From the beginning the firm has been an importer and maker of limited-edition plates.

World of Children, Reco International's first proprietary series, was introduced in 1977. A second series also with artwork by John McClelland, the *Mother Goose Series,* was introduced in 1979.

RECO INTERNATIONAL

(Port Washington, New York)

The World of Children Series

Artist: John McClelland. Artist's
  signature appears on front
China with 24k gold rim
Diameter: 26.5 centimeters
  (10½ inches)
No hanger
Edition size: As indicated
Numbered with certificate since
  1978

84-60-1.1
1977 *Rainy Day Fun.*
Artist: John McClelland.
Issue price: $50.00.
Edition size limited to 10,000.

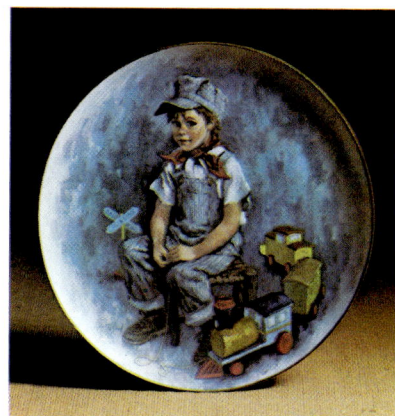

84-60-1.2
1978 *When I Grow Up.*
Artist: John McClelland.
Issue price: $50.00.
Edition size limited to 15,000.

84-60-1.3
1979 *You're Invited.*
Artist: John McClelland.
Issue price: $50.00.
Edition size limited to 15,000.

John McClelland's Mother Goose Series

Artist: John McClelland
China
Diameter: 22 centimeters
  (8½ inches)
No hanger
Edition size unannounced
Numbered with certificate

84-60-2.1
1979 *Mary, Mary.* 34.50
Artist: John McClelland.
Issue price: Unavailable at press time.

84-65-0.0

UNITED STATES
REED & BARTON
(Taunton, Massachusetts)

Reed & Barton Silversmiths traces its origin to a factory established by Isaac Babbitt in the early nineteenth century. In 1824 Babbitt developed an alloy, harder and more lustrous than pewter, which he named Britannia metal. Henry G. Reed and Charles E. Barton, artists working for Babbitt, acquired the firm in the 1830s and continued to manufacture Britannia ware. In the late 1840s, the factory began to produce plated silverware. Reed & Barton was incorporated in 1888 and started producing solid silver services. Sterling flatware and holloware soon replaced plated ware as their largest line. In 1903 the firm began reproducing colonial pewter ware.

Reed & Barton patented an electroplating process known as damascene silver that combines silver, gold, copper and bronze. The process was developed by artist Robert Johnson from a hand-done process perfected at Damascus in the middle ages. All Reed & Barton collector's plates are crafted in damascene silver.

In 1970 Reed & Barton began their *Christmas Series* which changes theme every three years. The first three plates are based on Christmas carols; the second three are based on fifteenth-century altar art; the next are based on American Christmas scenes; and the next depict nineteenth-century American illustrations.

Christmas Series

Artist: As indicated

Damascene silver

Diameter: 28 centimeters
(11 inches) through 1978;
thereafter, 20.3 centimeters
(8 inches)

No hanger

Edition size: As indicated

Numbered without certificate
through 1978; thereafter not
numbered accompanied with
numbered certificate

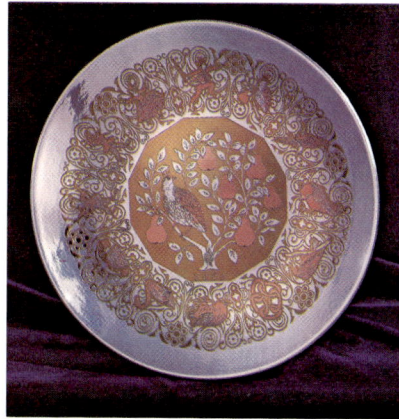

84-65-2.1
1970 *A Partridge in a Pear Tree.*
Artist: Robert Johnson.
Issue price: $55.00.
Edition size limited to 2,500.

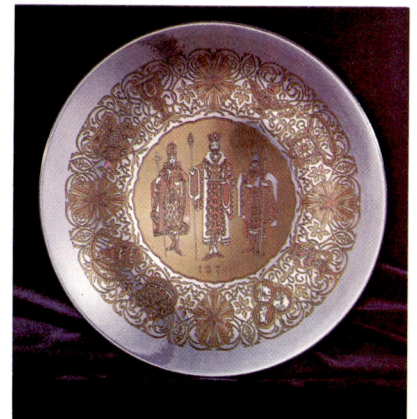

84-65-2.2
1971 *We Three Kings of Orient Are.*
Artist: Robert Johnson.
Issue price: $60.00.
Edition size limited to 7,500.

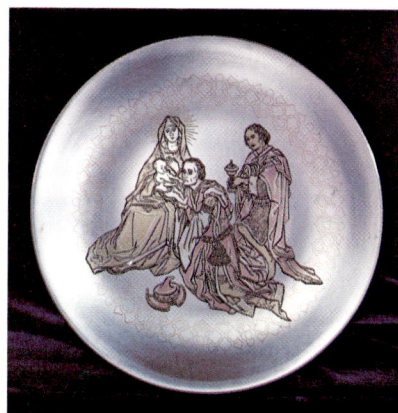

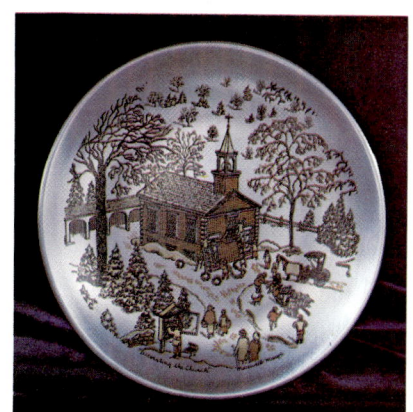

84-65-2.3
1972 *Hark! The Herald Angels Sing.*
Artist: Robert Johnson.
Issue price: $60.00.
Edition size limited to 7,500.

84-65-2.4
1973 *Adoration of the Kings.*
Artist: Rogier van der Weyden.
Issue price: $60.00.
Edition size limited to 7,500.

84-65-2.5
1974 *The Adoration of the Magi.*
Artist: Fra Angelico and Fra Lippi.
Issue price: $65.00.
Edition size limited to 7,500.

84-65-2.6
1975 *Adoration of the Kings.*
Artist: Steven Lochner.
Issue price: $65.00.
Edition size limited to 7,500.

84-65-2.7
1976 *Morning Train.*
Artist: Maxwell Mays.
Issue price: $65.00.
Edition size limited to 7,500.

84-65-2.8
1977 *Decorating the Church.*
Artist: Maxwell Mays.
Issue price: $65.00.
Edition size limited to 7,500.

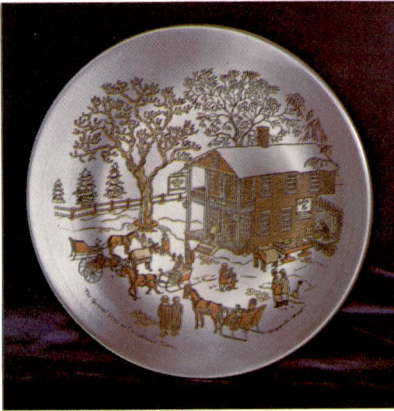

Maker had
no photo at
presstime

84-65-2.9
1978 *The General Store at
Christmas Time.*
Artist: Maxwell Mays.
Issue price: $65.00.
Edition size limited to 7,500.

84-65-2.10
1979 *Merry Old Santa Claus.*
Artist: Thomas Nast.
Issue price: $50.00.

UNITED STATES
RIVER SHORE, LTD.
(Caledonia, Michigan)

River Shore, Ltd.®

Creators of Museum Quality Limited Editions

River Shore Productions, established in 1975, specializes in the distribution of medallic art.

In 1976 River Shore began its *Famous Americans* series, the first collector's plates crafted in copper, based on artwork by Norman Rockwell.

RIVER SHORE, LTD.

(Caledonia, Michigan)

Famous Americans Series

Artist: Roger Brown (after works
   by Norman Rockwell). Artist's
   signature appears on front along
   with name of Norman Rockwell

Copper

Diameter: 20.5 centimeters
   (8 inches)

No hanger

Edition size limited to 9,500

Numbered with certificate

84-69-1.1
1976 Lincoln.
Artist: Roger Brown.
Issue price: $40.00.

84-69-1.2
1977 Rockwell.
Artist: Roger Brown.
Issue price: $45.00.

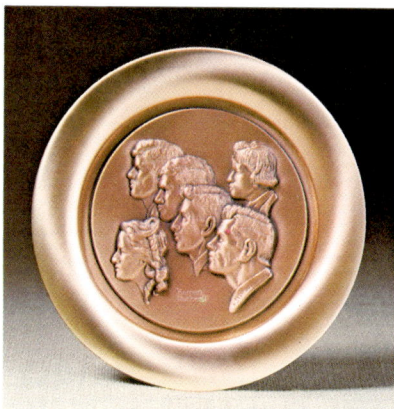

84-69-1.3
1978 Peace Corps.
Artist: Roger Brown.
Issue price: $45.00.

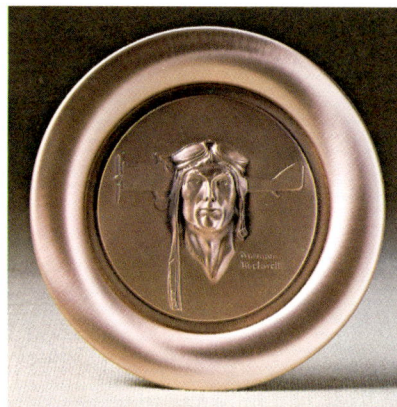

84-69-1.4
1979 Spirit of Lindbergh.
Artist: Roger Brown.
Issue price: $50.00.

UNITED STATES
ROCKWELL SOCIETY
(Stony Brook, New York)

The Rockwell Society of America is a chartered non-profit organization devoted to the study and appreciation of the works of Norman Rockwell. The Society's *Christmas Series* began in 1974, with the first issue manufactured by Ridgewood. Subsequent issues have been made by the Edwin M. Knowles China Company (see United States, KNOWLES). The *Mother's Day Series* started in 1976 and in 1977 The *Rockwell Heritage Series* began.

Christmas Series
Artist: Norman Rockwell. Artist's
  signature appears on front
China
Diameter: 21 centimeters
  (8½ inches)
Attached back hanger
Edition size undisclosed, limited
  by announced period of issue
Numbered with certificate

84-70-1.1
1974 *Scotty Gets His Tree.*
Artist: Norman Rockwell.
Issue price: $24.50.

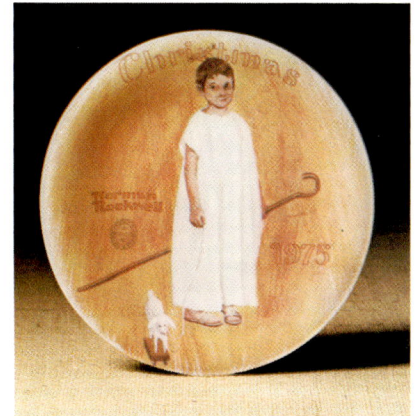

84-70-1.2
1975 *Angel with a Black Eye.*
Artist: Norman Rockwell.
Issue price: $24.50.

84-70-1.3
1976 *Golden Christmas.*
Artist: Norman Rockwell.
Issue price: $24.50.

84-70-1.4
1977 *Toy Shop Window.*
Artist: Norman Rockwell.
Issue price: $24.50.

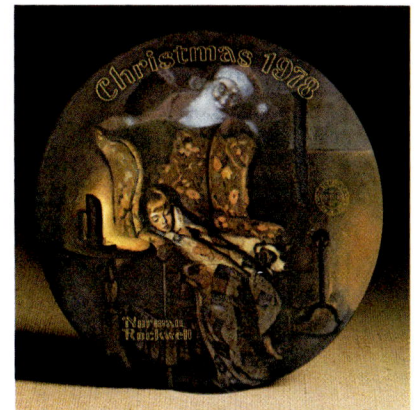

84-70-1.5
1978 *Christmas Dream.*
Artist: Norman Rockwell.
Issue price: $24.50.

Mother's Day Series

Artist: Norman Rockwell. Artist's
  signature appears on front

China

Diameter: 21 centimeters
  (8½ inches)

Attached back hanger

Edition size undisclosed, limited
  by announced period of issue

Numbered with certificate

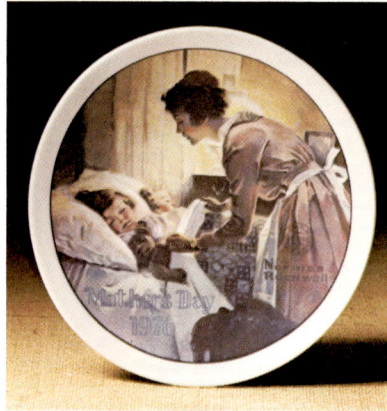

84-70-2.1
1976 *A Mother's Love.*
Artist: Norman Rockwell.
Issue price: $24.50.

84-70-2.2
1977 *Faith.*
Artist: Norman Rockwell.
Issue price: $24.50.

84-70-2.3
1978 *Bedtime.*
Artist: Norman Rockwell.
Issue price: $24.50.

84-70-2.4
1979 *Reflections.*
Artist: Norman Rockwell.
Issue price: $24.50.

Rockwell Heritage Series

Artist: Norman Rockwell. Artist's
  signature appears on front

China

Diameter: 21 centimeters
  (8¼ inches)

Attached back hanger

Edition size undisclosed, limited
  by announced period of issue

Numbered with certificate

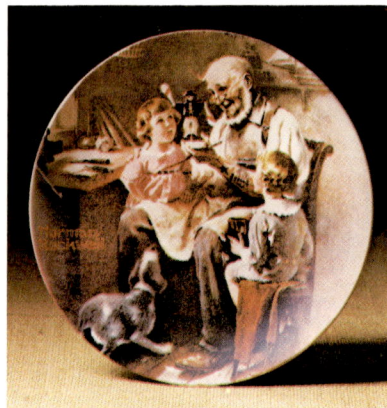

84-70-3.1
1977 *The Toy Maker.*
Artist: Norman Rockwell.
Issue price: $14.50.

84-70-3.2
1978 *The Cobbler.*
Artist: Norman Rockwell.
Issue price: $19.50.

84-70-3.3
1979 *Lighthouse Keeper's Daughter.*
Artist: Norman Rockwell.
Issue price: $19.50.

84-76-0.0

Royal Devon
MADE IN USA

Royal Devon plates are manufactured by
the Gorham Company (see United States,
GORHAM). Both the *Christmas Series* and
Mother's Day Series, bearing artwork by
Norman Rockwell, began in 1975.

(Providence, Rhode Island)

Christmas Series

Artist: Norman Rockwell. Artist's signature appears on front

China

Diameter: 21.5 centimeters (8½ inches)

No hanger

Edition size undisclosed, limited by year of issue

Not numbered; without certificate

84-76-1.1
1975 *Downhill Daring.*
Artist: Norman Rockwell.
Issue price: $24.50.

84-76-1.2
1976 *The Christmas Gift.*
Artist: Norman Rockwell.
Issue price: $24.50.

84-76-1.3
1977 *The Big Moment.*
Artist: Norman Rockwell.
Issue price: $27.50.

84-76-1.4
1978 *Puppets for Christmas.*
Artist: Norman Rockwell.
Issue price: $27.50.

Maker had
no photo at
presstime

84-76-1.5
1979 *One Package Too Many.*
Artist: Norman Rockwell.
Issue price: Not available at press time.

Mother's Day Series

Artist: Norman Rockwell. Artist's signature appears on front

China

Diameter: 21.5 centimeters (8½ inches)

No hanger

Edition size undisclosed, limited by year of issue

Not numbered; without certificate

84-76-2.1
1975 *Doctor and the Doll.*
Artist: Norman Rockwell.
Issue price: $23.50.

84-76-2.2
1976 *Puppy Love.*
Artist: Norman Rockwell.
Issue price: $24.50.

84-76-2.3
1977 *The Family.*
Artist: Norman Rockwell.
Issue price: $24.50.

84-76-2.4
1978 *Mother's Day Off.*
Artist: Norman Rockwell.
Issue price: $27.00.

84-76-2.5
1979 *Mother's Evening Out.*
Artist: Norman Rockwell.
Issue price: $30.00.

Royal Worcester is the American subsidiary of the English company of the same name. (See England, ROYAL WORCESTER). The firm was established in the United States after World War II.

In 1972 Royal Worcester initiated the *Birth of a Nation Series* of five annual pewter plates to commemorate the Bicentennial of the United States.

(Hudson, Massachusetts)

Birth of a Nation Series
Artist: Prescott Baston
Pewter with designs in bas-relief
Diameter: 26 centimeters
   (10¼ inches)
No hanger
Edition size limited to 10,000
Numbered without certificate

84-82-1.1
1972 *Boston Tea Party.*
Artist: Prescott Baston.
Issue price: $45.00.

84-82-1.2
1973 *The Ride of Paul Revere.*
Artist: Prescott Baston.
Issue price: $45.00.

84-82-1.3
1974 *Incident at Concord Bridge.*
Artist: Prescott Baston.
Issue price: $50.00.

84-82-1.4
1975 *Signing of the Declaration of
Independence.*
Artist: Prescott Baston.
Issue price: $65.00.

84-82-1.5
1976 *Washington Crossing the Delaware.*
Artist: Prescott Baston.
Issue price: $65.00.

FINE CHINA BY VILETTA

U.S.A.

Viletta China Company was started in 1959 in Roseberg, Oregon, by Viletta West who hand painted china and sold it through stores in the Pacific Northwest. The firm is involved in many areas of the giftware and fine china field, including commemorative china items and limited-edition collector's plates.

In 1978 Viletta China moved from Roseberg to Houston, Texas.

The *Zolan's Children Series* and the *Nutcracker Ballet Plate Collection* began in 1978.

VILETTA
(Houston, Texas)

Zolan's Children Series
Artist: Donald Zolan
China
Diameter: 21.5 centimeters
(8½ inches)
No hanger
Edition size undisclosed, limited
by period of issue
Numbered with certificate

84-91-1.1
1978 *Erik and Dandelion.*
Artist: Donald Zolan.
Issue price: $19.00.

84-91-1.2
1979 *Sabina in the Grass.*
Artist: Donald Zolan.
Issue price: $22.00.

Nutcracker Ballet Plate Collection
Artist: Shell Fisher
China
Diameter: 21.5 centimeters
(8½ inches)
No hanger
Edition size undisclosed, limited
by year of issue
Numbered with certificate

84-91-2.1
1978 *Clara and Nutcracker.*
Artist: Shell Fisher.
Issue price: $19.50.

84-91-2.2
1979 *Gift From Godfather.*
Artist: Shell Fisher.
Issue price: $19.50.

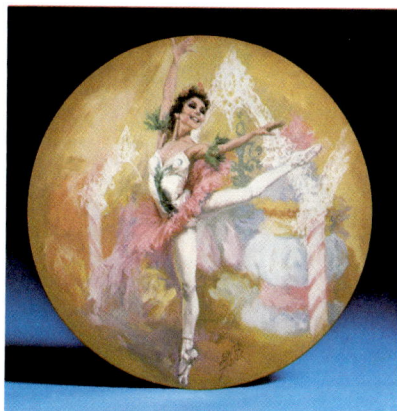

84-91-2.3
1979 *The Sugarplum Fairy.*
Artist: Shell Fisher.
Issue price: $19.50.

GLOSSARY OF COMMONLY USED TERMS

A

AFTERMARKET See MARKET.

ALABASTER A dense, fine-grained form of gypsum (calcium sulfate) stone, usually white to pink and slightly translucent. Alabaster stone can be carved in fine detail for ornamental objects and hardened by intense heat. Italian alabaster is also called Florentine marble. Ivory alabaster is composed of alabaster but is non-translucent and acquires a patina with age like that of old ivory.

ALLOTMENT A number of plates, all alike and usually at issue, allocated by a maker to a distributor or dealer. See LOT.

ALLOY Two or more metals combined while molten. Alloying is done to achieve hardness, toughness, or luster. See PEWTER.

ANNUAL A plate issued once each year as part of a series. The term is most often used when a plate does not commemorate a specific holiday.

ANNULAR KILN A round oven made from brick used to fire ceramic plates.

ART DECO, ART DECORATIF A style of decoration popular in Europe and America from 1920 to 1945. The Art Deco movement sought to glorify progress and the future by using as motifs such shapes as the cylinder, circle, rectangle, and cone.

ART NOUVEAU A style of decoration in Europe and America from 1890 to 1920. The Art Nouveau movement used twisting vegetable forms as its primary decorative motifs.

ASKED PRICE The price posted for a plate by a seller on the Exchange.

AT ISSUE A plate being offered for sale at the time of its manufacture and at the original price set by the maker.

B

BACKSTAMP The information on the back of a plate, usually including the maker's signature or name (logotype). It may also record serial number, title, artist's signature, explanation of the plate, sponsor, production techniques, awards, or release initials. It may be stamped, incised (cut or pressed), or applied as a decalcomania.

BAROQUE An elaborate style of decoration developed in Europe in the seventeenth and eighteenth centuries and noted for exaggerated gesture and line. Example: Dresden plates (22-15-0.0).

BAS-RELIEF See RELIEF SCULPTURE.

BAVARIA A province in the southwest corner of Germany long known as a center for porcelain factories. The region contains large deposits of kaolin, the key porcelain component.

BEDROOM DEALER A trade term for a small dealer who usually operates from his home, buys discounted plates and resells them for a small profit.

BID PRICE The amount a prospective buyer offers to pay for a plate on the Exchange.

BISQUE, BISCUIT A plate that has been fired but not glazed, leaving it with a matte texture. So called because of the biscuit-like appearance. Example: Lladró plates (72-46-0.0).

BLUE CHIP An established series by a well-known maker in which nearly every issue shows a steady sequence of price rises above issue price.

BODY 1. The formula or combination of substances that make up potter's clay, generally referring to stoneware and earthenware. 2. The basic plate form to which ornamentation is applied.

BONE ASH Calcium phosphate, a component of bone china, added to give whiteness and translucency. It is obtained by calcinating (reducing to powder by heat) animal bones, usually those of oxen.

BONE CHINA (BONE PORCELAIN) A type of china developed by Josiah Spode in England in the 1790s. By replacing part of the kaolin in the china formula with bone ash, greater translucency and whiteness is obtained at lower firing temperatures. The finest bone china contains up to 50% bone ash. It is the most commonly made china in England. Examples: Royal Doulton (26-69-0.0), Royal Worcester, England (26-78-0.0) plates.

BULLISH Marked by rising prices, either actual or expected, and optimistic atmosphere. A *bull market* is one of rising prices.

BUY ORDER A bid offered by an individual or dealer to purchase one or more plates of the same edition on the secondary market. See EXCHANGE.

C

CAMEO EFFECT Ornamentation in relief on a background of contrasting color to resemble a cameo. Examples: Wedgwood Jasperware plates (26-90-0.0) and Incolay Studios (84-31-0.0).

CELSIUS, CENTIGRADE The thermometric scale in which $0°$ represents the freezing point of water and $100°$ the boiling point. Celsius temperature is denoted by "C" after the number.

CERAMIC A general term applying to all of the various plates made from clay and hardened by firing.

CERTIFICATE An attestation of authenticity which may accompany each plate in an edition. A certificate authenticates a plate as being part of an issue and usually confirms the plate's individual number within the edition.

CHINA, CHINAWARE A hard, vitreous ceramic whose main components are kaolin and china stone fired at high temperature. Originally the term was used for these ceramics which only came from China. Later it was applied to all "hard" and "soft" *porcelain*. China is often used as a generic term which includes *porcelain*, but is properly distinguished from it by a high bisque firing temperature and a low glaze firing temperature. The main firing (bisque) of china is approximately 7% lower than the main firing (glaze) of *porcelain*. In china production, the glaze is applied after the main firing and fixed with a second lower-temperature firing. A typical china formula is 40% kaolin, 10% ball clay, and varying proportions of china stone, feldspar and flint. See PORCELAIN.

CHINA CLAY See KAOLIN.

CHINA STONE, PETUNTSE A feldspathic material in china formulas. China stone acts as a flux which helps dissolve and fuse the other components into a vitreous mass.

CHRISTMAS PLATES, CHRISTMAS SERIES Annual plates issued to commemorate Christmas, usually as part of a series. Plate names for Christmas include Noël (French), Weinachten (German), Jul (Danish), Navidad (Spanish and Portugese), and Natale (Italian). The oldest Christmas series is that of Bing & Grondahl, produced continuously since 1895 **(14-8-1.0)**.

CLAY Any of various plastic, viscous earths used to make plates. It is formed by the decomposition, due to weathering, of igneous rocks such as granite, feldspar, and pegmatite.

CLOSED-END SERIES A series of plates with a predetermined number of issues. Example: Haviland *Twelve Days of Christmas* series **(18-30-1.0)**. See OPEN-END SERIES.

COBALT BLUE Cobalt oxide in the form of a dark black powder which, when fired, turns a deep blue. It was the first known and is still the most commonly used ceramic underglaze color because of its ability to withstand high firing temperatures. It can produce a variety of shades. Examples: Kaiser cobalt blue **(22-42-0.0)**, Bing & Grondahl Copenhagen blue **(14-8-0.0)**, Royal Copenhagen Danish blue **(14-69-0.0)**, Rorstrand Scandia blue **(76-69-0.0)**.

COLLECTOR'S PLATE A decorative plate produced in a limited edition for the purpose of being collected. Although the earliest plates were not produced with this objective, they have since acquired the name by virtue of being collected and are now produced for this purpose.

COMMEMORATIVE PLATE A plate produced in remembrance of an event. Example: D'Arceau-Limoges *Lafayette Legacy* **(18-15-1.0)**.

COTERIE PLATE A collector's plate with a limited following whose trading is too infrequent to be listed on the Exchange but which may be traded over the counter.

CRYSTAL See LEAD CRYSTAL

CUT GLASS Glass decorated by the cutting of grooves and facets, usually done with a copper engraver's wheel.

D

DAMASCENE An electro-plating effect created and patented by Reed & Barton **(84-65-0.0)** of etching and then depositing layers of gold, copper and silver on bronze. Originally the term referred to the art, developed in Damascus, of ornamenting iron or steel with inlaid precious metals.

DEALER A marketer of plates who buys primarily from makers or distributors and sells primarily to the public.

DELFTWARE Earthenware covered with an opaque white glaze made of stannic oxide, an oxide of tin. Originally developed in Delft, Holland in the sixteenth century,

Delftware has the appearance of being covered with a thick white paint. Similar ware is the *Majolica* of Italy and *Faience* of France and Germany. See FAIENCE, MAJOLICA.

DISTRIBUTOR A marketer of plates who buys from manufacturers and sells to dealers. Some distributors also act as makers and as dealers.

DRESDEN, MEISSEN Nearby cities in eastern Germany where the first hard-paste porcelain outside of China was produced by Johann Fredrich Bottger in 1708.

E

EARTHENWARE A term for any ceramics which are not vitrified. Typical Components of earthenware are 43% ball clay, 24% kaolin, 23% flint and 10% pegmatite. Fired earthenware is normally covered with either a transparent or opaque glaze. *High-fired earthenware* is fired at a higher temperature to produce a harder ware. Example: Royal Doulton Christmas plates **(26-69-1.0)**.

EDITION The total number of plates, all with the same decoration, produced by a maker. Editions of collector's plates are normally limited to a fixed number and are not repeated.

ELECTRO-PLATING A process by which metal plates are coated with another metal by electrical charges.

EMBOSSED DESIGN Raised ornamentation produced by the plate mold or by stamping a design into the body of the plate. Example: BELLEEK plates **(26-8-0.0)**.

ENAMEL A glaze material colored with suspended mineral oxides for decorating plates.

ENGRAVED DESIGN Decoration produced by cutting into the surface of metal, glass or china plates with either a tool or acid, as in etching. Example: Veneto Flair plates **(38-84-0.0)**.

ETCHED DESIGN Decoration produced by cutting into the surface of a plate with acid. The plate is first covered with an acid-resistant paint or wax, and the design is carved through this coating. When the plate is immersed in acid, the acid "bites" into the plate surface in the shape of the design. Example: Franklin Mint silver plates **(84-19-0.0)**.

EXCHANGE A place where plates are traded, most commonly the Bradford Exchange, the world's largest trading center. Incorporated in 1962, it was formerly known as Bradford Galleries Exchange.

F

FAIENCE Tin-enameled earthenware from France, Germany, or Spain developed in the seventeenth century and named for the Italian town of Faenza, a center for *Majolica*, another name for this ware. See DELFTWARE.

FELDSPAR A mineral composed of aluminum silicates with either potassium, sodium, calcium, or barium. Feldspar decomposes to form kaolin, the key ingredient of china and porcelain. The addition of undecomposed feldspar to china formulas gives the ware greater hardness.

FIRE The heating process which hardens ceramic plates in a kiln. Ceramic clay begins to undergo chemical change at 500° C and vitrifies around 1300° C.

FIRST EDITION The first, and presumably the only, edition of a collector's plate. The term (or its abbreviation "FE") is sometimes used for the edition which is the *first*

issue in a series of collector's plates. However, since no edition is normally ever reopened and therefore no "second edition" is possible, all issues of collector's plates are properly termed first editions.

FIRST ISSUE Chronologically, the first plate in a series, i.e., the plates issued in the first year of an annual series.

FLUX Finely ground material added to porcelain formulas which lowers the vitrification temperature and helps fuse the components. Example: Feldspar.

G

GLAZE Glassy, hard surface coating on plates made of silicates (glass-forming compounds) and mineral oxides. Glaze is put on ceramic ware to make it wear-resistant, waterproof, decorative, and to seal the pores. Glaze material suspended in water is applied after the first firing and is heated to the glaze's vitrification point when it fuses to the plate body. Glaze is applied by dipping, spraying, or painting. Decorating is added under, over, or with the glaze layer. See UNDERGLAZE.

I

INCISED DESIGN Ornamentation cut into the body of the plate.

INCOLAY STONE The material from which the cameo-like plates produced by Incolay Studios are made. Incolay stone contains, among other minerals, both semi-precious carnelian and crystal quartz. See INCOLAY STUDIOS, **(84-31-0.0).**

INLAID Decoration on a plate created by etching, incising or engraving a design on the surface and filling with another material.

INTAGLIO Decoration created by cutting beneath the surface of the plate. See ENGRAVED DESIGN or ETCHED DESIGN.

IRIDESCENCE A rainbow effect on a plate's surface caused by the diffraction of light. True iridescent color effects are readily distinguished from a plate's inherent color because the pattern will change as the plate is moved. Example: BELLEEK plates **(26-8-0.0).**

ISSUE 1. The release for sale of an edition of plates by a maker. 2. A plate in an edition. 3. An edition within a series.

ISSUE PRICE Original or first price of plate established by the maker at the time the plate is released for sale.

J

JASPER WARE Hard, fine-grained, unglazed stoneware made by adding barium sulfate to clay, developed by Josiah Wedgwood in the 1770s. The term "jasper" does not indicate the presence of jasper stone but most likely denotes the varieties of colors in which Jasper ware can be produced. Though white in its original form, Jasper ware can be stained in blue, green, lilac, yellow, maroon, or black to serve as a background for embossments of white Jasper relief for a cameo effect. When stained throughout the body

it is called *solid Jasper ware.* Example: Wedgwood plates **(26-90-0.0).**

K

KAOLIN The only clay which yields a white material when fired and the indispensable element of porcelain and china plates. Also called *true clay* or *china clay,* it is formed by the complete decomposition by weathering of feldspar. Kaolin is a refractory clay which can be fired at high temperatures without deforming. It produces a vitreous, translucent ceramic when fired with fluxes (fusible rocks) such as feldspar. The components of kaolin clay are 50% silica, 33% alumina, 2% oxides, 1% magnesia, 2% alkali, and 12% water.

KPM The trademark on plates from Königliche Porzellan Manufaktur, Meissen, Germany. Plates made by this manufacturer date from as early as 1723.

L

LEAD CRYSTAL Extremely transparent fine quality glass, also called *flint glass* and *lead glass,* which contains a high proportion of lead oxide to give extra weight, better refractiveness, and a clear ringing tone when tapped. *Full lead crystal* identifies glass with a 24% or greater lead content. Example: Lalique **(18-46-0.0)** plates.

LIMITED-EDITION PLATES Plates produced in a fixed quantity, either predetermined or determined by a specific period of production. All true collector's plates are in limited editions.

LIMOGES A town in south central France famous for its porcelian production because of the discovering of nearby kaolin deposits in 1768. Limoges porcelain manufacturers have joined together to enforce quality standards. Examples: D'Arceau-Limoges **(18-15-0.0),** Haviland **(18-30-0.0),** Haviland Parlon **(18-32-0.0),** and Limoges-Turgot **(18-52-0.0).**

LISTED PLATE A plate listed and regularly quoted on the Bradford Exchange. See OVER-THE-COUNTER PLATE.

LOT A number of plates, all in the same edition and represented by a self order on the Exchange, usually on the secondary market and not at issue. See ALLOTMENT.

LUSTER Decoration applied to a plate surface by application of metallic oxides such as gold, silver, platinum, or copper over the glaze. When gently fired, this leaves a thin metallic film.

M

MAJOLICA, MAIOLICA Earthenware finished with opaque white enamel, similar to *Faience* and *Delftware,* but first made in the Spanish island of Majorca.

MAKER The name by which a plate is known or under which it is issued, e.g., manufacturer, distributor or sponsor. In most cases the "maker" is the actual manufacturer, i.e., Bing and Grondahl **(14-8-0.0).** However, it can also be a commissioner or distributor, e.g., Schmid **(22-85-0.0),** using a trade name, while the physical production is in fact done by a sub-contractor.

MARKET The structure within which plates are bought and sold. The *primary market* consists of new issues which are sold by the makers or their sales representatives to dealers and distributors. Dealers and distributors in turn normally sell the new issues to the public at issue price. The *secondary market* or *after-market* is the buying and selling of plates previously sold, and usually sold out, on the primary market. In many cases secondary market prices are higher than those of the primary market.

MARKET BRADEX A kind of "Dow Jones" index of the overall collector's plate market expressed as a percentage, determined by the current price/issue ratio of 12 key series.

MARKET PRICE The price at which a plate is currently traded regardless of its issue price. See ISSUE PRICE.

MARKET PRICE ORDER An open bid posted on the Exchange to purchase a top advancing issue at the price the market demands.

MEISSEN See DRESDEN.

MINT CONDITION A plate in new or like-new condition accompanied by any original certificates and packing materials included at issue.

MODELING The process of making the original pattern from which the master mold is made for a sculptured plate.

MOLD A general term for the form which gives a plate its shape. Clay, metal or glass is pressed into a mold to form a *blank* (without ornamentation). Intaglio decoration or raised ornamentation may also be formed in the mold. China or porcelain *slip-casting* is done in plaster of paris molds. Slip (diluted clay formula) is poured into the mold, and the excess water is absorbed into the plaster of paris.

O

OPEN-END SERIES A continuing series of annual plates with no established termination. Example: Royal Copenhagen Christmas series **(14-69-0.0)**. See CLOSED-END SERIES.

OPEN STOCK Plates available in or produced in unlimited numbers or for an unlimited time period (and therefore not considered collector's plates).

OVER-THE-COUNTER PLATE A collector's plate occasionally traded directly between specialized dealers but not listed on the Exchange and not normally traded through it. See LISTED PLATE.

P

PARIAN CHINA A highly vitrified, translucent china characterized by an iridescent luster and rich, creamy tint much like that of parian marble for which it is named. The process for parian ware was invented by the Copeland and Garrett firm in England in the mid-nineteenth century. See BELLEEK, **(26-8-0.0)**.

PASTE The combination of substances that make up potter's clay, generally that for porcelain or china.

PEWTER An alloy of tin with copper and antimony as hardeners. The greater the amount of copper and antimony, the harder the ware. *Fine pewter* is composed of 80% tin and 20% antimony and brass or copper. Examples: International **(84-34-0.0)** and Royal Worcester (U.S.A.) **(84-82-0.0)** plates. See ALLOY.

POINT, BRADEX POINT One percentage point of the Market Bradex.

PORCELAIN The hardest vitreous ceramic fired at the highest temperatures. Although the term *porcelain* is often interchanged with *china*, true porcelain as the term is used in the field is distinguished from china by its very high glaze firing and low bisque firing temperature compared with the high bisque firing and low glaze firing of china. The main firing (glaze) of porcelain is approximately 7% higher than the main firing (bisque) of china. The glaze fuses with the porcelain plate body and produces an extremely hard surface. *Hard-paste* or *true porcelain* is made from a formula whose primary components are kaolin and china stone (petuntse). When fired, the china stone vitrifies, producing a hard, glassy ceramic. True porcelain is translucent when thin, white unless colored, impervious to scratching, and transmits a ringing tone when struck. A typical porcelain formula is 50% kaolin, 25% quartz, and 25% feldspar. *Soft-paste porcelain* was developed in Renaissance Europe in an attempt to imitate the true porcelain of China. Soft-paste porcelain was a mixture of white sand, gypsum, soda, alum, salt, and niter, fired until it vitrified. It had a soft texture, great sensitivity to sudden temperature changes, was warmer to the touch than true porcelain, and could be scratched with a file. The terms "hard" and "soft" porcelain refer to the "hard" firing temperature (around 1450° C) required for true porcelain and the "soft" firing temperatures (around 1150° C) used for soft-paste porcelain. See CHINA.

POTTERY 1. A general term used for all ceramic ware but strictly speaking for earthenware and non-vitrified ceramics. 2. The place or kilns where ceramic objects are fired.

Q

QUEEN'S WARE An earthenware of ivory or cream color developed by Josiah Wedgwood. The name "Queen's Ware" was adopted by other potters for similar stoneware; also often referred to as "white ware."

QUOTE The current market value and selling price of a collector's plate on the Exchange.

R

RELIEF SCULPTURE Sculpture in which the design or figure is not free-standing but is raised from a background. There are three degrees of relief sculpture: *Alto-relievo* or high relief, where the design is almost detached from the background; *Basso-relievo* or bas-relief, where the design is raised somewhat; and *Relievo-stiacciato*, where the design is scarcely more than scratched. Relief designs on plates may be formed in the plate mold or formed separately and applied to the plate body.

S

SECOND, SECOND SORTING A plate judged to be a grade below first quality, usually indicated by a scratch or gouge through the glaze over the backstamp on the back.

SECONDARY MARKET See MARKET.

SELL ORDER An offer at an asked price given by an individual or dealer to sell one or more plates of the same edition on the secondary market, usually on the Exchange. See LOT.

SLIP Ceramic paste or body diluted with water to a smooth, creamy consistency used for *slip-casting*. See MOLD.

STEATITE, SOAPSTONE A natural rock whose primary component is talc. Steatite is used in porcelain formulas as a flux.

STERLING SILVER An alloy which, by United States law, must have the minimum fineness of 92.5% by weight of pure silver and a maximum of 7.5% by weight of a base metal, usually copper. Example: Franklin Mint plates **(84-19-0.0)**.

STONEWARE A hard ceramic fired to vitrification but not to translucency. Typical components of stoneware are 30% ball clay, 32% kaolin, 15% flint, and 23% cornish stone. Example: Wedgwood's Jasper ware plates **(26-90-0.0)**.

SUPERMARKET PLATE Common term for a plate edition of dubious limitations, cheaply produced, and not considered a true collector's plate.

T

TERRA COTTA A general term for any kind of fired clay. Strictly speaking, terra cotta is an earthenware produced from a clay which fires to a dull ochre or red color. The ware, left unglazed, is coarse and porous. Example: Veneto Flair plates **(38-84-0.0)**.

TIN GLAZE A glaze colored white by oxide of tin which produces a heavy, opaque surface when fired. See DELFTWARE.

TORIART The process by which wood shavings and resin are combined forming a wood material which is then molded and carved into three-dimensional forms. Example: Anri **(38-4-0.0)**.

TRANSLUCENT The qualify of transmitting light without transparence. In a plate, translucency depends on the quality of the china or porcelain, thickness of the plate, and firing temperature. Underfired porcelain is not translucent.

TRIPTYCH A set of three panels hinged side by side, bearing paintings or carvings usually on a religious theme; used as a portable altarpiece.

TRUE CLAY See KAOLIN.

U

UNDERGLAZE DECORATION Decoration applied after a plate has been fired once (bisque fired) but before it is glazed and fired a second time. Underglaze painting is most commonly done in cobalt blue pigment (although other colors can be used) because this is the most stable color and can withstand high firing temperatures. *"True underglaze technique"* means such painting was done by hand.

V

VITRIFICATION A fusion of potters clay at temperatures between 1250° C and 1450° C, to form a glassy, nonporous substance. With continued heating, the substance will become translucent.

INDEX OF PLATE MAKERS AND SPONSORS

NOTE: "Maker" is a general term for the name under which a plate is issued which is not necessarily the actual "manufacturer." A Maker can be a distributor, manufacturer, or occasionally a "sponsor." See GLOSSARY OF COMMONLY USED TERMS.

Alboth . . . . See Kaiser
Alvarez . . . . See Santa Clara
Anri 38-4-0.0
Anna Perenna 22-3-0.0
Arabia 16-5-0.0
Artists of the World 84-3-0.0
L'Association l'Esprit
 de Lafayette . . . . See D'Arceau-Limoges

B & G . . . . See Bing & Grøndahl
Bareuther 22-6-0.0
 See also Danish Church
Belleek 26-8-0.0
Berlin Design 22-8-0.0
Beswick, John Potteries . . . . See Royal Doulton
Bing & Grøndahl 14-8-0.0
Böttger 22-9-0.0

Giuseppe Cappe . . . . See King's
Carborundum Company . . . . See Spode
Chambre Syndicale de la Couture
 Parisienne . . . . See D'Arceau-Limoges
W. T. Copeland & Sons, Ltd. . . . . . See Spode
Creative World . . . . See Veneto Flair

Danish Church 22-13-0.0
D'Arceau-Limoges 18-15-0.0
Désirée . . . . See Svend Jensen
Dresden 22-15-0.0

Eslau . . . . See Grande Copenhagen;
 Georg Jensen

Fairmont 84-14-0.0
Franklin Mint 84-19-0.0
Fukagawa 42-23-0.0
Fürstenberg 22-23-0.0

Goebel 22-27-0.0
Gorham 84-24-0.0
 See also Royal Devon
Grande Copenhagen 14-26-0.0

Haviland 18-30-0.0
Haviland Parlon 18-32-0.0
Hibel Studio 22-30-0.0
Hummelwerk . . . . See Goebel
Hutschenreuther . . . . See Schmid (Germany)

Incolay Studios 84-31-0.0
International 84-34-0.0

Jasper ware . . . . See Wedgwood
Georg Jensen 14-38-0.0
Svend Jensen 14-40-0.0

Kaiser 22-42-0.0
Kern Collectibles 84-38-0.0

King's 38-43-0.0
Kirke Platten . . . . See Danish Church
Edwin M. Knowles 84-41-0.0
 See also Rockwell Society

Lafayette Society . . . . See D'Arceau-Limoges
Lalique 18-46-0.0
Lenox 84-47-0.0
Lihs-Lindner 22-47-0.0
Limoges-Turgot 18-52-0.0
Lladró 72-46-0.0
Lotus Ware . . . . See Edwin M. Knowles

Museo Teatrale alla Scala . . . . See di Volteradici

Orrefors 76-57-0.0

Pickard 84-50-0.0
 See also Kern Collectibles
Porcelana Granada 4-61-0.0
Porcellanas Verbano . . . . See Porcelana Granada
Porcellanzfabrik Tirschenreuth . . . . See Dresden
Porsgrund 54-61-0.0

R. C. . . . . See Royal Copenhagen
Reco International 84-60-0.0
Reed & Barton 84-65-0.0
River Shore Ltd 84-69-0.0
Rockwell Society of America 84-70-0.0
Rogers Brothers . . . . See International
Rörstrand 76-69-0.0
Rosenthal 22-69-0.0
Roskilde Church . . . . See Danish Church
Royal Bayreuth 22-73-0.0
Royal Copenhagen 14-69-0.0
Royal Devon 84-76-0.0
Royal Doulton 26-69-0.0
Royale 22-77-0.0
Royal Tettau . . . . See Royal Bayreuth
Royal Worcester . . . . (G.B.) 26-78-0.0
 (U.S.) 84-82-0.0

Santa Clara 72-72-0.0
La Scala . . . . See di Volteradici
Schmid . . . . (Ger.) 22-85-0.0
 (Jap.) 42-85-0.0
Silbermann Brothers . . . . See Kaiser
Spode 26-86-0.0
Staatliche Porcellanmanufaktur
 (KPM) . . . . See Royale

Veneto Flair 38-84-0.0
Verbano . . . . See Porcelana Granada
Viletta 84-91-0.0
di Volteradici, Studio Dante 38-90-0.0

Wedgwood 26-90-0.0

INDEX OF PLATE TITLES AND SERIES BY TYPE

NOTE: Plate titles are listed in alphabetical order and enclosed in quotation marks:
"Aabenraa Marketplace".......**14-69-1.14.**

Types of series are listed in bold face with individual makers indented and listed below:
Anniversary
Goebel *(Hummel)*......**22-27-3.1.**

INDEX OF PLATE ARTISTS

The editors acknowledge with gratitude the invaluable supplementary information supplied by:

Anna Perenna, Inc.
Klaus Vogt
Arabia of Finland
Kurt Poussar
Armstrong's
Dave Armstrong
Artists of the World
James LaFond
Bing & Grondahl Copenhagen Porcelain, Inc.
Joan Doyle
Creative World, Ltd.
Joseph Gabbe
Richard Gabbe
D'Arceau-Limoges
Gerard Boyer
Downs
Deborah Magnuson
Ebeling & Reusse
A. L. Goeldner
Mike Miller
Edward Marshall Boehm, Inc.
Frank J. Cosentino
Virginia Perry
Fairmont China
Thomas W. Hogan
Fisher, Bruce & Co.
Gerhard Heitler
The Franklin Mint
Herman Baron
Fukagawa Porcelain Manufacturing Ltd.
K. Nishiyama
Gorham Division of Textron, Inc.
David Bauver
Hackett American Collectors Co.
James Hackett
Haviland & Co., Inc.
Richard Coyle
Jean-Paul Narcy
Hibel Studios
William Hibel
Hummelwerk
Morris Kule
Helmut H. Lihs Imports
Helmut H. Lihs
International Silver Co.
Carl Aichler
Cindy Haskins
Jacques Jugeat, Inc.
Lloyd Glasgow
J.A.R. Publishers
Monica Fenton
William Hibel
Joy's Limited
Helene Dunn

Kaiser Porcelain Co.
Hubert E. W. Kaiser
Kern Collectibles
Matthew P. Brummer
Kosta Boda U.S.A. Ltd.
Raymond Zrike
Lenox China Co.
Karen Cohen
Pemberton & Oakes
John Huginin
Pickard China Co.
Henry Pickard
Larry D. Smith
Jay Voss
Porcelana Granada (Fennell Orchid Co.)
Trudy Fennell
Rasmussen Import Co.
R. D. Rasmussen
Reco International Corp.
Brigetta Moore
Heio Reich
Reed & Barton
Patrice Johnson
River Shore Productions
Richard Spiegel
Rosenthal U.S.A. Limited
Lilie Mahlab
Royal Copenhagen Porcelain Corp.
Ivar Ipsen
Royal Doulton & Co.
Christopher McGillivary
Royal Worcester/Spode
Sheri Gable
Joyce Hendlewich
Schmid
Charles Leitch
Donna M. Spink
Svend Jensen
Per Jensen
Erik Larsen
Trein's
Gordon Brantley
Viking Import House, Inc.
Pat Owen
Wara Intercontinental Co.
Walter A. Rautenberg
Waterford Glass Inc.
Dick Oster
Wedgwood, Incorporated
Claudia Coleman
Weil Ceramics & Glass, Inc.
Charles Morgan
Viletta China Co.
Tom O'Meara

Market BRADEX 338 (Up 1)
CANADIAN EDITION
The Market Bradex is the Bradford Index of overall market performance determined by the current quote-price/issue-price ratio of the 9 most significant plate series.

Advances	80
Declines	27
Unchanged	461

CURRENT TO
APRIL 30, 1981

The Bradford Exchange Ltd. Current Quotations

The Standard Comprehensive Market as Determined by the World's Largest Exchange in All Major Collector's Plates Currently Traded

All prices are in Canadian dollars; prices in other currencies to be at the dollar buying rate in Toronto on the day of transaction. Every effort is made to maintain a uniform international open market with the most precise quotations of actual available prices which are subject to market demand but may be generally relied upon to date shown.

All Prices other than Issue Prices Subject to Daily Market Fluctuations

DENMARK

PLATE		ISSUE PRICE	HIGH	LOW	QUOTE	CHANGE
Bing & Grondahl (14-B 36-1)						
14-B 36-1.1	95 Frozen Window	.50	6500.00	4000.00	**5200.00**	0.00
14-B 36-1.2	96 New Moon	.50	3250.00	2500.00	**3000.00**	+250.00
14-B 36-1.3	97 Sparrows	.75	2950.00	1500.00	**2400.00**	0.00
14-B 36-1.4	98 Roses and Star	.75	1000.00	500.00	**995.00**	0.00
14-B 36-1.5	99 Crows	.75	3500.00	1750.00	**1995.00**	+500.00
14-B 36-1.6	00 Church Bells	.75	1200.00	995.00	**1080.00**	+100.00
14-B 36-1.7	01 Three Wise Men	1.00	610.00	250.00	**560.00**	0.00
14-B 36-1.8	02 Gothic Church Interior	1.00	600.00	225.00	**450.00**	0.00
14-B 36-1.9	03 Expectant Children	1.00	425.00	300.00	**380.00**	+30.00
14-B 36-1.10	04 Frederiksberg Hill	1.00	195.00	100.00	**157.00**	0.00
14-B 36-1.11	05 Christmas Night	1.00	225.00	105.00	**185.00**	0.00
14-B 36-1.12	06 Sleighing to Church	1.00	175.00	125.00	**147.00**	+12.00
14-B 36-1.13	07 Little Match Girl	1.00	165.00	100.00	**160.00**	0.00
14-B 36-1.14	08 St. Petri Church	1.00	135.00	85.00	**130.00**	0.00
14-B 36-1.15	09 Yule Tree	1.50	120.00	80.00	**120.00**	0.00
14-B 36-1.16	10 The Old Organist	1.50	140.00	100.00	**130.00**	+5.00
14-B 36-1.17	11 Angels and Shepherds	1.50	130.00	90.00	**127.00**	0.00
14-B 36-1.18	12 Going to Church	1.50	180.00	115.00	**137.00**	0.00
14-B 36-1.19	13 Bringing Home the Tree	1.50	125.00	90.00	**115.00**	0.00
14-B 36-1.20	14 Amalienborg Castle	1.50	225.00	125.00	**160.00**	0.00
14-B 36-1.21	15 Dog Outside Window	1.50	175.00	110.00	**184.00**	+11.00
14-B 36-1.22	16 Sparrows at Christmas	1.50	150.00	75.00	**135.00**	0.00
14-B 36-1.23	17 Christmas Boat	1.50	140.00	85.00	**130.00**	0.00
14-B 36-1.24	18 Fishing Boat	1.50	130.00	50.00	**127.00**	0.00
14-B 36-1.25	19 Outside the Window	2.00	135.00	90.00	**129.00**	0.00
14-B 36-1.26	20 Hare in the Snow	2.00	150.00	65.00	**130.00**	0.00
14-B 36-1.27	21 Pigeons	2.00	135.00	80.00	**104.00**	0.00
14-B 36-1.28	22 Star of Bethlehem	2.00	80.00	60.00	**100.00**	+1.00
14-B 36-1.29	23 The Ermitage	2.00	135.00	70.00	**107.00**	0.00
14-B 36-1.30	24 Lighthouse	2.50	110.00	45.00	**88.00**	0.00
14-B 36-1.31	25 Childs Christmas	2.50	135.00	80.00	**107.00**	0.00
14-B 36-1.32	26 Churchgoers	2.50	125.00	65.00	**90.00**	0.00
14-B 36-1.33	27 Skating Couple	2.50	150.00	100.00	**140.00**	+15.00
14-B 36-1.34	28 Eskimos	2.50	95.00	45.00	**88.00**	0.00
14-B 36-1.35	29 Fox Outside Farm	2.50	100.00	69.00	**97.00**	0.00
14-B 36-1.36	30 Town Hall Square	2.50	190.00	115.00	**165.00**	0.00
14-B 36-1.37	31 Christmas Train	2.50	135.00	60.00	**125.00**	0.00
14-B 36-1.38	32 Lifeboat	2.50	150.00	90.00	**120.00**	0.00
14-B 36-1.39	33 Korsor-Nyborg Ferry	3.00	90.00	70.00	**84.00**	0.00
14-B 36-1.40	34 Church Bell in Tower	3.00	100.00	75.00	**89.00**	+4.00
14-B 36-1.41	35 Lillebelt Bridge	3.00	130.00	50.00	**105.00**	0.00
14-B 36-1.42	36 Royal Guard	3.00	125.00	65.00	**95.00**	0.00
14-B 36-1.43	37 Guests Arrival	3.00	150.00	105.00	**130.00**	0.00
14-B 36-1.44	38 Lighting the Candles	3.00	250.00	195.00	**216.00**	0.00
14-B 36-1.45	39 Ole-Lock Eye the Sandman	3.00	325.00	175.00	**295.00**	0.00
14-B 36-1.46	40 Christmas Letters	4.00	240.00	140.00	**240.00**	0.00
14-B 36-1.47	41 Horses Enjoying Meal	4.00	600.00	395.00	**425.00**	0.00
14-B 36-1.48	42 Danish Farm	4.00	275.00	175.00	**250.00**	+30.00
14-B 36-1.49	43 Ribe Cathedral	5.00	265.00	145.00	**250.00**	0.00
14-B 36-1.50	44 Sorgenfri Castle	5.00	225.00	120.00	**170.00**	0.00
14-B 36-1.51	45 The Old Water Mill	5.00	225.00	150.00	**180.00**	+30.00
14-B 36-1.52	46 Commemoration Cross	5.00	95.00	65.00	**95.00**	0.00
14-B 36-1.53	47 Dybbol Mill	5.00	155.00	110.00	**136.00**	0.00
14-B 36-1.54	48 Watchman	5.50	110.00	80.00	**101.00**	0.00
14-B 36-1.55	49 Landsoldaten	5.50	150.00	90.00	**120.00**	0.00
14-B 36-1.56	50 Kronborg Castle	5.50	300.00	225.00	**255.00**	−5.00
14-B 36-1.57	51 Jens Bang	6.00	195.00	150.00	**170.00**	0.00
14-B 36-1.58	52 Thorvaldsen Museum	6.00	160.00	110.00	**135.00**	0.00
14-B 36-1.59	53 Royal Boat	7.00	150.00	100.00	**120.00**	0.00
14-B 36-1.60	54 Snowman	7.50	220.00	150.00	**180.00**	0.00
14-B 36-1.61	55 Kalundborg Church	8.00	200.00	100.00	**160.00**	0.00
14-B 36-1.62	56 Christmas in Copenhagan	8.50	260.00	175.00	**210.00**	+15.00
14-B 36-1.63	57 Christmas Candles	9.00	225.00	180.00	**195.00**	0.00
14-B 36-1.64	58 Santa Claus	9.50	185.00	135.00	**171.00**	0.00
14-B 36-1.65	59 Christmas Eve	10.00	250.00	175.00	**205.00**	0.00
14-B 36-1.66	60 Village Church	10.00	460.00	320.00	**425.00**	0.00
14-B 36-1.67	61 Winter Harmony	10.50	245.00	190.00	**225.00**	+35.00
14-B 36-1.68	62 Winter Night	11.00	160.00	90.00	**135.00**	0.00
14-B 36-1.69	63 The Christmas Elf	11.00	275.00	195.00	**235.00**	0.00
14-B 36-1.70	64 The Fir Tree and Hare	11.50	115.00	85.00	**106.00**	0.00
14-B 36-1.71	65 Bringing Home the Tree	12.00	125.00	78.00	**100.00**	−3.00
14-B 36-1.72	66 Home for Christmas	12.00	110.00	68.00	**108.00**	0.00
14-B 36-1.73	67 Sharing the Joy	13.00	120.00	66.00	**91.00**	0.00
14-B 36-1.74	68 Christmas in Church	14.00	80.00	58.00	**69.00**	0.00
14-B 36-1.75	69 Arrival of Guests	14.00	65.00	45.00	**58.00**	+2.00
14-B 36-1.76	70 Pheasants in Snow	14.50	50.00	35.00	**46.00**	0.00
14-B 36-1.77	71 Christmas at Home	15.00	45.00	30.00	**39.00**	0.00
14-B 36-1.78	72 Christmas in Greenland	16.50	50.00	29.00	**41.00**	0.00
14-B 36-1.79	73 Family Reunion	19.50	59.00	40.00	**50.00**	+2.00
14-B 36-1.80	74 Christmas in the Village	22.00	45.00	30.00	**38.00**	0.00
14-B 36-1.81	75 Old Water Mill	27.50	40.00	35.00	**31.00**	0.00
14-B 36-1.82	76 Christmas Welcome	27.50	35.00	20.00	**34.00**	0.00
14-B 36-1.83	77 Copenhagan Christmas	29.50	40.00	35.00	**36.00**	0.00
14-B 36-1.84	78 Christmas Tale	35.00	45.00	35.00	**37.00**	+1.00
14-B 36-1.85	79 White Christmas	44.00	44.00	44.00	**44.00**	0.00
14-B 36-1.86	80 Christmas in Woods	50.00	50.00	50.00	**50.00**	0.00
Bing & Grondahl Mother's Day (14-B 36-3)						
14-B 36-3.1	69 Dog and Puppies	9.75	890.00	500.00	**810.00**	0.00
14-B 36-3.2	70 Birds and Chicks	10.00	80.00	50.00	**93.00**	0.00
14-B 36-3.3	71 Cat and Kitten	11.00	30.00	20.00	**29.00**	+3.00
14-B 36-3.4	72 Mare and Foal	12.00	44.00	27.50	**39.00**	−1.00
14-B 36-3.5	73 Duck and Ducklings	13.00	33.00	15.00	**28.00**	0.00
14-B 36-3.6	74 Bear and Cubs	16.50	60.00	27.00	**45.00**	0.00
14-B 36-3.7	75 Doe and Fawns	19.50	30.00	20.00	**27.00**	+1.00
14-B 36-3.8	76 Swan Family	22.50	30.00	15.00	**24.00**	0.00
14-B 36-3.9	77 Squirrel and Young	23.50	35.00	15.00	**24.50**	0.00
14-B 36-3.10	78 Heron	24.50	35.00	15.00	**24.00**	−1.00
14-B 36-3.11	79 Fox and Cubs	33.00	33.00	33.00	**33.00**	0.00
14-B 36-3.12	80 Woodpecker and Young	39.95	39.95	39.95	**39.95**	0.00
14-B 36-3.13	81 Hare and Young	42.95	42.95	42.95	**42.95**	0.00
Svend Jensen Christmas (14-J 21-1)						
14-J 21-1.1	70 H. C. Andersen House	14.50	200.00	100.00	**110.00**	−5.00
14-J 21-1.2	71 Little Match Girl	15.00	100.00	40.00	**60.00**	0.00
14-J 21-1.3	72 Mermaid of Copenhagen	16.50	100.00	50.00	**60.00**	0.00
14-J 21-1.4	73 The Fir Tree	22.00	80.00	55.00	**67.00**	0.00
14-J 21-1.5	74 The Chimney Sweep	25.00	80.00	40.00	**48.00**	0.00
14-J 21-1.6	75 The Ugly Duckling	27.50	80.00	50.00	**69.00**	0.00
14-J 21-1.7	76 The Snow Queen	27.50	50.00	25.00	**37.00**	0.00
14-J 21-1.8	77 Snowman	29.50	40.00	25.00	**35.00**	0.00
14-J 21-1.9	78 Last Dream of Old Oak	30.00	35.00	20.00	**20.00**	−5.00
14-J 21-1.10	79 The Old Lamp Post	35.00	35.00	35.00	**35.00**	0.00
14-J 21-1.11	80 Willie Winky	42.50	42.50	42.50	**42.50**	0.00
Svend Jensen Mother's Day (14-J 21-2)						
14-J 21-2.1	70 Bouquet for Mother	14.50	135.00	50.00	**75.00**	−3.00
14-J 21-2.2	71 Mothers Love	15.00	45.00	30.00	**35.00**	0.00
14-J 21-2.3	72 Good Night	16.50	45.00	30.00	**35.00**	0.00
14-J 21-2.4	73 Flowers for Mother	20.00	50.00	35.00	**40.00**	0.00
14-J 21-2.5	74 Daisies for Mother	25.00	35.00	25.00	**32.00**	0.00
14-J 21-2.6	75 Surprise for Mother	27.50	40.00	25.00	**37.00**	0.00
14-J 21-2.7	76 Complete Gardener	27.50	45.00	25.00	**40.00**	0.00
14-J 21-2.8	77 Little Friends	29.50	60.00	40.00	**42.50**	0.00
14-J 21-2.9	78 Dreams	32.00	45.00	30.00	**38.00**	0.00
14-J 21-2.10	79 Promenade	30.00	30.00	20.00	**28.00**	−2.00
14-J 21-2.11	80 Nursery Scene	39.95	39.95	39.95	**39.95**	0.00
Royal Copenhagen Christmas (14-R 59-1)						
14-R 59-1.1	08 Madonna and Child	1.00	3500.00	2500.00	**2830.00**	0.00
14-R 59-1.2	09 Danish Landscape	1.00	325.00	175.00	**255.00**	−5.00
14-R 59-1.3	10 The Magi	1.00	190.00	140.00	**182.00**	0.00
14-R 59-1.4	11 Danish Landscape	1.00	300.00	140.00	**260.00**	0.00
14-R 59-1.5	12 Christmas Tree	1.00	225.00	150.00	**205.00**	0.00
14-R 59-1.6	13 Frederik Church Spire	1.50	265.00	150.00	**245.00**	0.00
14-R 59-1.7	14 Holy Spirit Church	1.50	270.00	120.00	**195.00**	0.00
14-R 59-1.8	15 Danish Landscape	1.50	215.00	150.00	**190.00**	+2.00
14-R 59-1.9	16 Shepherd at Christmas	1.50	150.00	85.00	**130.00**	0.00
14-R 59-1.10	17 Our Savior Church	2.00	130.00	100.00	**130.00**	0.00
14-R 59-1.11	18 Sheep and Shepherds	2.00	135.00	80.00	**130.00**	0.00
14-R 59-1.12	19 In the Park	2.00	160.00	60.00	**130.00**	0.00
14-R 59-1.13	20 Mary and Child Jesus	2.00	210.00	90.00	**190.00**	0.00

Price Explanation: ISSUE: Price when first issued. HIGH: Highest known offering price during previous bi-monthly period. LOW: Lowest known offering price during previous bi-monthly period. QUOTE: Current selling price of the Exchange (subject to fluctuation). CHANGE: Increase or decrease in QUOTE price since previous bi-monthly period.

	PLATE	ISSUE PRICE	HIGH	LOW	QUOTE	CHANGE
14-R 59-1.14	21 Aabenraa Marketplace	2.00	160.00	80.00	**135.00**	0.00
14-R 59-1.15	22 Three Singing Angels	2.00	145.00	60.00	**127.00**	0.00
14-R 59-1.16	23 Danish Landscape	2.00	158.00	95.00	**137.00**	0.00
14-R 59-1.17	24 Sailing Ship	2.00	175.00	150.00	**175.00**	+20.00
14-R 59-1.18	25 Christianshavn	2.00	180.00	110.00	**147.00**	0.00
14-R 59-1.19	26 Christianshavn Canal	2.00	180.00	95.00	**140.00**	0.00
14-R 59-1.20	27 Ships Boy at Tiller	2.00	400.00	275.00	**390.00**	−5.00
14-R 59-1.21	28 Vicar's Family	2.00	140.00	90.00	**128.00**	0.00
14-R 59-1.22	29 Grundtvig Church	2.00	173.00	99.00	**145.00**	−3.00
14-R 59-1.23	30 Fishing Boats	2.50	175.00	90.00	**160.00**	0.00
14-R 59-1.24	31 Mother and Child	2.50	195.00	100.00	**165.00**	0.00
14-R 59-1.25	32 Frederiksberg Gardens	2.50	220.00	125.00	**210.00**	0.00
14-R 59-1.26	33 Great Belt Ferry	2.50	250.00	150.00	**218.00**	0.00
14-R 59-1.27	34 The Hermitage Castle	2.50	220.00	150.00	**185.00**	+5.00
14-R 59-1.28	35 Kronborg Castle	2.50	290.00	195.00	**265.00**	0.00
14-R 59-1.29	36 Roskilde Cathedral	2.50	285.00	175.00	**270.00**	0.00
14-R 59-1.30	37 Main Street Copenhagen	2.50	280.00	175.00	**260.00**	0.00
14-R 59-1.31	38 Round Church Ostelars	3.00	495.00	320.00	**465.00**	+5.00
14-R 59-1.32	39 Greenland Pack-Ice	3.00	490.00	350.00	**475.00**	0.00
14-R 59-1.33	40 The Good Shepherd	3.00	775.00	550.00	**700.00**	0.00
14-R 59-1.34	41 Danish Village Church	3.00	820.00	600.00	**720.00**	0.00
14-R 59-1.35	42 Bell Tower	4.00	800.00	600.00	**710.00**	+5.00
14-R 59-1.36	43 Flight to Egypt	4.00	750.00	590.00	**695.00**	0.00
14-R 59-1.37	44 Danish Winter Scene	4.00	400.00	250.00	**335.00**	0.00
14-R 59-1.38	45 A Peaceful Motif	4.00	810.00	600.00	**680.00**	−20.00
14-R 59-1.39	46 Zealand Village Church	4.00	350.00	200.00	**329.00**	0.00
14-R 59-1.40	47 The Good Shepherd	4.50	350.00	285.00	**365.00**	0.00
14-R 59-1.41	48 Nodebo Church	4.50	350.00	200.00	**320.00**	0.00
14-R 59-1.42	49 Our Lady's Cathedral	5.00	370.00	250.00	**300.00**	−5.00
14-R 59-1.43	50 Boeslunde Church	5.00	500.00	200.00	**425.00**	0.00
14-R 59-1.44	51 Christmas Angel	5.00	800.00	550.00	**730.00**	0.00
14-R 59-1.45	52 Christmas in Forest	5.00	235.00	150.00	**235.00**	0.00
14-R 59-1.46	53 Frederiksberg Castle	6.00	240.00	140.00	**225.00**	−5.00
14-R 59-1.47	54 Amalienborg Palace	6.00	310.00	209.00	**298.00**	0.00
14-R 59-1.48	55 Fano Girl	7.00	420.00	239.00	**420.00**	0.00
14-R 59-1.49	56 Rosenborg Castle	7.00	425.00	210.00	**420.00**	0.00
14-R 59-1.50	57 A Good Shepherd	8.00	260.00	200.00	**220.00**	+6.00
14-R 59-1.51	58 Sunshine over Greenland	9.00	370.00	190.00	**340.00**	0.00
14-R 59-1.52	59 Christmas Night	9.00	420.00	210.00	**335.00**	0.00
14-R 59-1.53	60 The Stag	10.00	480.00	350.00	**460.00**	0.00
14-R 59-1.54	61 Training Ship Danmark	10.00	510.00	329.00	**450.00**	0.00
14-R 59-1.55	62 Little Mermaid	11.00	495.00	300.00	**385.00**	+6.00
14-R 59-1.56	63 Hojsager Mill	11.00	244.00	150.00	**234.00**	0.00
14-R 59-1.57	64 Fetching the Tree	11.00	155.00	85.00	**155.00**	+6.00
14-R 59-1.58	65 Little Skaters	12.00	160.00	100.00	**124.00**	0.00
14-R 59-1.59	66 Blackbird	12.00	135.00	90.00	**115.00**	0.00
14-R 59-1.60	67 The Royal Oak	13.00	100.00	50.00	**97.00**	0.00
14-R 59-1.61	68 The Last Umiak	13.00	55.00	39.00	**69.00**	0.00
14-R 59-1.62	69 The Old Farmyard	14.00	60.00	35.00	**65.00**	0.00
14-R 59-1.63	70 Christmas Rose and Cat	14.00	95.00	42.00	**59.00**	0.00
14-R 59-1.64	71 Hare in Winter	14.00	75.00	40.00	**50.00**	+6.00
14-R 59-1.65	72 In the Desert	14.00	45.00	25.00	**45.00**	0.00
14-R 59-1.66	73 Train Homeward Bound	22.00	60.00	30.00	**46.00**	0.00
14-R 59-1.67	74 Winter Twilight	22.00	50.00	37.00	**46.00**	+1.00
14-R 59-1.68	75 Queens Palace	24.50	50.00	25.00	**43.00**	0.00
14-R 59-1.69	76 Danish Watermill	26.00	50.00	27.00	**43.00**	+7.00
14-R 59-1.70	77 Immervad Bridge	29.00	36.00	29.00	**30.00**	0.00
14-R 59-1.71	78 Greenland Scenery	35.00	35.00	35.00	**35.00**	0.00
14-R 59-1.72	79 Choosing a Christmas Tree	48.00	48.00	48.00	**48.00**	0.00
14-R 59-1.73	80 Bringing Home the Christmas Tree	56.00	56.00	56.00	**56.00**	0.00
Royal Copenhagen Mother's Day (14-R 59-2)						
14-R 59-2.1	71 American Mother	8.50	95.00	40.00	**52.00**	−2.00
14-R 59-2.2	72 Oriental Mother	14.00	30.00	10.00	**20.00**	0.00
14-R 59-2.3	73 Danish Mother	16.00	35.00	20.00	**23.00**	0.00
14-R 59-2.4	74 Greenland Mother	16.50	35.00	20.00	**23.00**	0.00
14-R 59-2.5	75 Bird in Nest	20.00	40.00	24.00	**30.00**	−2.00
14-R 59-2.6	76 Mermaids	20.00	35.00	25.00	**30.00**	0.00
14-R 59-2.7	77 The Twins	24.00	50.00	25.00	**36.00**	0.00
14-R 59-2.8	78 Mother and Child	25.50	35.00	20.00	**31.00**	0.00
14-R 59-2.9	79 A Loving Mother	38.00	38.00	38.00	**37.00**	0.00
14-R 59-2.10	80 An Outing With Mother	44.00	44.00	44.00	**44.00**	0.00

FRANCE

	PLATE	ISSUE PRICE	HIGH	LOW	QUOTE	CHANGE
D'Arceau Limoges Christmas (18-D 15-2)						
18-D 15-2.1	75 La Fruite en Egypte	31.62	195.00	160.00	**191.00**	0.00
18-D 15-2.2	76 Dans La Creche	31.62	45.00	33.00	**54.00**	0.00
18-D 15-2.3	77 Refus d'Hebergment	31.62	45.00	31.62	**51.00**	0.00
18-D 15-2.4	78 La Purification	40.57	45.00	34.85	**44.00**	0.00
18-D 15-2.5	79 L'Adoration des Rois	40.57	40.57	40.57	**40.57**	0.00
18-D 15-2.6	80 Tidings of Great Joy	43.57	43.57	43.57	**43.57**	0.00
D'Arceau Limoges Les Jeunes Filles de Saisons (18-D 15-4)						
18-D 15-4.1	78 La Jeune Fille d'Ete	150.00	195.00	160.00	**175.00**	+8.00
18-D 15-4.2	79 La Jeune Fille d'Hiver	150.00	200.00	150.00	**150.00**	0.00
18-D 15-4.3	80 La Jeune Fille du Printemps	150.00	150.00	150.00	**150.00**	0.00
D'Arceau Limoges Les Tres Riches Heures (18-D 15-5)						
18-D 15-5.1	79 Janvier	115.00	115.00	115.00	**115.00**	0.00
18-D 15-5.2	80 Avril	115.00	115.00	115.00	**115.00**	0.00
D'Arceau Limoges Les Sites Parisiens de Louis Dali (18-D 15-6)						
18-D 15-6.1	80 L'Arc de Triomphe	34.00	34.00	34.00	34.00	0.00
Limoges-Turgot Les Enfants de Durand (18-L 52-1)						
18-L 52-1.1	78 Marie-Ange	55.00	100.00	55.00	**57.00**	0.00
18-L 52-1.2	79 Emillie et Philippe	55.00	55.00	55.00	**55.00**	0.00
18-L 52-1.3	80 Christiane et Fifi	55.00	55.00	55.00	**55.00**	0.00

GERMANY

	PLATE	ISSUE PRICE	HIGH	LOW	QUOTE	CHANGE
Anna Perenna Triptychs (22-A 3-3)						
22-A 3-3.1	79 Byzantine Triptych	395.00	395.00	395.00	**395.00**	0.00
22-A 3-3.2	80 Jerusalem Triptych	450.00	450.00	450.00	**450.00**	0.00
Anna Perenna Romatic Loves (22-A 3-4)						
22-A 3-4.1	79 Romeo and Juliet	120.00	120.00	120.00	**120.00**	0.00
22-A 3-4.2	80 Lancelot and Guinevere	120.00	120.00	120.00	**120.00**	0.00
Anna Perenna Uncle Tad's Cats (22-A 3-5)						
22-A 3-5.1	79 Oliver's Birthday	95.00	125.00	95.00	**110.00**	+10.00
22-A 3-5.2	80 Peaches and Cream	95.00	95.00	95.00	**95.00**	0.00
Berlin Design Christmas (22-B 20-1)						
22-B 20-1.1	70 Christmas in Bernkastle	14.50	325.00	200.00	**245.00**	+10.00
22-B 20-1.2	71 Christmas in Rothenburg	14.50	65.00	40.00	**54.00**	0.00
22-B 20-1.3	72 Christmas in Michelstadt	20.00	65.00	40.00	**55.00**	0.00
22-B 20-1.4	73 Christmas in Wendelstein	25.00	90.00	60.00	**83.00**	+3.00
22-B 20-1.5	74 Christmas in Bremen	30.00	50.00	30.00	**46.00**	0.00
22-B 20-1.6	75 Christmas in Dortland	32.00	70.00	40.00	**50.00**	0.00
22-B 20-1.7	76 Christmas in Augsburg	32.00	60.00	40.00	**45.00**	−2.00
22-B 20-1.8	77 Christmas in Hamburg	40.00	40.00	30.00	**40.00**	0.00
22-B 20-1.9	78 Christmas in Berlin	45.00	45.00	35.00	**45.00**	0.00
22-B 20-1.10	79 Christmas in Greetsiel	54.00	54.00	54.00	**54.00**	0.00
22-B 20-1.11	80 Christmas in Miltenberg	59.00	59.00	59.00	**59.00**	0.00
Berlin Design Mother's Day (22-B 20-3)						
22-B 20-3.1	71 Grey Poodles	14.50	55.00	35.00	**47.00**	0.00
22-B 20-3.2	72 Fledglings	15.00	40.00	25.00	**35.00**	0.00
22-B 20-3.3	73 Duck Family	16.50	40.00	24.00	**38.00**	0.00
22-B 20-3.4	74 Squirrels	22.50	55.00	25.00	**44.00**	0.00
22-B 20-3.5	75 Cats	30.00	50.00	35.00	**49.00**	0.00
22-B 20-3.6	76 Doe and her Fawn	35.00	45.00	35.00	**38.00**	0.00
22-B 20-3.7	77 Storks	35.00	40.00	35.00	**40.00**	0.00
22-B 20-3.8	78 Mare with Foal	35.00	50.00	40.00	**47.00**	+3.00
22-B 20-3.9	79 Swan and Cygnets	54.00	54.00	54.00	**54.00**	0.00
22-B 20-3.10	80 The Goat Family	59.00	59.00	59.00	**59.00**	0.00
Christian Bell Preserving a Way of Life (22-C 13-1)						
22-C 13-1.1	80 Making Way For Cars	68.00	78.00	68.00	**68.00**	0.00
22-C 13-1.2	80 Atop the Hay Wagon	68.00	78.00	68.00	**68.00**	0.00
22-C 13-1.3	80 Turning the Sod	68.00	68.00	68.00	**68.00**	0.00
22-C 13-1.4	80 Winters Morning	68.00	68.00	68.00	**68.00**	0.00
Goebel Hummel Annual (22-G 54-1)						
22-G 54-1.1	71 Heavenly Angel	25.00	1250.00	750.00	**1150.00**	−75.00
22-G 54-1.2	72 Hear Ye, Hear Ye	28.00	200.00	125.00	**150.00**	0.00
22-G 54-1.3	73 Globe Trotter	32.50	400.00	250.00	**350.00**	0.00
22-G 54-1.4	74 Goose Girl	40.00	250.00	125.00	**175.00**	0.00
22-G 54-1.5	75 Ride into Christmas	50.00	150.00	100.00	**120.00**	0.00
22-G 54-1.6	76 Appletree Girl	50.00	150.00	100.00	**120.00**	0.00
22-G 54-1.7	77 Appletree Boy	52.50	325.00	150.00	**210.00**	−10.00
22-G 54-1.8	78 Happy Pastime	79.50	300.00	150.00	**200.00**	0.00
22-G 54-1.9	79 Singing Lesson	100.00	175.00	100.00	**130.00**	0.00
22-G 54-1.10	80 School Girl	120.00	120.00	120.00	**120.00**	0.00
22-G 54-1.11	81 Umbrella Boy	125.00	125.00	125.00	**125.00**	0.00
Goebel Hummel Anniversary (22-G 54-3)						
22-G 54-3.1	75 Stormy Weather	100.00	700.00	400.00	**565.00**	−20.00
22-G 54-3.2	80 Spring Dance	275.00	275.00	275.00	**275.00**	0.00
Heinrich, Villeroy & Boch Flower Fairy (22-H 18-2)						
22-H 18-2.1	79 The Lavender Fairy	45.00	50.00	45.00	**45.00**	0.00
22-H 18-2.2	80 Sweet Pea	50.00	50.00	50.00	**50.00**	0.00
22-H 18-2.3	80 Candy Tuft Fairy	50.00	50.00	50.00	**50.00**	0.00
22-H 18-2.4	80 Heliotrope Fairy	50.00	50.00	50.00	**50.00**	0.00
22-H 18-2.5	81 Blackthorn Farm	50.00	50.00	50.00	**50.00**	0.00
22-H 18-2.6	81 Apple Blossom Farm	50.00	50.00	50.00	**50.00**	0.00
Hutschenreuther Winther Christmas (22-H 82-1)						
22-H 82-1.1	78 Silent Night	300.00	600.00	300.00	**300.00**	0.00
22-H 82-1.2	79 Saint Lucia	365.00	365.00	365.00	**365.00**	0.00
22-H 82-1.3	80 Christmas Pavillion	395.00	395.00	395.00	**395.00**	0.00
Hutschenreuther Canada Christmas (22-H 82-9)						
22-H 82-9.1	73 Parliament Building	15.00	450.00	150.00	**295.00**	0.00
22-H 82-9.2	74 Moose	16.00	69.00	35.00	**43.00**	0.00
22-H 82-9.3	75 Basilica	21.00	50.00	30.00	**34.00**	0.00
22-H 82-9.4	76 Winter on the Prairies	23.00	50.00	25.00	**37.00**	0.00
22-H 82-9.5	77 Bluenose	25.00	50.00	25.00	**38.00**	0.00
22-H 82-9.6	78 Lost Lagoon	32.00	50.00	25.00	**32.00**	0.00
22-H 82-9.7	79 Yukon Highway Lodge	39.00	39.00	39.00	**39.00**	0.00
22-H 82-9.8	80 The Covered Bridge	45.00	45.00	45.00	**45.00**	0.00
Kaiser Christmas (22-K 4-1)						
22-K 4-1.1	70 Waiting for Santa Claus	12.50	75.00	45.00	**57.00**	0.00
22-K 4-1.2	71 Silent Night	13.50	60.00	35.00	**45.00**	0.00
22-K 4-1.3	72 Welcome Home	16.50	50.00	35.00	**42.00**	+5.00
22-K 4-1.4	73 Holy Night	18.00	65.00	35.00	**53.00**	0.00
22-K 4-1.5	74 Christmas Carolers	25.00	60.00	20.00	**48.00**	0.00
22-K 4-1.6	75 Bringing Home the Tree	25.00	60.00	45.00	**50.00**	0.00
22-K 4-1.7	76 Christ the Saviour	25.00	60.00	30.00	**45.00**	+20.00
22-K 4-1.8	77 Three Kings	25.00	40.00	25.00	**27.50**	0.00
22-K 4-1.9	78 Shepherds in the Field	30.00	35.00	20.00	**27.50**	0.00
22-K 4-1.10	79 Christmas Eve	32.00	32.00	32.00	**32.00**	0.00
22-K 4-1.11	80 Joys of Winter	35.00	35.00	35.00	**35.00**	0.00
Kaiser Mother's Day (22-K 4-2)						
22-K 4-2.1	71 Mare and Foal	13.00	50.00	30.00	**59.00**	0.00
22-K 4-2.2	72 Flowers for Mother	16.50	60.00	27.00	**43.00**	0.00
22-K 4-2.3	73 Cats	17.00	65.00	30.00	**49.00**	+14.00
22-K 4-2.4	74 Fox	22.00	40.00	20.00	**35.00**	0.00
22-K 4-2.5	75 German Shepherd	25.00	90.00	55.00	**60.00**	0.00
22-K 4-2.6	76 Swan and Cygnets	25.00	65.00	30.00	**45.00**	+16.00
22-K 4-2.7	77 Mother Rabbit and Young	25.00	60.00	35.00	**44.00**	+15.00
22-K 4-2.8	78 Hen and Chicks	30.00	50.00	30.00	**45.00**	+10.00
22-K 4-2.9	79 A Mother's Devotion	32.00	32.00	32.00	**32.00**	0.00
22-K 4-2.10	80 Raccoon and Babies	35.00	35.00	35.00	**35.00**	0.00
Kaiser Anniversary (22-K 4-3)						
22-K 4-3.1	72 Love Birds	16.50	60.00	35.00	**50.00**	+10.00
22-K 4-3.2	73 In the Park	18.00	30.00	20.00	**45.00**	+10.00
22-K 4-3.3	74 Canoeing Down River	22.00	37.50	15.00	**32.00**	0.00
22-K 4-3.4	75 Tender Moment	25.00	65.00	40.00	**46.00**	0.00
22-K 4-3.5	76 Serenade to Lovers	25.00	25.00	20.00	**28.00**	0.00
22-K 4-3.6	77 A Simple Gift	25.00	40.00	27.00	**29.00**	0.00
22-K 4-3.7	78 A Viking Toast	30.00	30.00	30.00	**30.00**	0.00
22-K 4-3.8	79 Romantic Interlude	32.00	32.00	32.00	**32.00**	0.00
22-K 4-3.9	80 Love at Play	35.00	35.00	35.00	**35.00**	0.00
Kaiser Nori Peter (22-K 4-4)						
22-K 4-4.1	78 Northern Lullabye	70.00	85.00	70.00	**75.00**	0.00
22-K 4-4.2	79 My Friend	75.00	75.00	75.00	**75.00**	0.00
22-K 4-4.3	80 Motherhood	75.00	75.00	75.00	**75.00**	0.00
Konigszelt Bavaria Hedi Keller Christmas (22-K 46-1)						
22-K 46-1.1	79 The Adoration	45.00	85.00	45.00	**73.00**	0.00
22-K 46-1.2	80 Flight Into Egypt	45.00	75.00	50.00	**60.00**	+15.00
Rosenthal Traditional Christmas (22-R 55-1)						
22-R 55-1.62	71 Christmas in Garmisch	66.00	125.00	90.00	**131.00**	0.00
22-R 55-1.63	72 Christmas in Franconia	66.00	130.00	85.00	**125.00**	−2.00
22-R 55-1.64	73 Lubeck-Holstein	84.00	140.00	90.00	**138.00**	0.00
22-R 55-1.65	74 Christmas in Wurzburg	85.00	145.00	90.00	**138.00**	0.00
Rosenthal Winblad Christmas (22-R 55-2)						
22-R 55-2.1	71 Maria and Child	100.00	2500.00	1850.00	**2350.00**	+100.00
22-R 55-2.2	72 Caspar	100.00	1750.00	1300.00	**1450.00**	0.00
22-R 55-2.3	73 Melchior	125.00	950.00	500.00	**870.00**	0.00
22-R 55-2.4	74 Balthazar	150.00	950.00	500.00	**860.00**	0.00
22-R 55-2.5	75 The Annunciation	200.00	410.00	300.00	**330.00**	0.00
22-R 55-2.6	76 Angel with Trumpet	225.00	425.00	275.00	**370.00**	0.00
22-R 55-2.7	77 Adoration of Shepherds	235.00	350.00	260.00	**350.00**	0.00
22-R 55-2.8	78 Angel with Harp	275.00	400.00	275.00	**350.00**	0.00
22-R 55-2.9	79 Exodus from Egypt	295.00	295.00	295.00	**295.00**	0.00
22-R 55-2.10	80 Angel with the Glockenspiel	360.00	360.00	360.00	**360.00**	0.00
Rosenthal Nobility of Children (22-R 55-6)						
22-R 55-6.1	76 La Contessa Isobella	150.00	425.00	300.00	**350.00**	+30.00
22-R 55-6.2	77 Le Marquis Maurice-Pierre	150.00	220.00	175.00	**190.00**	+8.00
22-R 55-6.3	78 Baroness	200.00	200.00	160.00	**160.00**	0.00
22-R 55-6.4	80 Chief Red Feather	210.00	210.00	210.00	**210.00**	0.00
Rosenthal Classic Rose Collection (22-R 55-11)						
22-R 55-11.1	74 Memorial Church in Berlin	75.00	220.00	100.00	**220.00**	0.00
22-R 55-11.2	75 Freiburg Cathedral	75.00	150.00	100.00	**126.00**	0.00
22-R 55-11.3	76 Castle of Cochem	115.00	150.00	100.00	**128.00**	0.00
22-R 55-11.4	77 Hannover Town Hall	150.00	150.00	95.00	**135.00**	−5.00
22-R 55-11.5	78 Cathedral at Aachen	150.00	150.00	150.00	**150.00**	0.00
22-R 55-11.6	79 Cathedral in Luxemburg	195.00	195.00	195.00	**195.00**	0.00
22-R 55-11.7	80 Christmas in Brussels	240.00	240.00	240.00	**240.00**	0.00
Royal Bayreuth Christmas (22-R 58-1)						
22-R 58-1.1	72 Carriage in Village	19.50	165.00	100.00	**150.00**	0.00
22-R 58-1.2	73 Snow Scene	21.50	65.00	40.00	**45.00**	0.00
22-R 58-1.3	74 The Old Mill	32.00	60.00	40.00	**50.00**	+10.00
22-R 58-1.4	75 Forest Chalet "Serenity"	35.00	60.00	40.00	**45.00**	0.00

PLATE		ISSUE PRICE	HIGH	LOW	QUOTE	CHANGE
22-R 58-1.5	76 Christmas in the Country	50.00	75.00	35.00	**47.00**	0.00
22-R 58-1.6	77 Peace on Earth	50.00	75.00	35.00	**50.00**	0.00
22-R 58-1.7	78 Peaceful Interlude	65.00	85.00	65.00	**75.00**	0.00
22-R 58-1.8	79 Homeward Bound	75.00	75.00	75.00	**70.00**	−3.00
Royal Bayreuth Mother's Day (22-R 58-2)						
22-R 58-2.1	73 Consolation	21.00	90.00	50.00	**65.00**	0.00
22-R 58-2.2	74 Young Americans	35.00	200.00	150.00	**185.00**	0.00
22-R 58-2.3	75 Young Americans II	35.00	250.00	175.00	**190.00**	+12.00
22-R 58-2.4	76 Young Americans III	40.00	195.00	100.00	**150.00**	0.00
22-R 58-2.5	77 Young Americans IV	50.00	150.00	90.00	**125.00**	+5.00
22-R 58-2.6	78 Young Americans V	55.00	100.00	80.00	**90.00**	0.00
22-R 58-2.7	79 Young Americans VI	80.00	160.00	110.00	**120.00**	+3.00
22-R 58-2.8	80 Young Americans VII	100.00	100.00	100.00	**100.00**	0.00
Royal Bayreuth Antique American Art (22-R 58-5)						
22-R 58-5.1	76 Farmyard Tranquility	75.00	125.00	55.00	**87.00**	0.00
22-R 58-5.2	77 Half Dome	85.00	80.00	45.00	**50.00**	−10.00
22-R 58-5.3	78 Down Memory Lane	100.00	100.00	100.00	**105.00**	0.00
Schmid Hummel Christmas (22-S 12-1)						
22-S 12-1.1	71 Angel	15.00	195.00	100.00	**130.00**	0.00
22-S 12-1.2	72 Angel with Flute	15.00	50.00	25.00	**50.00**	0.00
22-S 12-1.3	73 The Nativity	15.00	420.00	300.00	**385.00**	0.00
22-S 12-1.4	74 The Guardian Angel	18.50	75.00	40.00	**55.00**	+15.00
22-S 12-1.5	75 Christmas Child	25.00	49.00	25.00	**40.00**	0.00
22-S 12-1.6	76 Sacred Journey	27.50	120.00	50.00	**87.00**	0.00
22-S 12-1.7	77 Herald Angel	35.00	50.00	35.00	**50.00**	0.00
22-S 12-1.8	78 Heavenly Trio	39.00	75.00	30.00	**45.00**	0.00
22-S 12-1.9	79 Starlight Angel	42.00	60.00	42.00	**45.00**	+3.00
22-S 12-1.10	80 Parade into Toyland	48.00	48.00	48.00	**48.00**	0.00
Schmid Hummel Mother's Day (22-S 12-2)						
22-S 12-2.1	72 Playing Hooky	15.00	85.00	50.00	**74.00**	0.00
22-S 12-2.2	73 Little Fisherman	15.00	175.00	75.00	**152.00**	0.00
22-S 12-2.3	74 Bumblebee	18.50	60.00	50.00	**52.00**	+7.00
22-S 12-2.4	75 Message of Love	25.00	75.00	25.00	**58.00**	0.00
22-S 12-2.5	76 Devotion for Mother	27.50	35.00	30.00	**34.00**	0.00
22-S 12-2.6	77 Moonlight Return	35.00	45.00	25.00	**40.00**	0.00
22-S 12-2.7	78 Afternoon Stroll	35.00	75.00	35.00	**50.00**	0.00
22-S 12-2.8	79 Cherub's Gift	39.00	39.00	39.00	**39.00**	0.00
22-S 12-2.9	80 Mother's Little Helper	48.00	48.00	48.00	**48.00**	0.00
Schmid Ferrandiz Mother and Child (22-S 12-3)						
22-S 12-3.1	77 Orchard Mother and Child	65.00	225.00	150.00	**185.00**	0.00
22-S 12-3.2	78 Pastoral Mother and Child	95.00	200.00	115.00	**160.00**	0.00
22-S 12-3.3	79 Floral Mother	115.00	150.00	110.00	**120.00**	0.00
22-S 12-3.4	80 Avian and Child	125.00	125.00	125.00	**125.00**	0.00

GREAT BRITAIN

PLATE		ISSUE PRICE	HIGH	LOW	QUOTE	CHANGE
Aynsley Christmas (26-A 97-1)						
26-A 97-1.1	79 Mr. Fezziwigs Ball	36.95	49.95	36.95	**37.95**	0.00
26-A 97-1.2	80 Marley's Ghost	49.95	49.95	49.95	**49.95**	0.00
Belleek Christmas (26-B 18-1)						
26-B 18-1.1	70 Castle Caldwell	35.00	250.00	195.00	**225.00**	0.00
26-B 18-1.2	71 Celtic Cross	35.00	125.00	60.00	**98.00**	0.00
26-B 18-1.3	72 Flight of the Earls	35.00	60.00	35.00	**55.00**	0.00
26-B 18-1.4	73 Tribute to Yeats	35.00	55.00	35.00	**55.00**	0.00
26-B 18-1.5	74 Devenish Island	35.00	350.00	200.00	**260.00**	+20.00
26-B 18-1.6	75 The Celtic Cross	40.00	75.00	40.00	**49.00**	0.00
26-B 18-1.7	76 Dove of Peace	52.50	95.00	60.00	**81.00**	0.00
26-B 18-1.8	77 Wren	52.50	52.50	40.00	**52.50**	0.00
Belleek Irish Wildlife Christmas (26-B 18-2)						
26-B 18-2.1	78 Leaping Salmon	50.00	60.00	50.00	**57.50**	0.00
26-B 18-2.2	79 The Hare	71.95	71.95	71.95	**71.95**	0.00
26-B 18-2.3	80 Hedgehog	75.00	75.00	75.00	**75.00**	0.00
Royal Doulton Mother and Child (26-R 62-2)						
26-R 62-2.1	73 Colette and Child	40.00	1000.00	600.00	**700.00**	+15.00
26-R 62-2.2	74 Sayuri and Child	40.00	500.00	250.00	**265.00**	0.00
26-R 62-2.3	75 Kristina and Child	50.00	475.00	250.00	**275.00**	0.00
26-R 62-2.4	76 Marilyn and Child	55.00	450.00	200.00	**255.00**	0.00
26-R 62-2.5	77 Lucia and Child	60.00	250.00	100.00	**155.00**	0.00
Royal Doulton Log of the "Dashing Wave" (26-R 60-6)						
26-R 60-6.1	76 Sailing With Tide	65.00	225.00	150.00	**195.00**	+9.00
26-R 60-6.2	77 Running Free	70.00	200.00	120.00	**138.00**	+30.00
26-R 60-6.3	78 Rounding the Horn	70.00	140.00	80.00	**99.00**	0.00
26-R 60-6.4	79 Hong Kong	75.00	95.00	70.00	**85.00**	0.00
Royal Doulton Valentine's Day (26-R 62-7)						
26-R 62-7.1	76 Victorian Boy and Girl	25.00	150.00	90.00	**100.00**	0.00
26-R 62-7.2	77 My Sweetest Friend	25.00	25.00	10.00	**15.00**	−1.00
26-R 62-7.3	78 If I Loved You	25.00	75.00	40.00	**53.00**	0.00
26-R 62-7.4	79 My Valentine	30.00	75.00	40.00	**56.00**	+16.00
26-R 62-7.5	80 On A Swing	35.00	35.00	35.00	**35.00**	0.00
Royal Doulton Christmas (26-R 62-10)						
26-R 62-10.1	77 The Skater	25.00	150.00	60.00	**87.00**	0.00
26-R 62-10.2	78 Victorian Girl	30.00	30.00	30.00	**30.00**	0.00
26-R 62-10.3	79 Sleigh Ride	37.50	40.00	37.50	**40.00**	0.00
26-R 62-10.4	80 Victorian Christmas	49.50	49.50	49.50	**49.50**	0.00
Royal Worcester Doughty Birds (26-R 76-1)						
26-R 76-1.1	72 Redstarts and Beech	125.00	600.00	200.00	**375.00**	0.00
26-R 76-1.2	73 Myrtle Warbler	175.00	425.00	200.00	**350.00**	0.00
26-R 76-1.3	74 Blue-Grey Gnatcatchers	195.00	400.00	200.00	**300.00**	0.00
26-R 76-1.4	75 Blackburnian Warbler	195.00	400.00	220.00	**300.00**	0.00
26-R 76-1.5	76 Blue-Winged Sivas	195.00	400.00	195.00	**300.00**	0.00
26-R 76-1.6	77 Paradise Wydah	195.00	400.00	225.00	**225.00**	0.00
26-R 76-1.7	78 Bluetits and Witch Hazel	195.00	300.00	225.00	**225.00**	0.00
26-R 76-1.8	79 Mountain Bluebird and Pine	195.00	250.00	195.00	**225.00**	0.00
26-R 76-1.9	80 Cerulean Warblers Beech	500.00	500.00	500.00	**500.00**	0.00
26-R 76-1.10	81 Willow Warbler and Cranes Bill	575.00	575.00	575.00	**575.00**	0.00
Royal Worcester Christmas (26-R 76-3)						
26-R 76-3.1	79 God Rest Ye Merry Gentlemen	55.00	75.00	55.00	**57.00**	0.00
26-R 76-3.2	80 Christmas Morning	75.00	75.00	75.00	**75.00**	0.00
Spode Christmas (26-S 63-1)						
26-S 63-1.1	70 Partridge	25.00	150.00	100.00	**120.00**	0.00
26-S 63-1.2	71 Angels Singing	35.00	35.00	20.00	**32.00**	0.00
26-S 63-1.3	72 Three Ships A-Sailing	35.00	85.00	55.00	**72.00**	0.00
26-S 63-1.4	73 Three Kings of Orient	35.00	125.00	85.00	**93.00**	0.00
26-S 63-1.5	74 Deck the Halls	35.00	95.00	50.00	**91.00**	0.00
26-S 63-1.6	75 Christbaum	45.00	45.00	35.00	**45.00**	0.00
26-S 63-1.7	76 Good King Wenceslas	45.00	65.00	50.00	**65.00**	0.00
26-S 63-1.8	77 Holly and Ivy	45.00	35.00	30.00	**45.00**	0.00
26-S 63-1.9	78 While Shepherds Watched	45.00	45.00	45.00	**45.00**	0.00
26-S 63-1.10	79 Away in The Manger	50.00	50.00	50.00	**50.00**	0.00
26-S 63-1.11	80 Bringing in the Boar's Head	69.95	69.95	69.95	**69.95**	0.00
Wedgwood Christmas (26-W 90-1)						
26-W 90-1.1	69 Windsor Castle	25.00	675.00	425.00	**475.00**	+10.00
26-W 90-1.2	70 Trafalgar Square	30.00	50.00	20.00	**33.00**	+3.00
26-W 90-1.3	71 Piccadilly Circus	30.00	95.00	35.00	**60.00**	0.00
26-W 90-1.4	72 St. Paul's Cathedral	35.00	95.00	25.00	**50.00**	0.00
26-W 90-1.5	73 Tower of London	40.00	250.00	55.00	**77.00**	0.00
26-W 90-1.6	74 Houses of Parliament	40.00	120.00	48.00	**46.00**	0.00
26-W 90-1.7	75 Tower Bridge	45.00	45.00	30.00	**45.00**	0.00
26-W 90-1.8	76 Hampton Court	50.00	60.00	35.00	**48.00**	0.00
26-W 90-1.9	77 Westminster Abbey	55.00	80.00	40.00	**50.00**	0.00
26-W 90-1.10	78 Horse Guards	52.50	52.50	40.00	**52.50**	0.00
26-W 90-1.11	79 Buckingham Palace	59.95	59.95	59.95	**59.95**	0.00
26-W 90-1.12	80 St. James Palace	69.95	69.95	69.95	**69.95**	0.00
Wedgwood Mother's Day (26-W 90-2)						
26-W 90-2.1	71 Sportive Love	17.95	75.00	25.00	**35.00**	0.00
26-W 90-2.2	72 The Sewing Lesson	19.95	35.00	15.00	**20.00**	0.00
26-W 90-2.3	73 Baptism of Achilles	22.50	35.00	20.00	**22.00**	0.00
26-W 90-2.4	74 Domestic Employment	27.50	45.00	30.00	**35.00**	0.00
26-W 90-2.5	75 Mother and Child	27.50	45.00	30.00	**33.00**	0.00
26-W 90-2.6	76 The Spinner	32.50	45.00	29.00	**34.00**	0.00
26-W 90-2.7	77 Leisure Time	32.50	45.00	20.00	**35.00**	0.00
26-W 90-2.8	78 Swan and Cygnets	35.00	45.00	25.00	**32.00**	0.00
26-W 90-2.9	79 Deer and Fawn	39.95	39.95	39.95	**39.95**	0.00
26-W 90-2.10	80 Birds	45.00	45.00	45.00	**45.00**	0.00
Wedgwood Blossoming of Suzanne (26-W 90-4)						
26-W 90-4.1	77 Innocence	60.00	250.00	175.00	**180.00**	0.00
26-W 90-4.2	80 Cherish	80.00	80.00	80.00	**80.00**	0.00
Wedgwood Mary Vickers My Memories (26-W 90-5)						
26-W 90-5.1	81 Be My Friend	39.00	39.00	39.00	**39.00**	0.00
Wedgwood Calendar (26-W 90-6)						
26-W 90-6.1	71 Victorian Almanac	10.00	150.00	25.00	**40.00**	0.00
26-W 90-6.2	72 Carosel	12.50	50.00	10.00	**25.00**	0.00
26-W 90-6.3	73 Bountiful Butterfly	15.00	275.00	175.00	**240.00**	0.00
26-W 90-6.4	74 Camelot	17.50	225.00	175.00	**245.00**	0.00
26-W 90-6.5	75 Children's Games	25.00	100.00	60.00	**81.00**	0.00
26-W 90-6.6	76 Robin	25.00	60.00	35.00	**35.00**	0.00
26-W 90-6.7	77 Tonatuik	32.50	75.00	25.00	**35.00**	0.00
26-W 90-6.8	78 Samurai Warriors	35.00	35.00	35.00	**35.00**	0.00
26-W 90-6.9	79 Sacred Scareb	40.00	65.00	40.00	**47.00**	0.00
26-W 90-6.10	80 Safari	39.95	39.95	39.95	**39.95**	0.00
26-W 90-6.11	81 Horses	45.00	45.00	45.00	**45.00**	0.00

ITALY

PLATE		ISSUE PRICE	HIGH	LOW	QUOTE	CHANGE
di Volteradici Grand Opera (38-V 90-1)						
38-V 90-1.1	76 Rigoletto	49.00	200.00	107.00	**220.00**	+25.00
38-V 90-1.2	77 Madama Butterfly	49.00	90.00	40.00	**70.00**	0.00
38-V 90-1.3	78 Carmen	56.00	76.00	56.00	**55.00**	0.00
38-V 90-1.4	79 Aida	60.00	75.00	60.00	**63.00**	+3.00
38-V 90-1.5	80 Barber of Seville	60.00	60.00	60.00	**60.00**	0.00
di Volteradici Living Madonnas (38-V 90-2)						
38-V 90-2.1	78 The Pensive Madonna	67.50	75.00	60.00	**71.00**	0.00
38-V 90-2.2	79 The Serene Madonna	67.50	67.50	67.50	**67.50**	0.00
38-V 90-2.3	80 Beatific Madonna	67.50	67.50	67.50	**67.50**	0.00

JAPAN

PLATE		ISSUE PRICE	HIGH	LOW	QUOTE	CHANGE
Dave Grossman Annual (42-G 74-1)						
42-G 74-1.1	79 Leapfrog	75.00	150.00	80.00	**95.00**	+2.00
42-G 74-1.2	80 Lovers	90.00	90.00	90.00	**90.00**	0.00
Schmid Peanuts Christmas (42-S 12-1)						
42-S 12-1.1	72 Snoopy Guides the Sleigh	10.00	125.00	52.00	**85.00**	0.00
42-S 12-1.2	73 Christmas Eve at Doghouse	10.00	140.00	80.00	**107.00**	0.00
42-S 12-1.3	74 Christmas at Fireplace	10.00	135.00	75.00	**96.00**	0.00
42-S 12-1.4	75 Woodstock, Santa Claus	12.50	25.00	10.00	**25.00**	0.00
42-S 12-1.5	76 Woodstock's Christmas	13.00	35.00	20.00	**28.00**	0.00
42-S 12-1.6	77 Deck the Doghouse	13.00	40.00	25.00	**31.00**	0.00
42-S 12-1.7	78 Filling the Stocking	17.50	17.50	17.50	**17.50**	0.00
42-S 12-1.8	79 Christmas at Hand	19.95	19.95	19.95	**19.95**	0.00
42-S 12-1.9	80 Waiting for Santa	19.95	19.95	19.95	**19.95**	0.00
Schmid Peanuts Mother's Day (42-S 12-2)						
42-S 12-2.1	72 Linus	10.00	35.00	20.00	**25.00**	0.00
42-S 12-2.2	73 Mom?	10.00	35.00	20.00	**30.00**	0.00
42-S 12-2.3	74 On Parade	10.00	70.00	35.00	**43.00**	0.00
42-S 12-2.4	75 A Kiss for Lucy	12.50	35.00	25.00	**33.00**	0.00
42-S 12-2.5	76 Linus and Snoopy	13.00	35.00	20.00	**25.00**	0.00
42-S 12-2.6	77 Dear Mom	13.00	35.00	19.00	**27.00**	0.00
42-S 12-2.7	78 Thoughts that Count	17.50	30.00	17.50	**26.00**	0.00
42-S 12-2.8	79 A Special Letter	19.95	19.95	19.95	**19.95**	0.00
42-S 12-2.9	80 Tribute to Mom	19.95	19.95	19.95	**19.95**	0.00

SWEDEN

PLATE		ISSUE PRICE	HIGH	LOW	QUOTE	CHANGE
Rorstrand Christmas (76-R 54-1)						
76-R 54-1.1	68 Bringing Home the Tree	12.00	900.00	600.00	**752.00**	0.00
76-R 54-1.2	69 Fisherman Sailing Home	13.50	225.00	125.00	**180.00**	0.00
76-R 54-1.3	70 Nils with his Geese	13.50	49.00	35.00	**40.00**	0.00
76-R 54-1.4	71 Nils in Lapland	15.00	65.00	20.00	**37.00**	0.00
76-R 54-1.5	72 Dalecarlian Fiddler	15.00	55.00	30.00	**40.00**	0.00
76-R 54-1.6	73 Farm in Smaland	16.00	210.00	135.00	**154.00**	0.00
76-R 54-1.7	74 Vadstena	19.00	60.00	30.00	**40.00**	0.00
76-R 54-1.8	75 Nils in Vastmanland	25.00	50.00	35.00	**50.00**	0.00
76-R 54-1.9	76 Nils in Uppland	25.00	50.00	30.00	**38.00**	0.00
76-R 54-1.10	77 Nils in Varmland	35.00	35.00	20.00	**33.00**	0.00
76-R 54-1.11	78 Nils in Fjallbacka	39.00	39.00	39.00	**39.00**	0.00
76-R 54-1.12	79 Nils in Vaestergoetland	48.00	48.00	48.00	**48.00**	0.00
76-R 54-1.13	80 Nils in Sweden	57.00	57.00	57.00	**57.00**	0.00

UNITED STATES

PLATE		ISSUE PRICE	HIGH	LOW	QUOTE	CHANGE
Artists of the World Children of Aberdeen (84-A 72-1)						
84-A 72-1.1	79 Girl with Little Brother	70.00	90.00	70.00	**80.00**	+2.00
84-A 72-1.2	80 Sampan Girl	70.00	70.00	70.00	**70.00**	0.00
Fairmont Famous Clowns (84-F 4-2)						
84-F 4-2.1	76 Freddie the Freeloader	89.00	600.00	400.00	**535.00**	+100.00
84-F 4-2.2	77 W. C. Fields	89.00	175.00	90.00	**115.00**	+18.00
84-F 4-2.3	78 Happy	89.00	160.00	95.00	**95.00**	+6.00
84-F 4-2.4	79 The Pledge	89.00	89.00	89.00	**89.00**	0.00
Fairmont Classical American Beauties (84-F 4-8)						
84-F 4-8.1	79 Colleen	90.00	125.00	90.00	**95.00**	0.00
84-F 4-8.2	80 Heather	90.00	90.00	75.00	**85.00**	−2.00
84-F 4-8.3	81 Dawn	90.00	90.00	90.00	**90.00**	0.00
Gorham Rockwell Four Seasons (4 pc. set) (84-G 58-1)						
84-G 58-1.1	71 Boy and his Dog	50.00	1100.00	750.00	**875.00**	−25.00
84-G 58-1.2	72 Young Love	60.00	325.00	200.00	**285.00**	0.00
84-G 58-1.3	73 Ages of Love	60.00	700.00	450.00	**510.00**	0.00
84-G 58-1.4	74 Grandpa and Me	60.00	450.00	200.00	**260.00**	0.00
84-G 58-1.5	75 Me and My Pal	70.00	300.00	200.00	**250.00**	0.00
84-G 58-1.6	76 Grand Pals	75.00	370.00	250.00	**290.00**	+30.00
84-G 58-1.7	77 Going on Sixteen	100.00	320.00	195.00	**285.00**	0.00
84-G 58-1.8	78 Tender Years	125.00	180.00	100.00	**160.00**	0.00
84-G 58-1.9	79 A Helping Hand	200.00	200.00	200.00	**200.00**	0.00
84-G 58-1.10	80 Dad's Boy	250.00	250.00	250.00	**250.00**	0.00
Gorham Rockwell Christmas (84-G 58-3)						
84-G 58-3.1	74 Tiny Tim	17.50	120.00	75.00	**108.00**	0.00
84-G 58-3.2	75 Good Deeds	25.00	95.00	40.00	**69.00**	0.00
84-G 58-3.3	76 Christmas Trio	19.50	40.00	19.50	**37.00**	0.00
84-G 58-3.4	77 Yuletide Reckoning	29.50	60.00	35.00	**54.00**	0.00
84-G 58-3.5	78 Planning Christmas Visits	35.00	50.00	35.00	**45.00**	0.00
84-G 58-3.6	79 Santa's Helpers	35.00	35.00	35.00	**35.00**	0.00
84-G 58-3.7	80 Letter to Santa	40.00	40.00	40.00	**40.00**	0.00
Gorham Jansen Sugar & Spice (84-G 58-6)						
84-G 58-6.1	76 Dana and Debbie	50.00	175.00	125.00	**155.00**	+5.00
84-G 58-6.2	77 Becky and Baby	55.00	85.00	55.00	**70.00**	+10.00
84-G 58-6.3	78 Jeanette and Julie	70.00	100.00	75.00	**85.00**	+15.00
84-G 58-6.4	79 Ramona and Rachel	80.00	80.00	80.00	**80.00**	0.00

PLATE		ISSUE PRICE	HIGH	LOW	QUOTE	CHANGE
Gorham Prince Tatters (84-G 58-8)						
84-G 58-8.1	77 Johnny and Duke	50.00	100.00	65.00	90.00	0.00
84-G 58-8.2	78 Randy and Rex	55.00	125.00	55.00	90.00	0.00
84-G 58-8.3	79 Furry Friends	70.00	105.00	75.00	85.00	0.00
84-G 58-8.4	80 Benji's Burro	80.00	80.00	80.00	80.00	0.00
Kern Leo Jansen Young Professionals (84-K 20-7)						
84-K 20-7.1	80 Future Physician	80.00	80.00	80.00	80.00	0.00
Incolay Romantic Poets (84-I 31-1)						
84-I 31-1.1	77 She Walks in Beauty	84.00	525.00	300.00	445.00	0.00
84-I 31-1.2	78 A Thing of Beauty	84.00	120.00	69.00	98.00	0.00
84-I 31-1.3	79 To A Skylark	90.00	90.00	90.00	90.00	0.00
84-I 31-1.4	80 Phantom of Delight	90.00	90.00	90.00	90.00	0.00
Incolay Great Romances of History (84-I 31-3)						
84-I 31-3.1	79 Antony and Cleopatra	90.00	90.00	90.00	90.00	0.00
84-I 31-3.2	80 The Taj Mahal Lovers	90.00	90.00	90.00	90.00	0.00
Kern Runci Mother's Day (84-K 20-6)						
84-K 20-6.1	77 Darcy	75.00	175.00	90.00	107.00	+12.00
84-K 20-6.2	78 Moment to Reflect	85.00	100.00	60.00	90.00	0.00
84-K 20-6.3	79 Fulfillment	70.00	90.00	50.00	75.00	0.00
84-K 20-6.4	80 A Renewal of Faith	75.00	75.00	75.00	75.00	0.00
Edwin M. Knowles Wizard of Oz (84-K 41-1)						
84-K 41-1.1	77 Over the Rainbow	29.00	300.00	195.00	265.00	+40.00
84-K 41-1.2	78 If I Only Had a Brain	29.00	100.00	65.00	89.00	0.00
84-K 41-1.3	78 If I Only Had a Heart	29.00	75.00	39.00	60.00	0.00
84-K 41-1.4	78 If I Were King of the Forest	29.00	60.00	39.00	50.00	+3.00
84-K 41-1.5	79 The Wicked Witch of the West	29.00	29.00	29.00	29.00	0.00
84-K 41-1.6	79 Follow the Yellow Brick Road	29.00	29.00	29.00	29.00	0.00
84-K 41-1.7	79 Wonderful Wizard of Oz	29.00	29.00	29.00	29.00	0.00
84-K 41-1.8	80 We're Off To See The Wizard	36.00	36.00	36.00	36.00	0.00
Edwin M. Knowles Americana Holidays (84-K 41-2)						
84-K 41-2.1	78 Fourth of July	40.00	50.00	40.00	45.00	0.00
84-K 41-2.2	79 Thanksgiving	40.00	40.00	40.00	41.00	0.00
84-K 41-2.3	80 Easter	40.00	40.00	40.00	60.00	0.00
84-K 41-2.4	81 Valentine	40.00	40.00	40.00	40.00	0.00
Edwin M. Knowles Gone With The Wind (84-K 41-3)						
84-K 41-3.1	78 Scarlett	32.00	325.00	200.00	275.00	+35.00
84-K 41-3.2	79 Ashley	32.00	40.00	32.00	38.00	+4.00

PLATE		ISSUE PRICE	HIGH	LOW	QUOTE	CHANGE
84-K 41-3.3	80 Melanie	32.00	32.00	32.00	32.00	0.00
Edwin M. Knowles Csatari Grandparent (84-K 41-4)						
84-K 41-4.1	80 Bedtime Story	27.00	27.00	27.00	27.00	0.00
Pickard A Mother's Love (84-P 26-6)						
84-P 26-6.1	80 Miracle	145.00	250.00	175.00	220.00	+33.00
Reco Collection World of Children (84-R 60-1)						
84-R 60-1.1	77 Rainy Day Fun	75.00	425.00	250.00	340.00	+70.00
84-R 60-1.2	78 When I Grow Up	75.00	175.00	100.00	135.00	+15.00
84-R 60-1.3	79 You're Invited	75.00	150.00	100.00	130.00	+10.00
84-R 60-1.4	80 Kittens for Sale	75.00	75.00	75.00	75.00	0.00
Reco McClelland's Mother Goose (84-R 60-2)						
84-R 60-2.1	79 Mary, Mary	34.00	350.00	200.00	285.00	+30.00
84-R 60-2.2	80 Little Boy Blue	34.00	50.00	34.00	39.00	+5.00
Rockwell Society Christmas (84-R 70-1)						
84-R 70-1.1	74 Scotty Gets His Tree	37.00	310.00	225.00	250.00	−5.00
84-R 70-1.2	75 Angel with Black Eye	37.00	200.00	150.00	180.00	0.00
84-R 70-1.3	76 Golden Christmas	37.00	75.00	35.00	75.00	0.00
84-R 70-1.4	77 Toy Shop Window	37.00	103.00	35.00	87.00	0.00
84-R 70-1.5	78 Christmas Dream	37.00	60.00	37.00	41.00	0.00
84-R 70-1.6	79 Somebody's Up There	37.00	37.00	37.00	37.00	0.00
84-R 70-1.7	80 Scotty Plays Santa	37.00	37.00	37.00	37.00	0.00
Rockwell Society Mother's Day (84-R 70-2)						
84-R 70-2.1	76 Mother's Love	37.00	200.00	150.00	175.00	0.00
84-R 70-2.2	77 Faith	37.00	85.00	50.00	63.00	0.00
84-R 70-2.3	78 Bedtime	37.00	200.00	140.00	165.00	0.00
84-R 70-2.4	79 Reflections	37.00	40.00	37.00	39.00	0.00
84-R 70-2.5	80 A Mother's Pride	37.00	37.00	37.00	37.00	0.00
Rockwell Society Heritage (84-R 70-3)						
84-R 70-3.1	77 Toymaker	24.50	575.00	370.00	450.00	+25.00
84-R 70-3.2	78 Cobbler	29.50	150.00	70.00	110.00	0.00
84-R 70-3.3	79 Lighthouse Keeper's Daughter	29.50	125.00	70.00	80.00	+12.00
84-R 70-3.4	80 The Ship Builder	29.50	29.50	29.50	29.50	0.00
84-R 70-3.5	81 The Music Maker	29.50	29.50	29.50	29.50	0.00
Viletta Zolan's Children (84-V 36-1)						
84-V 36-1.1	78 Erik and Dandelion	29.00	225.00	125.00	195.00	+50.00
84-V 36-1.2	79 Sabina in the Grass	33.00	220.00	150.00	150.00	0.00
84-V 36-1.3	80 By Myself	36.00	36.00	36.00	36.00	0.00

MARKET NOTES

Market Bradex surges up 1 point to a record-high 338. Post Christmas trading up 40% to post another record trading period. Four of the nine key indicator series advance.

Gainers far outnumber losers 80 to 27 as new collectors still seek back-issues to round out newly started collections. Biggest gains posted by 1976 Kaiser Mother's Day up 55% to $45.00; 1977 Kaiser Mother's Day up 51% to $44.00; 1979 Royal Doulton Valentines up 40% to $56.00; 1974 Schmid Hummel Christmas up 37% to $55.00; 1980 Konigszelt up 31% to $60.00; 1978 Viletta Zolan's Children up 34% to $195.00; 1978 Kaiser Mother's Day up 28% to $45.00; 1973 Kaiser Anniversary up 28% to $45.00; 1977 Royal Doulton Log Of Dashing Wave up 27% to $138.00; 1977 Reco Collection Of Children up 26% to $340.00; 1972 Kaiser Anniversary up 25% to $50.00; 1974 Royal Bayreuth Christmas up 25% to $50.00; 1978 Gorham Rockwell Sugar & Spice up 21% to $85.00; and 1976 Royal Copenhagen Christmas up 19.9% to $43.00. Declines are negligible led by 1978 Svend Jensen Christmas down 20% to $20.00; 1977 Royal Bayreuth Antique American Art down 16.5% to $50.00; 1971 Goebel Hummel down 6.5% to $1150.00; 1977 Goebel Hummel down 4.5% to $210.00.

One new series is Bradex-listed-My Memories series by Wedgwood (26-W.90-6.1) with artwork by Mary Vickers. First issue - 1980 'Be My Friend', queensware; edition size - 100 firing days; issue price - $39.00.

Notable new series (not Bradex-listed): Pickard Children Of Mexico, edition size - 5,000; issue price - $127.50; first plate titled 'Maria' by noted Mexican artist Sanchez.

Kaiser's Romantic Portraits series by Gerda Neubacher; first issue in 1981 'Lilie', edition size - 5,000; issue price - $200.00.

Well-known American artist Leo Jansen died of heart failure December 21st 1980. Canadians will remember this artist for his Royal Bayreuth Mother's Day series, in which the 1979 Mother's Day plate was plate of the year in 1979. His new series 'Leaders Of Tomorrow' in which the first plate is titled 'Future Physician', will be completed as planned, as the remaining three pieces of artwork were completed before his death. Trading has increased substantially on all his series since his death. Analysts expect trading to increase a great deal more in the future.

CONVENTION NEWS: Collector Platemakers Association's second annual Plate Fair June 13 and 14 (dealers only June 12) at Calgary Convention Centre (Four Seasons Hotel) Calgary, Alberta. Artists attending will be: Roger Brown, Mary Ellen Wehrli, Lissa Calvert, John McClelland, Mary Vickers, Gerda Neubacher, Frances Taylor Williams, Thaddeus 'Uncle Tad' Krumeich and Murray Killman.